THE
GOLDEN AGE
OF
EMPIRE

VOLUME 1
1900-1914

THE
GOLDEN AGE
OF
EMPIRE

INTRODUCTION BY
ASA BRIGGS

HAMLYN

Project editor Peter Furtado
Project art editor Ayala Kingsley
Text editors Robert Peberdy, Mike March, Sue Martin
Cartographic manager Olive Pearson
Cartographic editor Zoë Goodwin
Designers Frankie Wood, Janet McCallum, Wolfgang Mezger, Gill Mouqué, Niki Overy, Linda Reed, Nicholas Rous, Tony de Saulles, Dave Sumner, Rita Wütrych
Picture research manager Alison Renney
Picture research Jan Croot, Diane Hamilton, Rebecca Hirsh, Angela Murphy, Diana Phillips, Linda Proud, Christine Vincent, Charlotte Ward-Perkins
Editorial assistants Elaine Welsh, Monica Byles

AN EQUINOX BOOK

Planned and produced by
Andromeda Oxford Ltd
9–15 The Vineyard
Abingdon
Oxfordshire OX14 3PX

© Copyright Andromeda Oxford
Ltd 1993

This edition published by
Hamlyn, part of Reed
Consumer Books Ltd, Michelin
House, 81 Fulham Road, London
SW3 6RB

ISBN 0 600 57989 1

Printed in Germany by
Mohndruck Graphische Betriebe
GmbH. Gutersloh.

CONTENTS

James Foreman-Peck
University of Hull
Brian Foss
Freelance writer
Michael Geyer
University of Chicago, USA
Robert Gildea
Merton College, Oxford
Anthony Glees
Brunel University
Roger Griffin
Oxford Polytechnic
Jennifer Hargreaves
Roehampton Institute,
London
Nathaniel Harris
Freelance writer
Nigel Harris
University College, London
Gundi Harriss
Birkbeck College, London
David Horn
University of Liverpool

Julian Jackson
University College of
Swansea
Keith Jeffrey
University of Ulster
Matthew Jones
St Antony's College, Oxford
Paul Kennedy
Yale University, USA
Ghislaine Lawrence
National Museum of Science
and Industry, London
Peter Lowe
University of Manchester
Keith Lyons
London School of Economics
Dermott MacCann
Brunel University
Peter Martland
Corpus Christi College,
Cambridge
Roger Morgan
London School of Economics

Lucy Newton
Leicester University
A. J. Nicholls
St Antony's College, Oxford
David Penn
Imperial War Museum,
London
Brian Holden Reid
King's College, London
Catherine Reilly
Freelance writer
Denis Ridgeway
Formerly of Royal Navy
Scientific Service
Gowher Rizvi
University of Warwick
Keith Sainsbury
University of Reading
Harry Shukman
St Antony's College, Oxford
Penny Sparke
Royal College of Art, London

Jill Stephenson
University of Edinburgh
Stanley Trapido
Lincoln College, Oxford
T.H.E. Travers
University of Calgary,
Canada
S.B. Whitmore
Formerly British Army of the
Rhine, Germany
Paul Wilkinson
University of Aberdeen
Elizabeth Wilson
North London Polytechnic
Roger Zetter
Oxford Polytechnic
Ronald Tamplin
University of Exeter
Ruth Pearson
University of East Anglia
Peter Lambert
University of East Anglia

INTRODUCTION

In retrospect, the period from 1900 to 1914 has a unity of its own. It stands out, particularly for Europeans, as an island in time. In another metaphor derived from nature, these were the years before the deluge. The surprising and horrifying magnitude of that deluge, the "Great War", a war that had its origins in European rivalries and antagonisms, swept away much that had been familiar, much that had been prized. For the privileged groups in society, including the rich middle classes on both sides of the Atlantic, the prewar years constituted a *belle époque*. Many 19th-century restraints were cast aside: the new century was, it was felt, made to be enjoyed.

Nostalgic reminiscence and harsher reality

Even in times of peace the 20th century was to provide far more surprises and horrors than most people had anticipated when it began, and far more had to be endured than enjoyed, particularly in the middle years of the century. Yet in 1920 the English economist JM Keynes provided a remarkable picture of what life viewed from London had been like on the eve of the Great War. "The inhabitant of London," he wrote, "could order by telephone, sipping his morning tea in bed, the various products of the whole earth in such quantity as he might see fit, and reasonably expect their early delivery on his doorstep; he could at the same moment and by the same means venture his wealth in the natural resources and new enterprises of any quarter of the world, and share, without execution, or even trouble, in their prospective fruits and advantages."

And that was only the beginning. His happy Londoner could also "secure forthwith, if he wished it, cheap and comfortable means of transit to any country or climate, without passport or other formality, could despatch his servant to the neighbouring office of a bank for such supply of the precious metals as might seem convenient, and could then proceed abroad to foreign quarters without knowledge of their religion, language or customs, having coined wealth upon his person, and would consider himself greatly aggrieved and much surprised at the least interference. But, most important of all, he regarded this stage of affairs as normal, certain and permanent, except in the direction of further improvements, and any deviation from it as aberrant, scandalous and avoidable."

If selective memory can play tricks with detail, such selective generalizations about the previous state of a society, including a recent period in its history, can just as effectively mislead posterity. There were strains and tensions that were present and perceived before 1914 that were not mentioned by Keynes, who was to establish his reputation in the years after the Great War and who was to influence public policy-making in the middle years of the century.

Even among the exceptionally privileged about whom Keynes was writing in 1920, there were some who were in doubt about whether the "normal" and the "certain" would remain "permanent", and amongst the less well-off middle classes, a very varied social group, there was a less clear sense either of security or of mobility. Meanwhile, sections of the industrial "working classes", whose standard of living had improved during the last decades of the 19th century, were worse off in 1914 than they had been in 1900. There was also a population of casual workers, migrant workers and paupers, and in years like 1908, when the trade cycle plunged to its trough, large numbers of unemployed.

It was clear to rich and poor alike before 1914 that increased wealth continued to be accompanied even in the richest countries and at peaks of the trade cycle by obvious poverty, poverty which, if not new, was far more publicized than it ever had been before. Writing as a businessman and a student of society, another Englishman, Seebohm Rowntree, estimated in 1901 that 31 percent of the population of York lived in primary poverty, and his book *Poverty, a Study of Town Life* was waved on political platforms, a sign at least that this situation was not deemed "normal".

The point at which Rowntree identified primary poverty was deliberately stringent. The person just above his primary poverty line had to live a life in total contrast to Keynes's happy Londoner. In order to remain above the line, he would have to be "prepared to abstain from beer and tobacco, to give no money to his wife for new clothes or to his children for dolls or sweets, never to spend a penny on railway fare or omnibus ... never to travel into the country unless [on foot], never to purchase a half-penny newspaper and spend a penny to buy a ticket for a popular concert." He would have had at his disposal no money to write a letter to absent children, to give to Church or Chapel, or to join a trade union or a sick club.

A poverty line so drawn in order to avoid philanthropic "sentimentality" was an exercise in model building. "Real life" could never so be lived. As a result "secondary poverty" was common. Drunkenness was rife. So also was gambling. Newspapers, including popular new newspapers, increased their circulations. Fashion was one of the main topics discussed in them. Meanwhile, collective pressure to change the distribution of property increased.

The conflicts of empire

Trade-union strength grew between 1900 and 1914, and there was a wave of strikes in many parts of Europe and the United States in the years from 1911 to 1914. Political parties had already emerged earlier that proclaimed the need to redistribute wealth, and the numbers of their supporters now grew. It was in the most autocratic country in Europe, a country that stretched far into Asia, czarist Russia, a country where strikes were outlawed, that Europe's most revolutionary political party, the Bolsheviks, was formed in 1903. It put its trust not in the advance of democracy but in a highly disciplined and centralized revolutionary leadership. VI Lenin, born in 1870, was its main theorist.

Such an approach to political action, an extension of Karl Marx's professed "scientific socialism", devised in industrializing Europe earlier in the 19th century, was to appeal far outside industrial Europe later in the 20th century. It was associated – after Lenin – with an attack not only on "capitalism" but on "imperialism". Before 1914, however, those parts of the world where it was to establish itself as the official ideology, were still largely economically dependent on industrial Europe. Indeed, the period from 1900 to 1914 is often called "the imperial age", and for most imperialists this was a matter not of shame but of pride. There was a continuing scramble for colonies and a continued pressure on tropical and other colonial territories both for raw materials, and for markets. Moreover, many countries that were not colonies were treated as if they were. A

quarter of British investments in 1914 were in Latin America, where there were no British colonies.

Not all colonies were equally profitable. Indeed, an agreed balance sheet of financial advantage is difficult to compile, and the quest for colonies was not dictated solely by the quest for profit. Nor was there unanimity even amongst the informed about their advantages. There were always arguments about empire, particularly in Britain: they were strongest when empires were being created or when colonial wars were being fought. Anti-imperialism as well as imperialism had its origins inside countries with overseas possessions – and inside the United States which had its own brand of imperialism then and later.

▲ **The Paris Exhibition of 1900 attracted visitors from many countries.**

The world was undoubtedly in the process of being opened up between 1900 and 1914, a process that inevitably involved clashes between cultures as well as greater economic interdependence. Africa – and the Pacific – were more vulnerable to pressure than Asia, where China, forced to make concessions to the "West", remained largely intact and where empire gave way to republic in 1912. The new century had begun with a government-inspired uprising in Beijing during which the German minister was assassinated and European property sacked.

Statistics, revealing when they dealt with movements of trade, were notoriously inadequate in relation to global population and standards of living, although it was plain that in 1914 a large majority of the world's peoples, including the poorest, lived outside industrial or industrializing countries and that their average incomes were only a third of those within the "advanced countries". Yet there were contrasts, within the latter group just as there were contrasts, sometimes picturesque contrasts, in any single country. The United States was already the richest country in the world by 1914. Indeed, average American incomes were five times greater than the European average and 25 percent higher than the British.

One Asian country, Japan, had already carried through the first critical stages of its own industrial revolution and had defeated in war one major European power, Russia. The treaty bringing the Russo–Japanese war to its end in 1905 was signed not in Europe or in Asia but in the United States; and the Russian revolution of 1905, which was a byproduct of the war, had farreaching repercussions. After 1907, however, most "crises" that hit the headlines involved the European Powers and Europe itself and the Mediterranean rather than distant parts of the globe.

The end of peaceful progress

When war broke out in 1914, it was a Balkan crisis that provided the trigger point, bringing into action an intricate system of alliances and treaties that was as complex as the economic system. Britain, France and Russia were on one side: Germany and Austria on the other. The conventions on which the international economic system were based were among the first victims of the war. Yet the contrast between a *belle époque* and a time of troubles after 1914 can be exaggerated. For all the 19th-century trust in "progress", there were voices prophesying a very different future from that hailed by the spokesmen of progress. Thus, the German philosopher Friedrich Nietzsche, who died in 1900, sensed that traditional values would soon disintegrate and that history would reach a point of crisis. "O my brothers," he asked in *Thus spake Zarathustra*, "where do you find the greatest danger for man's future; is it not with the good and the just? ... Whatever harm the evil may do, the harm done by the good is the most harmful harm."

Nietzsche's was not the only voice. In 1906 Frenchman Georges Sorel published his *Reflections on Violence* in which, quoting Nietzsche, he rejected "progress" as an illusion and parliamentary government as a game. For the quest for truth he substituted reliance on myth. A new order had to be created through "proletarian revolution", expressed in a general strike that would shatter the economy. "It is to violence that socialism owes those high ethical values by means of which it brings solution to the

world." Even in Britain, where such extreme philosophies were less acceptable, the philosopher Bertrand Russell wrote of "the barbaric substratum of human nature, unsatisfied in action" finding "an outlet in imagination".

Such passages stand out in the light of what was to come later. There were different strands, however, in the period between 1900 and 1914 that linked it with the years ahead. The amount of available leisure time increased for the working classes, who were now catered for increasingly by a more commercialized entertainment industry. These were the early years of the cinema, of holiday travel and of the gramophone. Across the Atlantic, they were the years too of the first automobile, the Model T Ford, deliberately designed for a mass market. The adjective "mass" now began to be applied to culture as well as to markets and politics.

Meanwhile, minority movements in the arts, some of them self-consciously *avant garde*, pointed to the "modernist" culture of the future. Pablo Picasso, born in 1881, developed Cubism after 1903. In music the first performance in 1913 of *Rite of Spring* by Igor Stravinsky, born in 1882, caused a near-riot in Paris's *Champs Elysées*. Three years ealier, the Italian poet FT Marinetti had launched a Futurist Manifesto, glorifying the machine and the achievements of modern science. In science there are direct links between the revolution in physics which had already taken place before 1914 and the post-1945 nuclear age. In 1914 Albert Einstein was still only in his mid-thirties, but he had already shaken the Newtonian world-system. Likewise, Sigmund Freud, explorer of the subconscious, was already in his late fifties. For all the discontinuities of the 20th century, among which the two wars are the most obvious, there have been continuities. The history of science spans the years of war.

The outcome of the new technology was now open. No one knew quite what air power would do to the world in peace or war when Louis Blériot crossed the Channel in 1909 in his new monoplane. Yet no one was in doubt that the world would never quite be the same again. There are historians who, ignoring one side of the balance sheet, have cheerfully contended that once an invention like his has been successfully launched improvements will follow "in a kind of geometric ratio". We now know that no improvement was unqualified.

▲ Many millions of Europeans set off for a new life in the Americas.

THE IMPERIAL AGE

Time Chart

	1900	1901	1902	1903	1904	1905	1906	1907
Europe/Mediterranean	• Start of armaments race in Europe, as construction of 38 new battleships approved in Germany to double navy within 20 years • Feb: Labour Representative committee formed in UK with Ramsay MacDonald as secretary (1906, Labour Party) • May: 1st trial of proportional representation in Belgian general election	• 22 Jan: Death of Queen Victoria and accession of Edward VII to UK throne • May: Limited franchise in local elections extended to Norwegian women • Jul, Taff Vale case: UK House of Lords ruled that trade unions could be sued for members' actions during strikes	• Sinn Féin (Irish republican party) founded by Arthur Griffith • Anglo–Japanese alliance broke UK's policy of "splendid isolation" • Jan: Protests in Malta at replacement of Italian by English as official language • 28 Jun: Renewal of Triple Alliance (Ger, Aut-Hung, Ita)	• Meeting in London, the Russian Social Democratic Party split into Bolsheviks (led by Lenin) and Mensheviks • Denmark granted Iceland responsible government • Worker's Educational Association (WEA) founded in UK by Albert Mansbridge • 10 Oct: Women's Social and Political Union founded (UK) by Emmeline Pankhurst	• 8 Apr: Anglo–French Entente Cordiale signed, ending overseas territorial rivalry	• 22 Jan (Old Style 9 Jan), Bloody Sunday: Demonstrators marching on the Russian Tsar's Winter Palace killed by Cossack troops • 7 Jun: Norway dissolved union with Sweden • Dec: French law decreed separation of Church and State	• May–Jul: 1st Russian *Duma* (parliament); dissolved by Tsar • Dec: UK Trades Dispute Act reversed 1901 Taff Vale ruling	• Mar: World's 1st women MPs elected in Finland • Jun: Limited female suffrage introduced in Norway • Sep: Signature of Anglo–Russian agreement on Asia, aligning Russia in Triple Entente with France, against Triple Alliance powers
The Middle East	• Dec: Secret Italo–French agreement over respective interests in Tripolitania and Morocco	• Persian oil concession granted to William Knox D'Arcy (later, Anglo–Persian Oil Co.) • Jul: Franco–Moroccan agreement, fixing frontier with French colony of Algeria and regulating police and trade policies		• Jan: UK King Edward VII proclaimed Emperor of India, in Delhi	• Apr: Anglo–French agreement over respective interests in Egypt and Morocco • Oct: Secret Franco–Spanish agreement on eventual partition of Morocco	• 31 Mar: German Kaiser's visit to Morocco perceived as threat to European interests in N Africa	• Muslim League founded in India • Jan–Apr, Algeciras Conference: Morocco's independence agreed • Protests led to convening of 1st Persian parliament (Oct) and authorization of constitution (30 Dec) by Persian Shah	• Aug: Following local uprisings, French troops occupied coastal areas (Mor) • Aug: Anglo–Russian Entente divided Persia into UK and Russian spheres of influence
Africa	• 24 May, Boer War: Britain annexed Orange River Colony (S Afr) • 25 Oct: Boer Republic of S Africa annexed by UK and renamed Transvaal	• Nov: Anglo–Italian agreement on frontier between respective colonies of Sudan and Eritrea (E Afr)	• 31 May: Peace of Vereeniging ended Boer War; Boers accepted British sovereignty; pledged representative government	• Jul: Uganda (E Afr) offered by UK government as site for Jewish homeland	• Beginning of Herero uprising in German SW Africa (to 1907)	• Beginning of Maji Maji rising in German E Africa (to 1907)	• 21 Mar: UK agreed to £9.5 million damages for Boer War • Apr: UK troops fought Zulu uprising (S Afr) • 6 Dec: Transvaal (S Afr) granted self-government by UK	• Mar: Indian immigration restricted in Transvaal; Mohandas Gandhi opened civil disobedience drive (*satyagraha*) • 1 Jul: Orange River Colony (S Afr) granted self-government by UK
The Americas	• 6 Mar: Social Democratic party (1901, Socialist Party) formed in US • 16 Dec: National Civic Federation formed in US, for arbitration of labor disputes	• 12 Jun: Cuba took on Platt Amendment; US right to military intervention confirmed • 6 Sep: US President William McKinley shot dead; succeeded by Theodore Roosevelt • 22 Oct (to Jan 1902): 2nd Pan-American Conference • 18 Nov: 2nd Hay–Pauncefoote treaty recognized US right to build C American shipping canal	• Dec: UK, Germany and Italy blockaded Venezuelan coast to procure payment for damage incurred during 1899 revolution	• Mar: US Congress moved to restrict immigration, imposing $2 per head tax • 3 Nov: Revolution in Panama and proclamation of independence from Colombia • 18 Nov: Treaty between US and Panama allowed for construction of Panama Canal, and US occupation and control of canal zone	• Dec: By Roosevelt Corollary to Monroe Doctrine, US claimed right to intervene in Latin American affairs	• Sep: Canadian provinces of Alberta and Saskatchewan established	• May: Last UK troops left Canada • 29 Sep: Following uprisings and invoking Platt Amendment, US proclaimed provisional government in Cuba (to Jan 1909)	• Feb: US Immigration Act limited entry of Japanese laborers • Feb–Dec: Conference of C American States, after war between Honduras and Nicaragua threatened regional stability • 1 Aug: 1st US military air force formed • 16 Dec: US Battle Fleet began round-the-world cruise
Asia and Pacific	• Russia occupied S Manchuria (Chn) • May: Tonga (formerly Friendly Is) annexed by UK • Jun–Aug, Boxer Rising (Chn): Foreign legations in Peking besieged; relieved by expeditionary force from 6 nations	• Australian Labor Party founded • 1 Jan: Federal constitution of new Commonwealth of Australia in force • Mar: Capture of Filipino rebel leader marked tougher US rule in Philippines. William H Taft installed as 1st US civil governor (Jul) • Sep: Peking Protocol marked end of Boxer Rising	• Australian women granted federal vote • Reforms in China of judiciary, government and education • 30 Jan, Anglo–Japanese Alliance: to protect interests in China and Korea • 8 Apr: Russo–Chinese accord to evacuate Manchuria • 7 Oct: French agreement with Siam on Indochinese frontier	• Jul–Aug: Japanese and UK protests at Russian failure to evacuate Manchuria	• 8 Feb: Outbreak of Russo–Japanese War, with Japanese naval attack on Russian fleet at Port Arthur, Manchuria, then invasion of Korea • Mar–Sep: 100s of Tibetans killed before UK military expedition forced trade treaty • 27 Apr: Australia's 1st (minority) Labor government	• New parliamentary government pledged by Chinese rulers • 27–8 May: Russian Baltic Squadron destroyed by Japanese navy • End of Russo–Japanese War. Pres. Roosevelt led way to peace talks in US (Aug) and signature of Treaty of Portsmouth (5 Sep): Manchuria to return to China; Russia recognized Japanese rights in Korea	• 1 Sep: British New Guinea declared an Australian federal possession and renamed Papua	• 26 Sep: New Zealand constituted a dominion within Commonwealth of Nations • 16 Oct: Philippines 1st elected legislature opened • 8 Nov: Harvester decision of Australian Arbitration Court established concept of basic wage
World	• Sep: 5th congress of 2nd International, Paris (Fr)	• International Federation of Trade Unions established	• 14 Oct: 1st decision by International Court of Arbitration at The Hague (Neth)	• Policy of preferential trading adopted within Commonwealth	• Aug: International Miners' Congress called for 8-hour day and minimum wage	• Industrial Workers of the World (IWW) founded in US		• 15 Jun: 2nd international peace conference opened at The Hague (Neth)

1908	1909	1910	1911	1912	1913	1914
• 23 Apr: Signature of [B]altic Conventions (Ger, [S]we, Den, Rus) and North [S]ea Conventions (Ger, [S]we, Den, UK, Neth, Fr) • 5 Oct: Bulgaria declared [in]dependence from Turkey • 7 Oct, Bosnian Crisis: [A]ustria-Hungary annexed [T]urkey's Balkan provinces [o]f Bosnia-Herzegovina	• 1-month general strike in Sweden, over economic conditions • Graduated rates of income tax introduced in UK • 30 Nov: Rejection by UK House of Lords of "people's budget", shifting taxation burden to wealthy, forced election on Liberal government	• Eleutherios Venizelos became Greek prime minister, beginning program of financial, administrative and constitutional reform • 6 May: Death of King Edward VII; George V succeeded to UK throne • 5 Oct: Portuguese monarchy overthrown; democratic republic proclaimed	• Assassination of Russian prime minister, P.A. Stolypin • Aug: Parliament Bill restricting power of House of Lords enacted (UK)	• Mar: Principle of minimum wage established in UK • Jul: UK decided to transfer Mediterranean warships to North Sea, to counteract German naval build-up • Oct: Outbreak of 1st Balkan War between Balkan League (Bulg, Serb, Gre, Montenegro) and Turkey	• Apr: UK suffragette leader Emmeline Pankhurst sentenced to 3 years' imprisonment • 30 May: 1st Balkan War ended by Treaty of London; Turkey surrendered most of its European empire • 29 Jun: Outbreak of 2nd Balkan War, between Bulgaria and Romania, Greece, Serbia and Turkey • Aug, Treaty of Bucharest: 2nd Balkan War ended, with loss of territory by Bulgaria	• 28 Jun: Assassination of Austro-Hungarian heir, Archduke Franz Ferdinand, at Sarajevo (Bosnia); Serbs suspected of plot • 28 Jul: Austria-Hungary declared war on Serbia • 1–3 Aug: Germany declared war on Russia and France, and invaded Belgium • 4 Aug: UK and Commonwealth declared war on Germany
• Jun: Successful [c]ounter-revolution by new [P]ersian shah, Mohammad [A]li, who ordered bombing [o]f *majlis* (parliament) • Young Turk Revolution: [A]rmy rebellion (Jul) forced [O]ttoman sultan to restore [1]876 constitution and [c]onvene parliament (Dec) • Aug: In Morocco, Sultan [A]bdel Aziz overthrown by [b]rother, Mulay Abdel Hafid	• India Act (Morley–Minto Reforms) gave Indians share in legislative councils of British India • Jul: Persian shah deposed by nationalist forces • Nov: Attempted assassination of UK viceroy, Lord Minto, in India	• Feb: Egypt's Coptic Christian premier, Butros Ghali, assassinated by nationalist	• Jul–Nov, Agadir Crisis: Franco–German rivalry over Morocco threatened to erupt into war • 29 Sep: Italy began war with Turkey over latter's N African provinces of Tripolitania and Cyrenaica	• Protectorates set up by French in S Morocco (Mar), Spain in N Morocco (Nov) • Aug: Abdication of Moroccan sultan in protest at French rule • 15 Oct: Treaty of Ouchy: Italo–Turkish war ended with Turkey ceding Tripolitania and Cyrenaica	• Jun: Young Turks formed cabinet and assumed power over Turkish empire	• Nov: Turkey entered war on side of Central Powers (Ger, Aut-Hung) • 17 Dec: Egypt declared a UK protectorate
• 15 Nov: Congo (C Afr) [f]ormally annexed by [B]elgium	• Aug: S Africa Act passed in UK, approving union of Cape Colony, Natal, Orange River Colony (renamed Orange Free State), Transvaal	• Gabon, Middle Congo and Ubangi-Shari-Chad federated as French Equatorial Africa • 1 Jul: Union of S Africa became dominion within Commonwealth under Louis Botha (Sep)	• Nov: Franco–German agreement, recognizing French rights in Morocco; French Togoland (W Afr) given to Germany	• African National Congress (ANC) formed in S Africa	• Afrikaner Nationalist Party formed by James Hertzog (S Afr)	• 1 Jan: Union of N and S Nigeria as UK protectorate and colony • Aug: Anglo–French colonial troops invaded German protectorate of Togoland (W Afr) and forced German surrender
• In US, Federal [E]mployers' Liability Act [c]overed industrial injury [o]n interstate carriers • 25 May: C American [C]ourt of Justice [e]stablished, in Chile	• General Juan Gómez established dictatorship in Venezuela (until 1935) • Jun: National Negro Committee founded in US (from 1910, National Association for the Advancement of Colored People, NAACP)	• Revolutionary movement instituted in Mexico by Francisco Madero; supported by Emiliano Zapata and Pancho Villa	• 25 May: Mexican dictator Porfiro Diaz forced to resign, ending 35-year rule	• Jul–Oct: Civil war in Nicaragua; beginning of US military intervention (to 1933), as US forces intervened to support President Adolfo Díaz • 5 Nov: Woodrow Wilson elected 1st Democrat president of US in 20 years	• 25 Feb: Collection of income tax constituted in US, by 16th Amendment • Feb: Overthrow of Mexico's President Madero heralded military dictatorship of Victoriano Huerta and civil war • 31 May: Election of US senators instituted, by 17th Amendment	• Clayton Act legalized US trade unions • US took military control of Haiti • Apr: US support for restoration of constitutional government in Mexico implemented by landing of troops and capture of Veracruz • 4 Aug, WWI: US President Wilson issued proclamation of neutrality • 15 Aug: Panama Canal opened to shipping
• Foundation of Indonesian [c]ultural society Budi [U]tomo gave focus to [e]arly nationalism (Dutch [In]dies) • Nationalist movement [in] French Indochina began [w]ith rising in Tonking • Invalid and Old-Age [P]ensions Act passed [by] Australian federal [g]overnment • 14 Nov: Death of [C]hinese Empress Tzu Hsi [a]nd succession of boy [e]mperor, Pu Yi	• Assassination of Japanese resident-general in Korea • Mar: Anglo–Siamese treaty placed unfederated states in north of Malay peninsula under UK control	• 1st national assembly met in China; half members elected, half appointed by throne • Feb: Chinese army occupied Lhasa (Tib); Dalai Lama fled to India • Aug: Korea annexed by Japan	• 10 Oct: Revolution began in China, led to overthrow of Manchu dynasty • Dec: Sun Yat-sen elected president of provisional Chinese government (to Feb 1912)	• In New Zealand, new Reform Party gained power under leadership of W. Ferguson Massey, ending 42 years of Liberal government • 12 Feb: Emperor Pu Yi forced to abdicate; provisional republic of China declared • Jul: Death of Meiji emperor, Mutsuhito; accession of his son Yoshihito began Taishō era in Japan	• Dalai Lama returned to Tibet, following withdrawal of Chinese occupying force • 8 Apr: 1st Chinese elected parliament	• Following outbreak of WWI, German possessions of New Guinea captured by Australia, W Samoa by New Zealand, Pacific Is (Marianas, Carolines, Marshalls) and territory in Shandong province (China) by Japan (all formally ceded as mandates by League of Nations after 1919) • Aug: Japan, Australia and New Zealand declared war on Germany
• Nov: World's 1st aerial [b]ombing raid, by Italians [in] N Africa					• Apr: International Women's Peace Conference, The Hague (Neth)	

13

Datafile

The pursuit of power has always been closely linked with economic development. Growth in industry, agriculture and transportation supports an expanding population, creates trade opportunities and provides the economic surplus necessary for expansion and war. The wars of the early 20th century drew their rationale and their economic support from the industrializing economies of the Great Powers, and their outcome was determined as much by economic strength as by military prowess. At the turn of the century, the rapid industrial growth of Germany was the most important factor in the upsetting of the European balance of power, while in the Far East Japan emerged as the dominant industrial power.

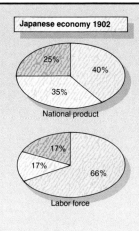

Japanese economy 1902

National product: 40%, 35%, 25%

Labor force: 66%, 17%, 17%

- Agriculture
- Services
- Manufacturing

◀ In the mid-19th century, the Japanese economy was almost entirely agricultural. Some 50 years later, the manufacturing and service sectors together accounted for more than half the national product while employing only a third of the labor force – evidence that Japan was developing into a well-articulated industrial state with the economic strength to make an impact on the world political scene.

▼ Russia entered the 20th century with an overwhelmingly agricultural economy. Industrialization was beginning to gather momentum in the western cities, deriving strength from the development of a national rail network to bring food and raw materials to the cities and distribute goods around the huge but largely unexploited domestic market. The predominance of the railway sector is clear – levels of employment in other industries were low compared to both the total Russian population and other European industrial Powers.

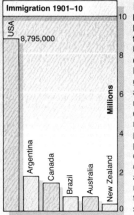

Immigration 1901–10

USA 8,795,000; Argentina; Canada; Brazil; Australia; New Zealand

(Millions, 0–10)

▶ By 1900 the United States had already emerged as the largest industrial nation in the world. Within Europe the UK still maintained a lead over Germany, but the latter's far greater rate of growth was fast eroding that advantage. The other four major European Powers could match neither the UK nor Germany, and excepting possibly Russia, did not possess the resources to close the gap. Economic competition in Europe was a matter of Anglo-German rivalry, but both were threatened on the world scene by the United States.

Manufacturing output 1900

24%, 22%, 18%, 13%, 9%, 7%, 7%, 2%

- USA
- Other
- UK
- Germany
- Russia
- France
- Austria–Hungary
- Italy

Employment in Russia 1904

Rail transport; Other factories; Cotton; Metallurgy; Other textiles; Other metalworking; Water transport; Mineral mining; Sugar; Coal mining

(Thousands, 0–800)

▲ World industrialization was attended by a mass migration – largely from Europe to the Americas. Early industrialization in western Europe produced a surplus working population, while agricultural improvement to the east produced a whole generation of unemployed people with no factories into which to move. The huge underdeveloped hinterlands of the Americas and Australasia served as a magnet for these jobless millions. In economic terms, the major beneficiary was the United States.

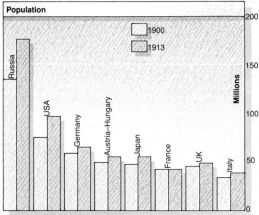

Population

- 1900
- 1913

Russia; USA; Germany; Austria–Hungary; Japan; France; UK; Italy

(Millions, 0–200)

◀ Population growth was essential to economic growth at this stage of industialization, and in an era when military might depended upon the ability to mobilize mass conscript armies, the birth rate was also a matter of strategic importance. With the exception of France, all the Great Powers were experiencing dynamic population growth, although in the case of Russia, Italy and Austria-Hungary, retarded industrial development made if difficult to translate people into economic or military power.

▼ Railway development provided the support system for economic growth, transporting raw materials and produce to industrial cities, and manufactured goods to inland markets or to ports for export overseas. It was also critical to the development of military capacity, through the mass mobilization of armies and the ability to supply those armies at the front. The effectiveness of Russian rail development is distorted by the geographical scale of the nation; of the major powers Germany had the most advanced rail network.

▶ Industrialization was attended by the large-scale movement of population from the countryside to the factories of the city. At the turn of the century, well over half the populations of the Great Powers still lived in the country, but the proportion of city dwellers was steadily rising, giving a useful indication of industrial might. One other aspect of urbanization was soon to play a central role – the collection of workers into factories and industrial slums would accelerate the emergence of class consciousness.

Urban population

- 1900
- 1913

Russia; USA; Germany; Austria–Hungary; Japan; France; UK; Italy

(Total population (percent), 0–40)

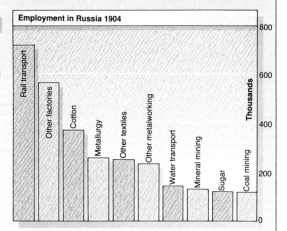

Building railroads

- 1890
- 1910

Russia; Germany; France; UK; Italy; Spain; Belgium; Switzerland

(Kilometers (thousands), 0–80)

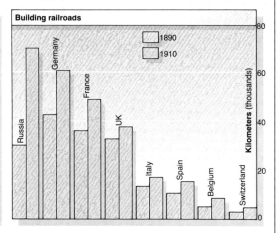

POWERS AND EMPIRES

The first years of the 20th century were marked by the scramble for colonial possessions. In the previous decades new imperial states, such as Germany and Italy, had emerged to rival the traditional colonial powers of Britain, France and Russia. They were soon followed by the United States and Japan. By 1900 sub-Saharan Africa and many of the Pacific regions had been conquered.

Except for Russia, whose armies marched across Asia, the Great Powers of Europe gained access to their colonies by sea. Accordingly, this was a period in which the major instrument of national power was seen to be the navy. Each country with imperial ambitions strove to build large fleets of battleships and, especially in the Far East, to secure coaling stations and naval bases.

Increases in the armies of Europe were comparatively insignificant and considered far less urgent. Earlier rivalries between military blocs – the Dual Alliance of France and Russia on the one hand and the Triple Alliance of Germany, Austria-Hungary and Italy on the other – still

existed, but the tension was much less than it had been a decade earlier. The great-power states could thus afford to direct their attention largely outside Europe, in pursuit of what the Germans called *Weltpolitik*, or world politics. Only Austria-Hungary did not take part in the race for the colonies and seek "a place in the sun".

How effectively a government pursued its colonial ambitions became important for electoral success at the national polls. Canvassing in the British general elections of 1900 focused on the war in South Africa to quell the Boers, while the American election of the same year dwelled on the conquest of the Philippines. In Germany, the 1907 election was dubbed the "Hottentot election" because the government's handling of uprisings by Hottentot tribes in German-controlled southwest and east Africa was a major electoral issue. Later, colonial clashes in Morocco, annexations of Bosnia and Tripoli and the race to build battlefleets to safeguard or further imperial ambitions colored the domestic politics of the great-power states.

▼ European sovereigns gathered for the funeral of Britain's King Edward VII in 1910. The period before the World War I represented an Indian summer for Europe's royalty, who ruled vast empires in grand style, but within a decade war and revolution would destroy their power for ever.

▶ **The idyllic face of imperialism – George V of Britain on an Indian tiger shoot. To many eyes, the European imperial experience was a great endeavor, at once romantic and worthy. Exotic lands provided a playground for the wealthy and a challenge to civilized nations intent on shouldering the "white man's burden" and bringing enlightenment and improvement to the "uncivilized" and (hopefully) grateful natives.**

▲ **The darker side of imperialism – a Congolese child mutilated by Belgian colonial soldiers. Everywhere in Africa and Asia the imposition of European rule destroyed traditional patterns of life and was backed by the brutal suppression of any form of resistance.**

▶▶ **A poster advertising a French colonial exhibition. European governments used imperialist propaganda to distract their people from domestic problems. The government of France, a country defeated in the Franco-Prussian war, beset by political instability, and fearful of the rising power of Germany on its frontier, tried to foster national pride in colonial expansion in Africa. Imperial policies undoubtedly brought short-term political gains, but did little to strengthen the nation and involved an already unstable Europe in a furious competition for overseas influence that heightened the risk of war.**

Imperialist Propaganda

In the industrial age of mass-production and increasing literacy, the press played an important part in swaying public opinion to support colonial expansionism. Imperial enthusiasts described the "opening up" of the nation's latest overseas acquisitions in glowing terms. Some colonial territories were said to be important as future markets, or as sources of raw materials or precious metals. Others – especially those that adjoined existing colonies or lay along major sea routes – had "strategic value". Sometimes protecting the lives of missionaries or explorers was given as a justification for intervention or conquest. Often more emotional arguments were used, although wrapped up in pseudo-scientific language. The Social-Darwinists, who analyzed historical trends in terms that derived from Charles Darwin's theory of natural evolution, claimed that any country that did not expand its power beyond its frontiers would face decline.

Imperial rivalries also produced nationalist arguments. The British referred to the Anglo-Saxon genius for colonial rule. The French had a "civilizing mission" to perform, the Americans a "manifest destiny" in Latin America and the Pacific, and the Russians something similar in the Balkans and in Asia.

The arguments from ethnic and cultural identity used to justify imperial expansion were, however, double-edged. They also aroused passions among the peoples who had been conquered. In Ireland, for instance, a culturally-driven "Celtic revival" was under way. Similar movements were stirring among the Czechs, Poles, Finns, and Balkan peoples, and nationalist circles were growing up in Egypt and India. In Budapest, Theodor Herzl (1860–1904) began promoting Zionism, an ideological movement calling for the return of Jews to a national, territorial homeland in Palestine.

▲ **German cartoon of imperial growth.**

Patterns of colonialism

By far the richest and most powerful of the colonial empires was the British Empire. It sprawled over almost a quarter of the Earth's land mass and included about a quarter of the world's population. Some parts of it were made up of self-governing Dominions like Canada and Australia. Others included the British Raj in India – the "jewel in the imperial crown" – and an array of older Crown Colonies and naval bases as well as newer acquisitions in northeast, central and southern Africa. In effect, there were really four British empires under the Crown, each governed differently.

France's colonial empire, occupying some ten million square kilometers (four million square miles), was administered much more uniformly. Heavily centered upon northwest and equatorial Africa, it also included territories in the West Indies, southeast Asia, and the Pacific. Germany held territories in Africa and the Pacific covering an area about a quarter the size of France's colonies. However, as a latecomer Germany had acquired chiefly tracts of jungle and desert. Italy, Portugal and Belgium also had colonies in Africa. Russia's colonial expansion had been achieved by a persistent push eastward across Asia. Of the

China, the Near East or North Africa, the colonizer risked provoking rivals to join forces in opposition.

Even Britain, the greatest of the traditional world powers, began to experience the strain of maintaining its erstwhile policy of "splendid isolation". While the bulk of the British army was pinned down in South Africa in the war against the Boers (1899–1902), it could not intervene to settle any dispute that might arise in the colonies. Moreover, foreign battlefleets presented a growing challenge to Britain's naval power, increasing the pressure in areas of the world such as China and Persia where Britain had important commercial or strategic interests. Consequently, the foreign secretary, the Marquess of Lansdowne and his colleague A.J. Balfour (who became prime minister in 1902) were forced to reconsider the question of making regional agreements, or forming alliances, with other countries.

In 1901 Britain conceded to the United States its rights to a half-share in the control of the future Panama Canal, and two years later accepted American territorial claims along the Alaska-British Columbia border. Britain reasoned that it was better to secure American goodwill through concessions than to risk a quarrel when so many serious interests were at stake elsewhere.

Similar considerations prompted other deals throughout Europe. The French and the Italians were secretly beginning to sink their differences over colonial territories in North Africa, while at the same time some of the French politicians hoped to secure British agreement to a takeover of Morocco. German entrepreneurs also looked to Britain for financial and diplomatic aid to develop the Baghdad railway. With international relations in an unusual state of flux, European foreign ministries warily watched each other for potential rivals or potential partners.

Powers outside Europe, Japan had acquired overseas territories in the Pacific and Far East following a victorious war with China 1894–95, as had the United States after the Spanish-American war of 1898.

Despite the jingoism of the age, many radicals and liberals in Europe were opposed to this imperialism. They believed that annexing other peoples' territories was morally indefensible, and the arms race a waste of the nation's resources. Colonial policies, they argued, served the interests of the armed forces, the financiers, the munitions manufacturers and the press barons, not the people – a view that found support among the rising forces of organized labor. Trade union leaders contended that passions over empires were being aroused to divert attention and resources away from pressing domestic issues. Opponents of imperialism in the United States also stressed that colonization opposed the country's own heritage of being born out of an anti-imperial revolt.

Great-power alliances
As the jostling for colonies and spheres of influence increased, it became harder for any of the powers involved to act alone. Whether in

Trouble in the Far East

A crisis looming in the Far East brought about changes in the diplomatic scene. In China, irregular nationalist groups known as the Boxers rose up against foreign missionaries and diplomats, prompting the dispatch of an international army to Peking in 1900. These events seriously weakened the Manchu empire and left foreign forces in charge of key areas. Britain, worried by Russia's desire to maintain its grip on Manchuria and northern China, sought the cooperation of Germany to uphold the territorial status quo in the region. The government in Berlin, however, wanted neither to antagonize Russia nor to help Britain out of a jam, and the Anglo-German alliance talks of 1901 petered out by the end of the year.

The Japanese, on the other hand, were keen to help to check Russian expansion into Manchuria and especially Korea. Under the terms of the Anglo-Japanese alliance signed in January 1902, Britain and Japan agreed to come to each other's aid if its ally was at war with more than one enemy over Far Eastern issues, but to stay neutral if its ally was fighting only one foe. This treaty, which commited Britain, under certain circumstances, to fight for another Power, virtually ended the country's policy of "splendid isolation". It also reduced the need for an alliance with Germany, which was emerging as an ever more dangerous rival. By 1902–03 an Anglo-German press war was raging and many Britons viewed with alarm the massive expansion of Admiral Alfred von Tirpitz's High Seas Fleet in the North Sea.

The French too were worried about the German buildup. After the British King Edward VII's highly successful visit to Paris in May 1903, voices in both Britain and France urged an end to their countries' long-standing colonial quarrels in Africa, stressing the need to hold together against Germany. The new mood suited the ambitions of the able French foreign minister Théophile Delcassé to gain a free hand for his country in Morocco by befriending Britain and at the same time detaching Italy from the Triple Alliance. The German chancellor von Bülow proved to be no match for Delcassé, and his bungled attempts to play off the powers against each other, coupled with Kaiser Wilhelm II's impulsiveness, only further compromised German diplomatic efforts.

The Russo-Japanese war

Japan had sought to contain Russian expansion in the Far East by diplomacy, but influential circles around Czar Nicholas II seemed more determined to make Russia the dominant power in the Orient than to negotiate seriously. In February 1904 the Japanese, unable to ignore Russian actions in the Far East any longer, launched a preemptive strike at Russian warships anchored in Port Arthur.

At the outset of the Russo-Japanese war, many believed that Russia would be the eventual victor. It had the largest army in the world and a mighty fleet too. Moreover, a European Power would allegedly always be superior to an Asiatic one. Realistically, however, Japan had an important strategic advantage in being much closer to the

The Boxer Rising

The Chinese Boxer rising of 1900 was both the long-term result of progressive European penetration of the Chinese economy together with the steady disintegration of the corrupt and inefficient Qing dynasty, and the short-term consequence of the Chinese government's attempt to use popular unrest to oppose colonial settlements.

Colonial exploitation of China gained momentum in the 1890s. In the same decade a feeble modernization program of the Chinese government received a serious blow when its forces were crushed in the Sino-Japanese war (1894–95). Losing power to mount direct opposition, the regime of the dowager-empress Cixi secretly encouraged the growth of a popular resistance movement, The Society of Harmonious Fists (popularly known as the Boxers), and helped to whip up anti-European feeling among its youthful members. The Boxer movement was fired by a hatred of anything foreign, particularly the Christian religion being preached by missionaries, and developed a semi-mystical ideology which included the belief that its members were immune to foreign bullets. Small-scale attacks on foreign nationals and their

▲ US soldiers at the foot of China's Great Wall. After the rebellion the imperial government were unable to prevent foreign troops from moving at will throughout the country.

▲ ◄ European governments used graphic accounts of Boxer atrocities to whip up popular support for intervention.

◄ The foreign powers collaborated against the Boxer rebellion – the soldiers and marines in this photograph represent eight different fighting forces.

Chinese associates grew in number all over north China, and even British reinforcements on their way to Beijing to protect resident nationals came under fire.

On 14 June 1900 a government-inspired uprising broke out in Beijing. The German minister was assassinated, European property sacked and foreign legations besieged as frenzied mobs ran riot. As a result, six foreign nations, in a rare exercise, collaborated in a joint military relief mission to Beijing. The Boxers fought bravely to oppose the march, but, lightly armed and poorly organized, they succumbed to superior firepower and the legations were relieved in mid-August. A wave of brutal repression followed all over the affected area, until resistance finally collapsed. In 1901 the

foreign powers imposed the Peking Protocol, forcing China to pay an annual indemnity, accept the stationing of troops in its territory and submit to foreign control of the capital's diplomatic quarter. This settlement intensified antiforeign feeling and totally discredited the old Qing dynasty. Anti-imperial nationalist and republican movements attracted scores of new recruits, and when fresh unrest broke out in 1912 it rapidly developed into a full-scale revolution which destroyed the Chinese imperial government in a matter of months. A republic was set up, and a National Assembly met in February 1913, at which the Nationalists (Guomindang) were the majority party. Yuan Shikai was appointed president, and forced through a new constitution in 1914.

combat zones. To reach the Far East, Russia had to send its troops along the 10,000-kilometer (6,000-mile) single-track trans-Siberian railway, and its reserve fleet had to steam from the Baltic and around Africa and the East Indies. Japan also enjoyed superior organization. The Japanese navy was especially highly trained in gunnery, and the army drilled in making fearless assaults on enemy machine-gun posts, trenches and barbed wire. The Russian troops fought hard, but suffered from poor leadership and at home the war became increasingly unpopular.

Eventually, at the end of 1904, Port Arthur fell to the besieging Japanese, who advanced irresistibly on to Mukden. Worse was to follow. The Russian Baltic fleet, after an epic round-the-world voyage around the world full of incidents (including firing on British trawlers on the Dogger Bank, which almost sparked off an Anglo-Russian war), sailed into the straits of Tsushima in May 1905, to be annihilated by the Japanese navy.

In Russia itself, the hardships caused by the war and the increasing unpopularity of the czarist regime led to widespread riots, strikes and demands for reform. Moreover, the government could no longer count on the loyalty of the armed forces to quell unrest. Throughout 1905 the whole country trembled on the brink of a full-scale revolution. Russia had lost its status as a Great Power, the treasury was bankrupt, and it had become impossible to raise the huge foreign loans needed to continue the war.

Following mediation by the US president

▼ **Japanese soldiers survey the sunken Russian warships in Port Arthur. The Russian loss of the harbor was the product of Japanese superiority on land and sea. The Russian fleet was unable to break the blockade imposed by the better-trained Japanese navy while the heroic resistance of the Port Arthur garrison could only delay defeat, because the Japanese army blocked the way for any military relief force. Unwilling to face certain loss at sea, Russian warships were eventually sunk at their mooring by land-based siege artillery.**

The 1905 Revolution

As Russia faced defeat by Japan, public opinion voiced open criticism of the government and political parties expressed sectional discontents. The workers were partly organized by Marxists as the Russian Social Democratic Labor party, the Socialist Revolutionaries claimed to represent the peasants, and the Constitutional Democrats (Kadets) called for democratic reform.

Matters came to a head with the "Bloody Sunday" episode of 22 January 1905. A strike in St Petersburg begun in December 1904 gave rise to a demonstration in which the priest Father Gapon (himself a police agent) was persuaded by socialists to present a political petition to the czar. The huge crowds that amassed were fired on by troops, causing about 200 deaths. Strikes and demonstrations ensued throughout the year. The humiliating Portsmouth Treaty, which ended hostilities with Japan, sustained the dual mood of protest and nationalist outrage. In October 1905 the czar was forced to concede a national assembly (Duma).

Basic freedoms were introduced and gradually the opposition parties, including the Kadets, who had boycotted the elections, and the socialist Soviet of Workers' Deputies, who had called for an armed uprising, took part in the Duma. Having divided the forces of revolution, the government, under prime minister Stolypin, proceeded to carry out a dual policy of reform and repression.

▶ **Bloody Sunday, 1905, at St Petersburg.**

▼ Crude imagery to glorify Japanese success. The blockade of Port Arthur and the role of Russia's navy are parodied here as stakes are driven in to seal Russian mouths and render them toothless. Such propaganda made a direct appeal to a susceptibly bellicose public.

▲ Racist imagery to bolster Russian resistance. The depiction of the noble, upright Russian, beleaguered by a host of subhuman Asiatics typified European incredulity at the successful expansion of an Eastern culture hitherto seen as barbarous and backward.

Theodore Roosevelt, in August 1905 Russia and Japan signed the Treaty of Portsmouth, under which Japan gained a protectorate over Korea and southern Manchuria. The war had launched Japan as a great power, but had been a profound humiliation for Russia. The outcome was ideal for Britain, whose interests in China were safeguarded by Japan's victory. The British could now recall their Far Eastern battleships to join the growing force being assembled to keep watch on Germany's powerful High Seas Fleet nearer home. Not surprisingly, Britain hastened to renew its 1902 alliance with Japan.

The Franco-British settlement

During the Russo-Japanese war the great fear of Britain and France, as respective allies of Japan and Russia, was that they might be drawn in to fight on opposite sides, just at a time when relations between them were improving. This fear grew with suspicions of intrigue by Germany to escalate the war in order to enhance its own position and weaken that of the combatants.

Thus, in 1904, in a move to resolve their outstanding differences and seek closer cooperation, the governments of London and Paris announced a wide-ranging colonial settlement. The French agreed to recognize Britain's claims in Egypt and the Nile valley in exchange for British support for France's position in Morocco. The agreement also committed the signatories to helping each other to achieve their aims. The French foreign minister, Delcassé, anticipating problems with Germany over Morocco, was keen that the new

entente cordiale should have an anti-German thrust, but his British counterpart, Lansdowne, was less enthusiastic about this. Delcassé also managed to secure the Spaniards' support for his country's policy, by offering them a sphere of influence in Morocco.

The collapse of Russia in 1905, however, represented a serious setback to France's plans. Since the early 1890s there had been a power balance in Europe between the Dual Alliance (France and Russia) and the Triple Alliance (Germany, Austria-Hungary and Italy). While Italy's commitment to the alliance was half-hearted, and Austria-Hungary was riven with internal conflict between ethnic groups, imperial Germany more than made up for the weaknesses of the other two member states. The industrial powerhouse of Europe, it had a modern battlefleet and a large, efficient army, and was growing stronger year by year.

Before 1905 Germany's ability to dominate Europe had been checked by the military and economic expansion of Russia. But with its ally now weakened by war and revolution, France alone was not strong enough to oppose Germany. Kaiser Wilhelm II and his advisers, many of whom had a diplomatic score to settle with Delcassé, read the situation only too well. In a move to thwart French efforts to take over Morocco, the German foreign ministry first encouraged the kaiser to pay a symbolic visit to Tangiers in March 1905, and then backed this up by making veiled threats to settle the dispute with France by force. How serious a threat this was remains unclear, but in military terms it would have been an opportune time for Germany to attack France. Fearing the worst, the French premier dismissed Delcassé in June 1905 and agreed to attend an international conference to settle Morocco's future. On the German side, Chancellor von Bülow was made a prince for his great diplomatic victory.

Anglo-German rivalry

Germany's diplomatic successes were, however, short-lived. In July 1905 the kaiser met the czar in Björkö, Sweden, to seek a new German–Russian alliance, but the proposal was rejected by the Russian government, who preferred to maintain the older ties with France. Germany's diplomatic initiatives and naval policies were the cause of growing concern to Britain, which already suspected that ministers in Berlin had been secretly plotting to involve the British Empire in the war in the Far East. Any agreement that the Germans made with the Russians, Britain believed, would be directed against British interests. Moreover, under Admiral von Tirpitz Germany was building a battlefleet, apparently to challenge the Royal Navy's control of the North Sea.

In late 1904 and early 1905 some extreme politicians in Britain had argued that the German High Seas Fleet should be "copenhagened" – sunk in port before it could grow any bigger. The British government dismissed the idea as absurd but the possibility still alarmed the kaiser. In this atmosphere of growing suspicion and mistrust, some British officials drew up contingency plans to help France in the event of an attack by Germany over the Morocco dispute. For almost a century Britain had avoided a policy of what it called "the continental commitment", since any military intervention in Europe would break with Britain's liberal traditions and be unpopular at home.

Now, voices within the newly formed Imperial General Staff argued that, if Britain did nothing while Germany overran France, then Britain too would suffer a serious strategic setback. How to support the French without involving unacceptable levels of commitment was a problem that

▲ Colonial postage stamps reflect the scale and variety of the imperial experience. European rule was underpinned by a massive colonial bureaucracy and a communications system in which the steamship and the mail service were central.

▼ The German kaiser leads his troops through Tangiers in 1905. Colonial rivalries reflected more deep-set European antagonisms, and the series of diplomatic crises away from the European continent increased the likelihood of war in Europe.

Imperial Powers in 1900

ALASKA (US)

CANADA

UNITED STATES OF AMERICA

NEWFOU

PACIFIC OCEAN

BAHAMAS (Br)

CUBA US occ

BRITISH HONDURAS

JAMAICA

Leeward Islands

Windward Islands

TRINIDAD

BRITISH GUIANA
DUTCH GUIA
FRENCH

European empires
- Belgian
- British
- Dutch
- French
- German
- Italian
- Portuguese
- Spanish
- Other important power

Scale 1:115 000 000
0 — 3000 km
0 — 2000 mi

Falkla

Balfour's Conservative government bequeathed to its Liberal successor at the end of 1905.

The Moroccan and Persian settlements

An international conference held at the Spanish town of Algeciras early in 1906 decided the future of Morocco. The settlement gave France and its junior partner Spain effective control of the Moroccan police and finances, and was a bitter diplomatic blow to the Germans. Only Austria-Hungary supported the German claim, and did so reluctantly. Britain strongly backed the French, and was determined to improve Anglo-Russian relations in Asia, a move much encouraged by the French, who sought to bring together its new entente partner, Britain, and its old ally, Russia, in an alliance that would hold Germany in check.

After tough, difficult negotiations, Britain and Russia concluded an agreement in August 1907. Sometimes referred to as the Asian entente, it

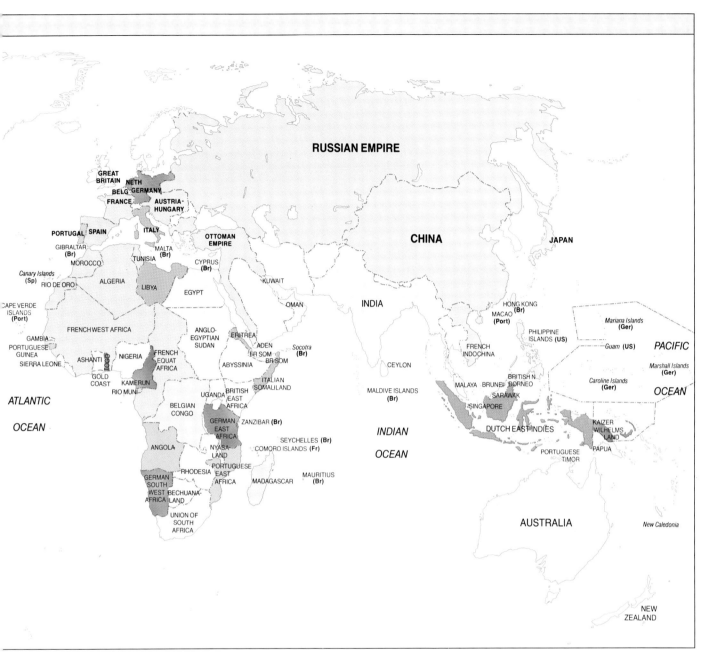

RUSSIAN EMPIRE

GREAT
BRITAIN NETH
BELG GERMANY
FRANCE AUSTRIA-
HUNGARY
PORTUGAL SPAIN ITALY
GIBRALTAR MALTA OTTOMAN
(Br) (Br) EMPIRE
MOROCCO TUNISIA CYPRUS
(Br)
Canary Islands
(Sp) RIO DE ORO ALGERIA LIBYA
EGYPT
CAPE VERDE OMAN
ISLANDS KUWAIT
(Port)
GAMBIA FRENCH WEST AFRICA ANGLO-
PORTUGUESE EGYPTIAN ERITREA
GUINEA SUDAN ADEN
SIERRA LEONE ASHANTI NIGERIA FRENCH ER SOM Socotra
GOLD EQUAT BR SOM (Br)
COAST KAMERUN AFRICA ABYSSINIA
RIO MUNI UGANDA BRITISH ITALIAN
EAST SOMALILAND
BELGIAN AFRICA
CONGO GERMAN ZANZIBAR (Br)
EAST
AFRICA SEYCHELLES (Br)
ANGOLA NYASA- COMORO ISLANDS (Fr)
LAND
PORTUGUESE
RHODESIA EAST MAURITIUS
GERMAN AFRICA MADAGASCAR (Br)
SOUTH BECHUANA-
WEST LAND
AFRICA
UNION OF
SOUTH
AFRICA

CHINA JAPAN

INDIA HONG KONG
MACAO (Br)
(Port) Mariana Islands
PHILIPPINE (Ger)
ISLANDS (US) Guam (US) PACIFIC
FRENCH
INDOCHINA Marshall Islands
CEYLON (Ger)
BRITISH N Caroline Islands
MALAYA BRUNEI BORNEO (Ger) OCEAN
MALDIVE ISLANDS SARAWAK
(Br) SINGAPORE
KAIZER
DUTCH EAST INDIES WILHELMS
INDIAN LAND
PORTUGUESE PAPUA
OCEAN TIMOR

ATLANTIC

OCEAN

AUSTRALIA New Caledonia

NEW
ZEALAND

divided Persia into spheres of Russian and British influence in the north and south respectively, with a neutral "buffer zone" in the middle. The treaty also stabilized the status of the Indian border territories of Tibet and Afghanistan and marked the end of a century of Anglo-Russian rivalry in central Asia.

The end of *Weltpolitik*
The year 1907 also marked the end of the era of "world policy" and a return to the European political arena. After Roosevelt's energetic presidency, in which the United States had helped to end the Russo-Japanese war and participated in the Algeciras conference, the country returned to a more isolationist diplomacy under President William H. Taft. By then, the position of the United States as the strongest power in the Western Hemisphere was unchallengeable.

Affairs in the Far East had also stabilized, Japan and Russia having secretly agreed, in 1907, on

zones of influence in Manchuria. The "scramble for Africa" too seemed virtually complete, and Britain's fears over the defense of India were partly allayed by its Asian entente with Russia.

As for Germany, events had dealt a series of blows to its colonial ambitions and hopes of achieving the status of a great world power. The United States blocked any German expansion in Latin America, and Japan did the same in the Far East. France and Britain held the initiative in Morocco and Egypt. Russia and Britain exercised joint influence in Persia, and opposed the Germans' Baghdad railway project in Mesopotamia. It seemed to Germany that Britain, France and Russia, despite their ideological differences, were drawing closer together and eyeing Germany with hostile intent. The cry arose that the Fatherland was being "encircled" by jealous foes, and the time had come, Prussian conservatives argued, to forget about distant colonies and to prepare to engage enemies much closer to home.

▲ The map of the world in 1900 shows the effects of several decades of frenetic imperial expansion. Africa and large parts of Asia were either under direct imperial rule or had been heavily penetrated by foreign economic interests. The export of European rivalries to a wider stage had carried the flags of Britain, France, Germany, Russia and others across the desert, jungle and mountains with little regard for economic or political rationality. Many colonies were unstable, underdeveloped hinterlands which cost more to maintain than they returned to European treasuries – and whose very existence threatened the stability of the international political order.

POWERS AND GREAT POWERS

The Great Powers were the states around which the deadly game of international diplomacy revolved in the years before 1900. They were not necessarily large in size. China, though an enormous country, was not considered a Great Power while Japan, a group of small islands, was. Another group of small islands, the United Kingdom, was arguably the world's leading Power for most of the 19th century.

There were five main conditions of great-power status. First, military strength. A Great Power required land armies to ensure continental dominance and naval power to gain and defend overseas colonies. Second, an industrial base. Guns and battleships presupposed coal, iron, steel and engineering industries. A railway network was needed for the swift mobilization of troops. Third, colonies. These provided raw materials such as oil, rubber and metals, markets for exports and investment opportunities for capital. They were also training-grounds and garrisons for troops. Areas such as China or the Ottoman Empire, which were themselves being colonized, were "sick men" rather than Great Powers. Fourth, a certain degree of social cohesion. One way to check social unrest and the progress of socialism was social reform; another, and commoner, way was the official encouragement of nationalism by mass education, jingoistic organizations and the popular press. Politicians and generals could not expect to mobilize men and resources for war without the services of nationalism. Fifth, national cohesion. States with one dominant nationality tended to be in a strong position. Those possessing numerous national minorities, or evenly balancing national minorities, were nstable, with the conflict of loyalties and confusion of languages extending into the army itself.

In the mid-19th century, when Britain was evidently the most powerful nation, there was a certain tranquility on the international scene. Then came serious challenges for great-power status, particularly from Germany, Russia, the United States and Japan, and immense rivalry for recognition as the greatest Power. Worst of all, there was the fear of demotion from the "league-table" of Powers, and of annihilation in the event of war. No effective European or global organizations existed to keep the peace; the Powers were driven into a relentless arms race. There was a scramble for colonies, first in Africa, then in the Far East and Middle East, to win extra points for the league-table, but the scramble multiplied instances of contact between powers and possibilities of conflict. Safety was sought in numbers. Ententes and alliances were formed to isolate enemies and increase military strength by proxy. But the effect was to divide the world into two armed camps, from which before 1917 only the United States stood aloof. The system was unstable, the stakes were repeatedly raised, and in the end national honor excluded any kind of retreat, the only alternative to fullscale war.

◀ Theodore Roosevelt inspecting progress on the construction of the Panama Canal. Even at the turn of the century such "photo opportunities" generated symbols of state power: advanced technology plus political authority.

▶ When "your country needs you" the abstract forces of state authority and military might are transformed into the expendable flesh and blood of able-bodied men. Here young Russians undergo medical examination before being sent to the front in 1905.

▶ At the level of international diplomacy states act as individuals writ large as well as having a unique cultural and political history which give them a mythical personality. This French cartoon vividly expresses the natural tendency for European nations to be stereotyped in various states of passivity, submission or aggression. It also dramatizes the dynamic, precarious nature of the balance of power.

▲ The Great War dramatically exposed the sinister relationship between military might and productive capacity at the heart of modern state power. This accumulation of army stores was needed to sustain the "war of attrition" of 1914–18.

▼ Military hardware, formed by an alliance between state and industry, underpins the political initiatives of modern states. Without the guns rolling off the Krupp assembly lines, Wilhelmine Germany could never have behaved as a "Great Power".

Datafile

The decade and a half before the outbreak of World War I witnessed an unprecedented build-up of armaments. As alliances and antagonisms hardened, and as commercial competition added heat to existing political rivalries, governments devoted larger amounts of economic output to expanding armies and navies. Europe was experiencing a huge arms race, and as much attention was paid to the numbers of men under military training and warships under construction as to industrial output or social welfare.

Germany was a military threat to its European neighbors because it could exploit its coal and iron resources and efficiently mobilize a growing population. Britain remained predominant at sea because the government could justify heavy expenditure on warship construction to a population which equated maritime supremacy with national greatness. The other Powers, however, could only maintain the pace at the cost of putting great strain on their weaker economies.

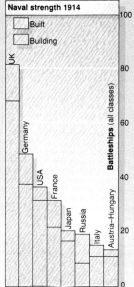

Naval strength 1914

◀ Britain was unusual among the European powers in devoting the bulk of defense expenditure to the navy. Because it did not maintain a huge conscript army, Britain never lost the lead in the naval building race, despite German efforts to create a rival battlefleet. The US fleet cmerged as the third largest but was not yet a factor in world politics.

▼ By 1910 the European Powers were maintaining large armies and had the capacity to call up many more trained reservists. The bare figures distort the reality of the situation, as the Russian army could not be efficiently deployed and the French army was maintained at too great a cost — the German army was more effective than either.

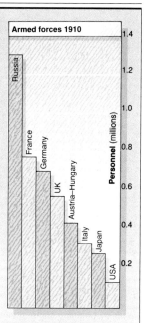

Armed forces 1910

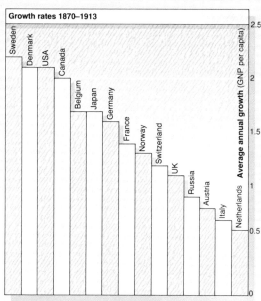

Growth rates 1870–1913

◀ Growth rates, which show how the economic balance was changing, were in many ways more significant than annual output figures. The US was continuing to get stronger, while Germany was outstripping France and overtaking a flagging UK — Japan was a rising force in the East, but in Europe itself Russia, Austria and Italy were sluggish performers.

▶ Arms expenditure varied only over a spread of about 15 million pounds equivalent among the five major spenders, but the relationship between that expenditure and total mobilizable resources showed the US, UK and Germany to be stronger than France or Russia, who would have severe problems in continuing the war.

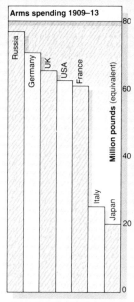

Arms spending 1909–13

▼ While it is extremely difficult to measure an "industrialization coefficient" of the rival Powers, the key manufacturing outputs, available horsepower and railway mileage in relation to population give a fair idea of overall economic strength. The US, UK and Germany had achieved a relatively high level of industrial resources in terms of their available human resources, but the other Powers lagged well behind. Even if the latter could find the men to send into the field in time of war, they did not have the raw materials, the manufacturing capacity or the transportation infrastructure to arm and supply them. The war would show that in Europe only the UK and Germany could sustain the effort of prolonged warfare.

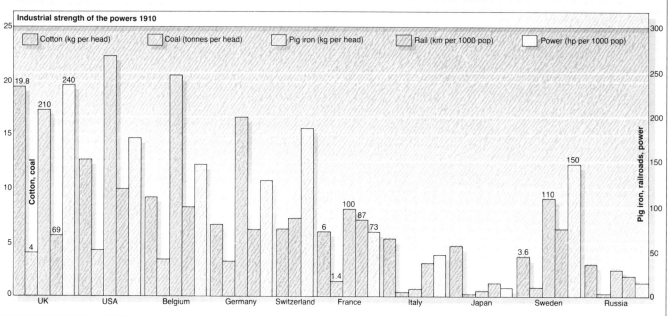

Industrial strength of the powers 1910

GREAT POWER RIVALRIES

The rivalries among the Great Powers of Europe over colonial possessions had for the most part been settled diplomatically, without the need to resort to war. The situation within Europe itself, however, proved to be less tractable. Germany's imperial aspirations abroad had been thwarted, largely by Anglo-French cooperation, and now Germany looked to the power struggle within Europe as a means of reasserting itself and restoring German pride.

From 1907 the political climate of Europe steadily worsened. At the second Hague Peace Conference of that year the Great Powers failed to agree on any substantial reduction in armaments or on the control of their use in war. Each of the participants supported proposals that would bring advantage to themselves, but fiercely resisted schemes that would hamper their freedom of action. Thus the British Liberal government's proposal for all-round cuts in naval expenditure and for a freeze on building new warships was opposed by Germany because it would leave Britain's Royal Navy with an unapproachable

The failure of arms control negotiations

Build-up of the British and German navies

Slav nationalism and the Balkan crises

The resurgence of Turkey

Mobilization in Europe

▼ A banner at the Hague Peace Conference of 1907 proclaims "Down with War". Intensifying political rivalries and rearmament programs alarmed many, but the failure of the Hague conference proved that nationalism remained a more potent force than pacifism.

superiority over the German High Seas Fleet.

Germany also rejected plans to enforce binding arbitration upon quarreling states, which it regarded as a ploy to neutralize the logistical advantages the German army enjoyed over its neighbors. The kaiser's government gained a particular notoriety by its opposition to proposals to limit war, but, despite appearances, it was not alone in preferring to defend national interests by force rather than by negotiation. The imperialist fervor, which in earlier decades had focused upon colonial disputes in Africa and the Pacific, now concentrated increasingly upon naval and military rivalries in Europe. Rightwing organizations such as naval and national-service leagues, who sought to mobilize public opinion behind larger armament expenditures, issued grim warnings about the evil intentions of jealous enemies. The press, appealing to patriotic emotions, fanned the flames of hostility. Against the barrage of nationalist propaganda, the opposition of peace societies, churchmen, left-liberals and socialists could make little headway.

The Anglo-German naval race

Britain and Germany were not alone in investing more and more money in battlefleets. Following its losses in the war with Japan, Russia plunged itself into a costly shipbuilding program, while in the Mediterranean, Italy and Austria-Hungary both sought to create modern navies, provoking a similar response from France. Outside Europe, Japan and the United States already possessed powerful navies.

By 1908 Britain and Germany, urged on by their naval lobbies, were building warships faster than anyone else. Admiral von Tirpitz, the head of the German navy, was making a determined bid to challenge the world's number-one maritime power in its own home waters.

The rivalry had sharpened after 1906, when the British Admiralty unveiled a new and much more powerful Dreadnought-class battleship, which made all earlier types obsolete. The Germans responded by announcing in their 1908 fleet program that, from then on, they would launch four Dreadnought-class vessels each year. Britain's Liberal government had hoped to hold down defence spending, but by early 1909 the allegation – vigorously denied by von Tirpitz – that Germany was laying down ships faster than permited by its own Navy Law – caused such outrage in Britain that H.H. Asquith's government was forced to order eight new battleships in one year.

By this time, too, almost all of the major warships of the Royal Navy, apart from a Mediter-

Early 20th-century Nationalism

Nationalism had become a powerful political force in the 19th century, drawing its inspiration from the French Revolution and the experience of Napoleonic conquest in Europe. Initially it was regarded as subversive, aiming at the overthrow of conservative dynasties, but by 1900 – after the successful unification of Germany and Italy – the nation state seemed to be the most successful form of political organization. Multinational empires, such as those of the Habsburgs or the Ottoman Turks, were in decline, at least within Europe. By this time nationalism had lost some of its revolutionary edge and become associated with conservative social forces – a useful cement binding different classes together in a national community, in opposition to the divisive influences of Marxist socialism, which emphasized class conflict. Nationalism stressed the importance of linguistic and historic communities, implying an organic connection between their members.

Nationalism appealed to large nations trying to eliminate the nationhood of smaller ones, for example the Germans and the Russians in their attitude towards the Poles, as well as to separatist movements within smaller nationalities rebelling against hegemony, such as the Irish or the Norwegians. During World War I nationalism received a strong boost as the result of the damage done to large central and east European empires. The defeat of czarist Russia paved the way for independence for the Poles, the Finns and the Baltic peoples. The Ukrainians also emerged as a nationality, although their attempts to gain political independence from their Russian masters failed.

After the United States entered the war, President Wilson announced, early in 1918, that he wished to see a peace based on the principle of national self-determination. This was encouraged at the negotiations to produce a postwar settlement, which reinforced disintegrating tendencies in the Habsburg monarchy, and in 1918 the Czechs and Slovaks gained national independence, as did the peoples of Yugoslavia. Hungary and Austria became small but independent states. The Ottoman Empire collapsed and a new, nationalistic Turkish state emerged under the charismatic leader Atatürk.

▶ Military training in Russia in the 1900s.

▲ A British postcard asserting that the *Pax Britannica* still prevailed in 1906.

▶ The German navy firing a ceremonial salute during a British royal visit. Britain had enjoyed unchallenged naval supremacy since the Napoleonic wars, and it was on the might of the Royal Navy that the security of the empire rested. German naval expansion threatened this security, pulling Britain directly into the highly-charged alliance politics of the continent. To Britain, the new German navy was a weapon purpose-built for use against it.

ranean fleet much reduced in size, were concentrated in the North Sea to shadow the German navy. Moreover, in accordance with Admiral J.A. Fisher's drastic reforms, dozens of small cruisers and gunboats deployed overseas – the naval symbol of a former age of *Pax Britannica* – were scrapped to release crews for the North Sea squadrons.

Crisis in the Balkans
A renewal of trouble in the Balkans, the scene of so many international disputes in the 19th century, was a further cause of rising tension in Europe. However, with the exception of spasmodic interest in reforming Turkish rule in Macedonia, the regions had been relatively peaceful since 1897, when Russia and Austria-Hungary had agreed that they would put Balkan issues "on ice".

That situation changed, beginning with a coup d'état in Serbia in 1903, which put into power a strongly nationalistic faction who looked to St Petersburg for guidance rather than to Vienna. These events encouraged many southern Slavs in Austria-Hungary, especially those suffering under the harsh rule of the Magyars. The overthrow of the regime of Sultan Abdul Hamid by the "Young Turks" in 1908 further stimulated Balkan nationalism, causing concern among other states that a reinvigorated Turkey might thwart their ambitions in the Balkans.

Russia, halted in its far-eastern drive, now showed renewed interest in the Balkans, though its military weakness forced it to proceed with caution. The Austrians were the first to make a move. Politicians and generals in Vienna, unable to solve the problem of the differences between

the Hungarians and the southern Slavs, feared that the Habsburg Empire might disintegrate unless the Serbian threat was checked. Foreign minister Alois von Aehrenthal tried to warn off the Serbs by threatening to annex the provinces of Bosnia and Herzegovina, which were already governed by the Empire. In exchange for granting this concession, the Russian foreign minister, Alexander Isvolsky, hoped to secure Vienna's support for Russian claims in the Black Sea Straits, the lifeline of its southern and western trade.

In October 1908, however, Austria-Hungary annexed Bosnia and Herzegovina without further warning. The Serbs were taken by surprise, but so too were the Russians, who now felt forced to defend the Slavic cause. Russia received only token support from its allies Britain and France, both of whom opposed Russian claims in the Straits, whereas Austria-Hungary had the strong backing of Germany. Given the state of its own armed forces, Russia had little choice but to concede without a fight. In fact, the Austro-

German action did not solve the problem of the south Slavs. It succeeded only in temporarily driving the opposition underground.

The repercussions of the Balkan crisis were felt across Europe. Italy was alarmed by Austria-Hungary's aggression, as was Britain by Germany's habit of diplomatic blackmail. When, over the next two years, the new German chancellor Bethmann Hollweg tried to make a neutrality treaty with Britain in exchange for slowing down the naval race, the government in London was unresponsive. Although, generally, the Liberal government favored arms reductions, it did not want to give Germany a free hand in Europe by committing itself not to intervene in any continental conflict.

The second Moroccan crisis

In 1911, a new crisis flared up in Morocco. In response to a rebellion by the Berbers, France dispatched a military expedition to Fez, then Morocco's capital. The Germans, fearing for their own colonial ambitions, sent a a warship to the Moroccan port of Agadir, to warn off the French from taking over the whole of the country. France and its prime minister Joseph Caillaux were eager to compromise. Britain, however, was alarmed at what it perceived to be a further example of Germany's browbeating diplomatic tactics.

In his famous "Mansion House" speech of 21 July 1911, the British Chancellor of the Exchequer, David Lloyd George, sent what was widely seen as a warning to Germany and a message of support to France. The speech infuriated German nationalists, who regarded it as another example of Britain jealously blocking Germany's legitimate overseas claims. However, the Berlin government was not prepared to go to war over the issue, and later that year accepted a compromise settlement that included part of the French Congo. French patriotism was so revived that, in January 1912, Caillaux was swept out of office and replaced by the strongly nationalistic Raymond Poincaré. The Moroccan crisis, though soon forgotten, added to the overall international tension.

Preparing for war

Until the Balkan and Moroccan crises the existence of rival alliance blocs had little direct influence on military or naval planning. Now, diplomacy and operations plans began to interact. At the time of the annexation of Bosnia and Herzegovina, the German and Austro-Hungarian general staffs had each found that the other had a plan that complicated its own operational scheme. Conrad, the Austrian chief of staff, hoped to eliminate Serbia early in the war, at the same time as Germany tied down the Russian armies. The Germans, however, were committed to the Schlieffen plan. This involved three-quarters of the German army launching a swift westwards strike, across Belgium, against France while Austria-Hungary kept Russia busy.

Since then the two general staffs had moved towards a closer cooperation, and had made contingency plans for a coalition war. Moreover, Germany, unlike in Chancellor Otto von Bismarck's time, was prepared to give the Habsburg Empire unconditional support. Thus, if Austria-Hungary went to war in the Balkans and Russia responded, German troops would be marching over the Belgian frontier a few days later.

In the other camp, too, military arrangements were being strengthened. France was pouring loans into Russia's strategic railway network to facilitate the transportation of the enormous Russian army towards the German and Austro-Hungarian borders. France had also replaced its earlier defensive war-plan with a scheme to launch assaults into Alsace-Lorraine (but keeping its armies out of Belgium). The Moroccan crisis had caused British defence planners to reconsider how best to assist France and Belgium in the event of a European war and a German push westwards. They rejected the idea of using naval operations alone, but favored, in principle, sending an expeditionary force across the Channel. All these decisions further strained international relations and increased the prospect of war.

The French government, encouraged by the nationalist revival, forced through a law extending the period of compulsory military service from two years to three, in a bid to create an army as large as Germany's. Russia, too, by 1912, had announced enormous increases in its armed forces for the following few years, provoking Germany to draw up its own army expansion plan of 1913. Moreover, the German Admiral von Tirpitz, despite opposition from the chancellor and army, managed to increase the size of the High Seas Fleet and its preparedness for battle.

When the British admiralty learned how many German warships would be kept in a state of readiness on the other side of the North Sea, it decided that, to meet the German challenge, there was no alternative but to withdraw the remainder of its large vessels from the Mediterranean. In

▲ The Balkan wars of 1912–13 were a curtain-raiser for the far larger war to follow. The Bulgarian capture of the Turkish fortress of Adrianople was an example of the heavy casualties that modern weaponry could inflict.

◄ The cost borne by the civilian population through brutality and requisition showed that war endangered the lives of not only soldiers.

► Cartoon showing the Russian and Austrian emperors wrenching possessions from a sullen and helpless Turkish sultan. The Great Powers came into direct and dangerous rivalry for influence in the unstable patchwork of small states left behind by the collapse of Ottoman power in an area controlled from Constantinople since the Middle Ages.

LE REVEIL DE LA QUESTION D'ORIENT
La Bulgarie proclame son indépendance. — L'Autriche prend la Bosnie et l'Herzégovine

▶▶ The Balkan wars of
1912–13 saw a jockeying for
position among the new states
of the region that left a legacy
of bitterness quite apart from
the dangers implicit in
great-power involvement.

▼ Military failure and
political corruption produced
a nationalist revolution in
Turkey, which transformed the
country into an important
player in the European
diplomatic game. The Young
Turks ruthlessly swept aside
the discredited old regime,
executed opponents and
turned to Germany for military
and economic assistance. The
presence of another dynamic
political force in an unstable
area posed a further threat to
peace because it suggested
an extension of German power
into the Entente Powers' areas
of interest in the Middle East.

view of Britain's imperial interests in the region, and the presence of Italian and Austro-Hungarian Dreadnought fleets, it was a very controversial decision to take. After much hesitation, Britain made an agreement with France in November 1912, whereby the French navy would protect British interests in the Mediterranean in exchange for British guarantees of French maritime security in the Channel and southern North Sea. Although there was still no formal military alliance between Britain and France, moral, political and strategic ties drew them closer together.

The Balkan wars
The wars that broke out in the Balkans in 1912 and 1913 represented the most serious consequence of the Morocco crisis. In September 1911, Italy, envious of French colonial gains in Morocco, but powerless to press its own territorial claims in the region, declared war on Turkey with a view to seizing Tripoli as compensation. When this attempt failed, Italy set its sights on the Dode-

canese, bringing the conflict nearer to the Balkans and causing the Turks to close the Straits.

These events worried the Russians and excited the Balkan states – Serbia, Montenegro, Bulgaria, Greece – which for a long time had wished to drive Turkey out of Europe altogether. By October 1912 the Balkan states were at war with Turkey. Austria-Hungary feared that Serbia would expand as far as the Adriatic, while Russia was afraid that Bulgaria would reach Constantinople. Both Great Powers were concerned at the volatility of the small Balkan states and resolved to settle the issue diplomatically. The first Balkan war formally ended at a conference in London in May 1913, with neither Serbia nor Bulgaria achieving its distant objective.

Within a month, however, war broke out again. Bulgaria quarreled with Serbia and Greece over territorial gains, and was in turn attacked by Romania and Turkey. The second Balkan war, which ended in October 1913, stripped Bulgaria of all that it had won earlier. The animosity

The Balkan Wars

Scale 1 : 10 000 000

▲ **Enver Pasha (1881–1922),** a leader of the Young Turks, with a a key role in modernizing the army and forging links with Germany.

1912

March
Bulgaria and Serbia form alliance against Ottoman Empire; Greece and Montenegro join in October, to form Balkan League.

October 8
Montenegro declares war on Ottoman Empire

October 17
Ottoman Empire declares war on Serbia and Bulgaria, after refusing to make reforms in its Balkan territories, as proposed by the Great Powers.

December 3
After Ottoman defeats at the hands of Bulgaria (Kirk Kilisse), and Serbia (Kumanovo), an armistice is called.

1913

May 30
Treaty of London ends first Balkan war; an independent Albania is formed, chiefly to deny Serbia access to the Adriatic. The next day Serbia and Greece sign a secret pact against Bulgaria

June 29
Serbia and Greece attack Bulgaria. Ottoman Empire separately attack Bulgaria.

August 10
Balkan states sign Treaty of Bucharest.

September 30
Ottoman Empire and Bulgaria sign Treaty of Constantinople.

between Austria-Hungary and Serbia was greater than ever before, and they had come close to the brink of war. Politicians in Berlin felt obliged to stand by their allies in Vienna, but were eager to avoid a war with others of the Great Powers, at least until the summer of 1914. By then, the widening of the Kiel Canal to take Dreadnought-sized battleships would be complete, and the 1913 army increases would have taken effect.

Meanwhile, the news that a German military mission was reorganizing the Turkish armed forces, and a German general was to take command at Constantinople, greatly disturbed the Russians. After extreme tension, both sides accepted a compromise solution in 1914, but the St Petersburg government concluded from the incident that, from then on, not only Austria-Hungary but also Germany would oppose Russia's Balkan interests.

War or peace

Anglo-German relations improved publicly after 1912. Liberals in the British cabinet and Parliament were eager to head off a war, and Britain renegotiated an old agreement about the future disposal of Portugal's colonies in Africa.

However, any similarities to the earlier period of *Weltpolitik* were only superficial. In reality, all non-European controversies were of marginal im-portance. Despite Britain's discussions with Germany over colonial issues, the two powers could never properly restore harmonious relations so long as the naval race in the North Sea continued unabated and British worries about a German attack upon France and Belgium persisted. Earlier colonial hotspots such as the Far East, Venezuela, the south Pacific, the Transvaal, and the upper Nile, had all faded from the headlines. As both Britain and Germany and their respective allies increased their armaments and streamlined their mobilization schedules, they concentrated their attention on the traditional cockpits of Europe – the Belgian plain, Lorraine and the Balkans.

Of course, a major war was by no means inevitable. The Great Powers had already avoided being drawn into the two earlier Balkan crises, while at home attention focused on domestic issues, such as taxation, social reform and, in Britain, the troubles in Ulster. Diplomatic relations between states proceeded as normal and many felt that the prospects for peace had actually improved. However, it was clear that if there were to be a war in Europe it would involve many countries. The tightening alliance system, the joint military plans, and a plethora of national rivalries would convert any single clash of arms into a massive coalition war, with large and small powers ranged on either side.

THE MISSIONARY MOVEMENT

Reflecting a belief that "the white man" was in the vanguard of history spiritually as well as materially, the 19th century saw a revival of the missionary movement. Organizations both Protestant and Catholic operated from the United States, Britain, Holland, Scandinavia, Germany, Switzerland, France, Belgium and Portugal and competed to turn vast areas of Southeast Asia and Central and southern Africa into parishes of their national churches. The "scramble" for foreign possessions went hand in hand with the contest for the souls and minds of their inhabitants, so that by the turn of the century the missionary movement was well established as a integral part of the "development" of colonies, and was given an international dimension by the setting up in 1910 of the World Missionary Conference (superseded in 1921 by the International Council of Missionaries).

Many missions provided elementary medical services and rudimentary social welfare which from a humanitarian perspective were essential; but the imposition of an alien religion had profoundly disruptive consequences on the integrity of the subject peoples. This was especially the case when it was accompanied by the imposition of an alien language in both spoken and written form. Most devastating of all, Christian evangelism might undermine the basis of the complex ritual and symbolism through which tribes and nations had evolved and maintained their identity, their sense of place and origins.

The cultural imperialism of the missionaries, unwittingly or otherwise, prepared for or colluded with the depredations wrought by commercial and military imperialism. The Ethiopian Emperor Theodore was prompted to comment wryly, "First it's traders and missionaries. Then its ambassadors. After that, they bring the guns. We shall do better to go straight to the guns." The contamination of colonial cultures, generally carried out within artificially imposed territorial boundaries, was perpetuated by the attempts of the more "enlightened" nations to fill minor bureaucratic positions with officials recruited from the indigenous population. In practice this meant the formation of an elite indoctrinated with the Eurocentric vision of history which underpinned imperialism, so that the very people best placed to help their own societies develop autonomously complied with the unraveling of the fine tissue of their native history.

▶▶ The colonizer as a blend of Christ and doctor. It was widely assumed by 19th-century Europeans that as the alleged incarnation of a superior culture "the white man" had a mission to bring spiritual and physical succour to "primitive" peoples.

▶ A white teacher in an African missionary school looks sternly but benignly over her black "flock". Only in the recent decades have anthropologists come to recognize the extraordinary complexity, richness and ecological sanity which tribal cultures possessed before being forcibly "educated" into adopting Western notions of "progress".

▼ Devout missionaries were sufficiently blinded by their own religious convictions to reject native belief systems wholesale and seek to replace them with European creeds and icons.

▶ Even after decolonization the states created by Europeans have generally been retained, along with the alien religion they implanted. Though the stamp with the "present cathedral" is of lower numismatic value than the earlier one, it is presented as more "modern".

◀ Zimbabwe is another nation-state superimposed over existing tribal territories. Though the remaining settlers eventually submitted to black majority, the ceremonial opening of its parliament still celebrates the continuity with British legal institutions, and indirectly the superiority of "white" civilization.

▲ Natives were taught to read and write, ostensibly for philanthropic purposes, but primarily to be more susceptible to European rule. Recently, however, gifted writers have emerged using the colonial *lingua franca* they learned to express instead the unique history of their "ethnic" culture.

Datafile

Behind the growth of the industrial economies and the build-up of national armories, another development was unfolding which would have an equally dramatic effect on 20th-century politics. Economic, demographic and social trends had combined to produce a large, politically-aware industrial workforce that was beginning to articulate its desire for full political representation and a fair share in the general rise in prosperity.

British electorate 1914

30%

70%

Total population (20+) 24,969,210

☐ Non-eligible

▨ Electorate

US representation 1901–13

☐ Republican ▨ Democrat

Seats (percent)
House of Representatives
Senate

100
75
50
25
0

1901 1903 1905 1907 1909 1911 1913

▲ In almost undisputed control since the end of the American Civil War, the Republicans began to lose ground as new working class voters, many of them recent arrivals, sought a new kind of government.

US Presidents
1901 T H Roosevelt R
1905 T H Roosevelt R
1909 W H Taft R
1913 W Wilson D

▼ As the new century unfolded, working-class protest began to manifest itself in increasing industrial radicalism. The number of hours lost through strikes rose steeply as workforces sought better pay and conditions, and a larger say in their destinies. Britain suffered the most dramatic rise in strike activity.

UK elections 1900–10

☐ Conserv & Unionist
☐ Liberal & Lib Union
☐ Irish Nationalist
▨ Labour

Seats in Commons (percent)

100

75

50

25

0

Oct 1900 | Jan 1906 | Jan 1910 | Dec 1910

▲ A slow process of electoral reform had given a proportion of the British working class the vote by 1914, but the majority of the population remained unenfranchised. Despite the rising tide of working class protest, the established political parties maintained their power, though each was forced to adopt social reform policies.

Days lost through industrial militancy 1901–15

☐ 1901–05 ☐ 1906–10 ▨ 1911–15

Millions

16
12
8
4
0

UK Germany France Belgium

Trade union membership

☐ 1904 ☐ 1910 ▨ 1914

Millions

3
2
1
0

UK Germany France Italy

▲ High levels of trade union membership in Britain and German were reflections of both the spread of working-class consciousness and the high level of industrialization. In France and Italy forms of working-class association remained smaller and more traditional, and radicalism manifested itself in different forms.

► In Russia, the connection between politics and industrial action was more profound than elsewhere in Europe. With its relatively small workforce clustered in the western cities, Russia experienced a rapid politicization of the working class. This manifested itself in high strike activity in times of national crisis.

Strikes in Russia

Thousands / Hundreds / Tens

Total strikes

Political strikes

1905 1908 1911 1914

Apart from Russia, Turkey and tiny Montenegro, all the European nations had some form of parliamentary system. However, the workings of that institution varied from country to country and did not fit any overall democratic pattern. By 1900 the German empire had universal adult male suffrage, whereas in Britain voting was still limited by complicated residence qualifications, so that many working-class men (and, of course, all women) could not vote. On the other hand, the British Parliament had far greater powers than the German Reichstag; and Britons considered their system much more liberal in regard to the freedom of the press, police actions, monarchical privileges, conscription, state controls over the economy, and so on.

In France and the United States, professional, middle-class politicians, once elected, had total control of the country. whereas in Britain, Italy, Germany and Austria-Hungary that power was shared, to different degrees, with a nonelected upper house and the monarchy. In Russia, even after the Duma was set up in 1905 as a consultative-legislative body, control still rested very firmly with the czarist autocracy.

From about the beginning of the century, however, all of these systems came under pressure for changes, which could not easily be effected by constitutional means. While women suffragettes, non-Magyar elements in Hungary, and other groups disadvantaged by the restricted franchises of the day still agitated for electoral reform, newer pressures for social and economic reform from organized labor joined, and often overshadowed, this traditional concern about political rights.

Russia

In 1900 czarist Russia represented the bastion of autocracy. Nicholas II's power was supported by a reactionary aristocracy (who were almost absolute monarchs on their own estates) and mediated by an elaborate array of government inspectors, judicial officials, tax-collectors, and the police. Dissenters either fled abroad or were punished with death or deportation to Siberia. Ethnic minorities were "russified", Jews were persecuted, and the press and intelligentsia came under the constant scrutiny of the secret police.

The widespread unrest and revolutionary upheaval of 1905 shook the regime to its very foundations. Never before had there been so much united opposition and so much pressure for change from so many different groups, including liberal parliamentarians, the St Petersburg workers' soviet (council), peasants, and ethnic minorities in the Baltic states and in Finland, Poland, and Georgia. Yet, despite the concession of a national legislative assembly (Duma) and

POLITICS AND PEOPLE

some civil liberties, within a few years the autocracy had reasserted itself. By 1914, Russia seethed with discontent.

Germany

The unification of Germany had taken place with the support of many of the middle classes, who had been rewarded with a national constitution, a code of laws, and a legislative assembly. However, Bismarck deliberately widened the franchise to include all males over 25 in order to curb the influence of liberal intellectuals and businessmen. Moreover, the individual German states still retained their own very considerable prerogatives and, in Prussia and other states, a restricted three-class franchise ensured that real power remained with the traditional elites. The German parliament, the Reichstag, had no control over the Kaiser or his ministers in matters of foreign policy, military affairs, or war and peace. Frustrated critics termed Prussia-Germany a *Scheindemokratie* ("bogus democracy"). In fact, the Reichstag did possess the power to vote taxes, and included different political parties, even if it was a very restricted form of parliamentary rule, and came under growing pressure from below as Germany became more industrialized. In the few years before 1914, the chancellor, Bethmann Hollweg, found it increasingly difficult to form a coalition of pro-government parties in the Reichstag because of the intransigence of the conservative right and the stated policy of having no dealings with the large Social Democratic party.

Austria-Hungary

Compared with the Habsburg monarchy, Germany was a model of constitutional efficiency. Austria-Hungary was a great conglomeration of

▼ The Russian royal family in the early years of the century exemplified the world of inherited privilege.

37

The Duma, Russia's concession to parliament, failed to make the czarist autocracy more democratic

territories and ethnic groups sharing allegiance to a "common monarchy" but with little else in common. When war came, the mobilization posters had to be prepared in 15 languages.

Pressure from the Magyars in 1867 had forced the government in Vienna to make widespread concessions to the kingdom of Hungary, which, as its price for not breaking up the Austro-Hungarian duocracy, opposed both centralization of the empire and the granting of rights to other nationalities. Whereas in Hungary a ruthless "Magyarization" policy continued to deny representation to ethnic minorities, the *Reichsrat*, the constitutional assembly of Austria (and, in effect, of all the other lands in the empire) was multinational and included Poles, Czechs, Ruthenes and others, as well as Germans. The emperor, his ministers and the imperial bureaucracy had overall charge of Austria-Hungary, including the powers of war and peace, albeit with the need to secure Hungarian support.

Italy

Italy had a monarchy with very considerable powers of appointment, both of ministers and of life-members of the Senate, the upper house. However, central government could not function without control of the Chamber of Deputies, the lower house, whose members were elected on a limited suffrage, though this rose as literacy increased. The most successful prime ministers, such as Giuseppe Zenardelli and Giovanni Giolitti, used widespread bribery and political favors to "oil" the electoral system, and preferred to work with the various factions in the Chamber rather than challenge parliamentary powers, as Luigi Pelloux had tried to do in 1899–1900.

The political malaise that, despite Giolitti's reforms, prevailed in Italy during this period was caused not so much by constitutional idiosyncrasies, as by cynicism at the overt jobbery and electoral corruption, and, in particular, by economic failure and the widening gap between the north and the south. Loyalty to the Italian state was less deep-rooted than loyalties to the family, church, village or region.

Britain

In contrast to Italy, Britain, another constitutional monarchy, possessed a strong sense of national unity (except in Ireland) that dated back hundreds of years. The king's role was much more honorific, and the complex relationships between the political parties and the executive and legislature were well established. General elections were free of corruption, and victory in them by one or other of the two major parties, Liberals or Conservatives, allowed the administration to carry out, unhindered, its electoral pledges. Politics centered very tightly upon Westminster, and was an honored profession. The British constitution (which was never committed to paper) was widely praised for its balance and utility, which was why Britons felt justified in passing it on to the self-governing Dominions. Whether, however, its delicate mechanisms and gradual adjustment to change could easily withstand new social and fiscal pressures, or a revived Irish nationalism, was still not clear.

The years 1909–14, in particular, placed great strains upon Britain's traditional Parliament-based solutions to problems. For example, in 1910 Asquith's Liberal government called two general elections over the question of the House of Lords' unprecedented obstruction of a money bill. In theory, Britain's unwritten constitution was intended to be very flexible, but in practice, it did not always prove to be so.

The Birth of Bolshevism

By the late 1890s some German Social Democrats, inspired by Eduard Bernstein, had begun to question Marxist predictions about revolution in capitalist society. This so-called "revisionist" school of thought was formally denounced at party conferences, but in fact many Social Democratic politicians leaned towards compromise with the institutions of the German empire. Such apparent backsliding disgusted more radical figures like Rosa Luxemburg, a refugee from czarist oppression and a passionate believer in proletarian revolution.

Inside Russia, gradual progress toward democracy – let alone socialism – seemed unlikely. In 1903 V.I. Lenin split the Russian Social Democratic Labor party by insisting on the need for a highly disciplined revolutionary organization rather than a mass membership movement modeled on those in the west. Lenin's breakaway party, which received majority support, were called Bolsheviks, from the Russian for "more". The other faction were known as Mensheviks (from the Russian for "less"). The Bolshevik party schooled a cadre of professional revolutionaries who were to be the future rulers of the Soviet Union.

◀ Russian poster of Karl Marx, c. 1920.

France and the United States

Constitutionally, France and the United States distinguished themselves by being democratic republics, which had universal male suffrage. (Few countries in the world at that time gave the vote to women.) There were significant differences between the two constitutions, however. Fundamentally, the United States exercised a much stricter division of powers between the executive and the legislature. Compared with the powers of the US Senate, the rights of the upper house in France were limited, as in Britain's House of Lords. The center of politics in France was the Chamber of Deputies, elected from single-member constituencies. Both houses chose the president, but government ministers felt responsible to the Deputies, where voting numbers were really significant.

In both France and the United States the lack of strong party discipline helped to produce individual senators or deputies who were powerful independent figures who had to be wooed by governments that needed their vote. Ideology did affect politics in the legislative assembly (especially, in France, over church–state relations or social issues), but it was very much the place where regional and sectoral interest groups struggled for influence and hammered out compromises over such issues as tariffs. As in Italy or Austria, the effective political figures were those who could, whether by patronage or concession, get together a majority to vote on the matters of the day.

The labor movement

The root cause of the pressure for social and economic reform was industrialization. It had herded workers into factories, steel-mills and shipyards, created mushrooming urban slums close to the workplaces, and given rise to the formation of organizational bodies to protect the interests of the new urban proletariat.

By far the most important of these organizations was the trade union. Trade unions brought together workers of a particular skill into a body to negotiate improvements in wages, hours and working conditions, and which, by the concerted action of withdrawal of labor – the strike – could threaten to bring industrial production to a halt. Such combinations clearly challenged the industrialists' *laissez-faire* creed, as well as their profits, and many factory owners fought to suppress them. The setting up of trade unions was often accompanied by strikes, lockouts, street violence, clashes with the police and legislation, which generally favored the established orders.

In Russia, trade unions were outlawed and strikes were put down by force. In the United States, where some ferocious industrial struggles occurred, trade unions were restrained by the sheer power of the factory owners, as well as the size of the country and the mobility of labor. Italy and France were predominantly agrarian societies in which the unions were really only significant in the industrialized towns and cities of the north. There, they developed syndicalist ideas of using trade unions as a revolutionary force. In Britain and Germany, which were more industrialized, trade-union membership grew rapidly in the

▲ An American socialist delivers an unequivocal message to his government. In the decades before the Great War, the rise of international socialism and other working-class movements seemed to threaten the international political order. Socialists and syndicalists, with their tens of thousands of members, possessed the power to halt the arms race and deny conscript armies the mass manpower needed for war. When war occurred, however, national pride proved stronger than international class consciousness, and the workers of the world shouldered arms to fight against each other.

Votes for Women

The motives of women campaigners for the vote were complex and varied. Some wanted the vote to achieve social reform. Others demanded the vote for working women to bargain for pay and conditions and the right to work. Women of liberal persuasion sought to extend the traditional quest for political democracy to women, and in so doing they came into conflict with intransigent male politicians. Even emergent socialist movements campaigned only for the enfranchisement of the working classes. In the United States women suffragists became distanced from the antislavery movement, which concentrated on registering the black vote.

Means were as varied as motive. Suffragists, such as the 50,000 strong membership of the British National Union of Women's Suffrage Societies, formed the largest groups and followed constitutional means such as non-payment of taxes and extensive lobbying. Much smaller, but better publicized, were the groups of militant suffragettes who used violence against property in their cause; these included the 5,000-member Women's Social and Political Union run by Emmeline and Christabel Pankhurst in Britain and the National Women's Suffrage Association led by Susan Anthony in the United States.

Much of the international contact between these groups was loosely based in the international labor movement, whose priority was working-class emancipation, rather than votes for women. At the 1910 Labor and Socialist International meeting at Copenhagen. British women were condemned for supporting the enfranchisement of propertied women. Yet, the eventual winning of the parliamentary vote owed much to these contacts, as socialists pressed for electoral reform, which included the enfranchisement of women.

New Zealand led the way with a new constitution and women's franchise in 1893; Australia followed in 1901. Finland was the European pioneer (1906) when a new diet was empowered; then Norway (1907). Revolutions in the Soviet Union (1917), Germany and Austria (1918) and China (1925) enfranchised women. British women over 30 gained the vote in 1918, but 21–30-year-olds had to wait till 1928. By 1920 American women had been enfranchised, but out of 20 European states, six (including France) still partially or wholly denied women the vote.

▲ A British suffragette is led away by police in 1914 after participating in an attack on Buckingham Palace. Such militant tactics alienated some liberal support for the cause of women's suffrage, but the sense of crisis generated, together with changes wrought by the impact of the World War, led to a consensus for change in 1918.

▶ British suffragettes endured prison and forcible feeding while on hunger strike for their cause. After the election of a Liberal government in 1906, seven suffrage bills failed in Parliament and tactics such as hunger-strikes became more common and won a degree of public support, despite male fears about the rationality of women.

◀ A Hungarian suffragist puts her cause to men in a Budapest street in the early 1900s. Women's suffrage was a worldwide cause during this period; in Hungary, too, women won the vote in the new republic set up in 1918.

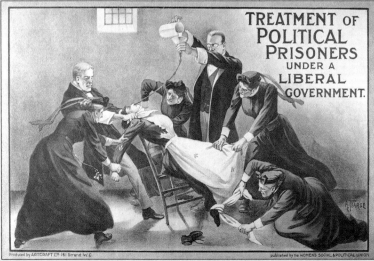

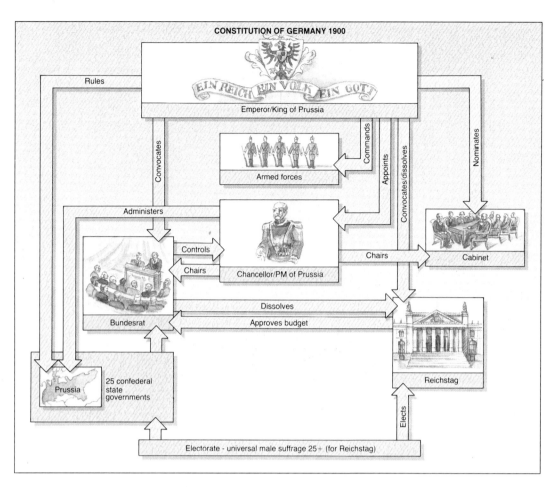

CONSTITUTION OF GERMANY 1900

EIN REICH EIN VOLK EIN GOTT

Emperor/King of Prussia

Rules

Convocates

Commands

Appoints

Nominates

Convocates/dissolves

Armed forces

Administers

Controls

Chairs

Chancellor/PM of Prussia

Chairs

Chairs

Cabinet

Dissolves

Approves budget

Bundesrat

Prussia

25 confederal
state
governments

Reichstag

Elects

Electorate - universal male suffrage 25+ (for Reichstag)

◄ The German empire was a classic example of a constitution that sought to provide a strong central authority by focusing power in the hands of two men – the emperor (president) and his chancellor. Both men usually held equivalent positions within Prussia, and the dominance of that state within Germany assured their authority throughout the empire. The crucial role of chairmanship of the Bundesrat (federal council), at which members of all the German states approved imperial policy. The Reichstag had been set up in 1871 as a concession to democracy, and could vote on legislation and exercised a degree of budgetary control over the Bundesrat. Some of the state governments also included a small democratic element within them. By the early 1900s opposition in the Reichstag was growing more effective with the development of liberal and socialist parties. This constitution was swept away in 1918.

years before 1914, among both unskilled and skilled workers, making them a new, if uncertain force in national politics.

The reaction of the aristocratic or middle-class governing elites to the rise of trade unionism, and to the industrial proletariat as a whole, was usually hostile. The movement received some support, however, from among French radicals, American Democrats and certain British Liberals, who argued for social and economic reforms and regarded the growing workforce as a potential source of electoral support. By broadening the political agenda to include socioeconomic issues, they hoped to absorb this new class within the system and so preserve its essential stability.

In many countries of Europe (less so in Britain and the United States) organized labor had long been influenced by the socialist ideas of Karl Marx and Friedrich Engels, and by their vision of a complete transformation of political and economic relationships along egalitarian lines. Such programs (and even more, the anarchist doctrines of Pierre Proudhon and Mikhail Bakunin) called for the revolutionary overthrow of the existing order. Nevertheless, many trade-union leaders began to accept the utility of electing working-class representatives into their national assemblies, to influence legislation.

The newly formed Labour party in Britain gained 29 members of parliament in the 1906 election, while its counterpart in Germany, the Social Democratic party, though professedly revolutionary Marxist, worked through the existing quasi-democratic structures to become the largest single party in the Reichstag at the 1912 elections.

To many among the older elites, the growth of trade unions and socialist parties posed the greatest threat to the internal order of the country. Even more alarming to them was the fact that the various national organizations were also members of the International, committed to the advance of the working classes everywhere. On their side, the labor movements encountered enormous difficulties, quite apart from harassment by the police and tough measures by employers to resist their influence. Most trade unionists, in fact, wanted improved pay and conditions, not social revolution. Many were strongly patriotic, and unlikely to join in any international strike that might be called to oppose a war. Moreover, socialist programs did not appeal to peasant smallholders across Europe or to the American farmer, and they were attacked by anarchists and other revolutionaries. Neither did they win the support of ethnic minorities to whom they seemed irrelevant.

Some of the more desperate and reactionary elites wanted to imitate the czarist regime by using force to quash trade union and socialist movements. Most governments, however, looked for more subtle ways to keep them in check and reduce their revolutionary appeal. Significantly, in many Western countries, state spending on education and health, and in other domestic areas, rose steadily in this period, as did taxes. Labor's rise had brought social issues to the fore, and greatly added to the problems that confronted politicians in the decade after 1900.

▲ US president Theodore Roosevelt on the campaign trail in 1903. The growth of democracy meant that politicians were increasingly forced to defend their actions to the public; Roosevelt in particular brought a fresh populism to the US political scene.

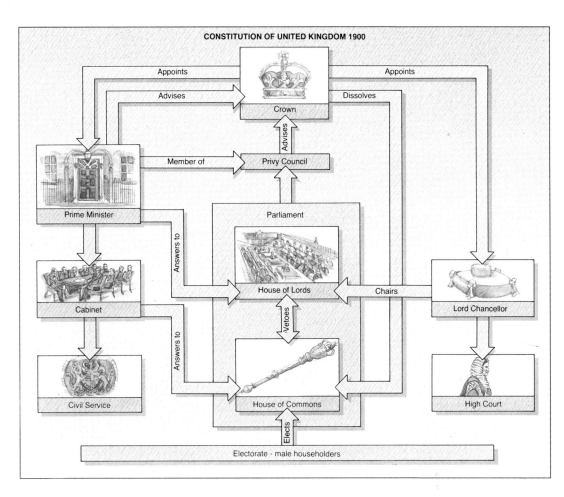

CONSTITUTION OF UNITED KINGDOM 1900

◀ The British system has never been formalized in the same way as the German or US constitutions, and the division of power between the branches of government is more pragmatic than theoretical. By the early 20th century the power of the Crown played a role that was advisory and ceremonial, with most power in the hands of Parliament. The prime minister, though appointed by the Crown, was the person, usually leader of the majority party in the Commons, who could command a majority in the Commons. The House of Lords retained a veto over decisions of the Commons until 1911, when its powers were limited to delaying legislation. From the same date, the maximum term of a Parliament before fresh elections were called was reduced from seven years to five. Universal male suffrage was introduced in 1918, with women given identical voting rights in 1928.

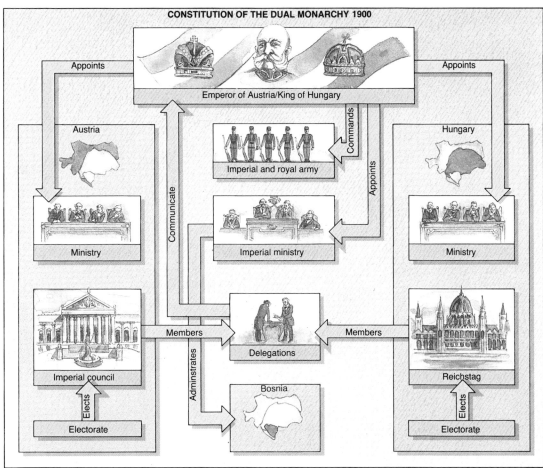

CONSTITUTION OF THE DUAL MONARCHY 1900

◀ Under the Dual Monarchy arrangement of 1867, the imperial crown of Austria and royal crown of Hungary were vested in the same person (Francis Joseph). Each had its own ministers responsible for its own affairs, but for many questions a "common concern" was invoked that allowed the emperor-king considerable power. These especially included foreign and military affairs. Direct universal suffrage for parliamentary elections was introduced in Austria in 1907; a similar proposal had been made in Hungary two years earlier but had been rejected by the ruling Magyar group.

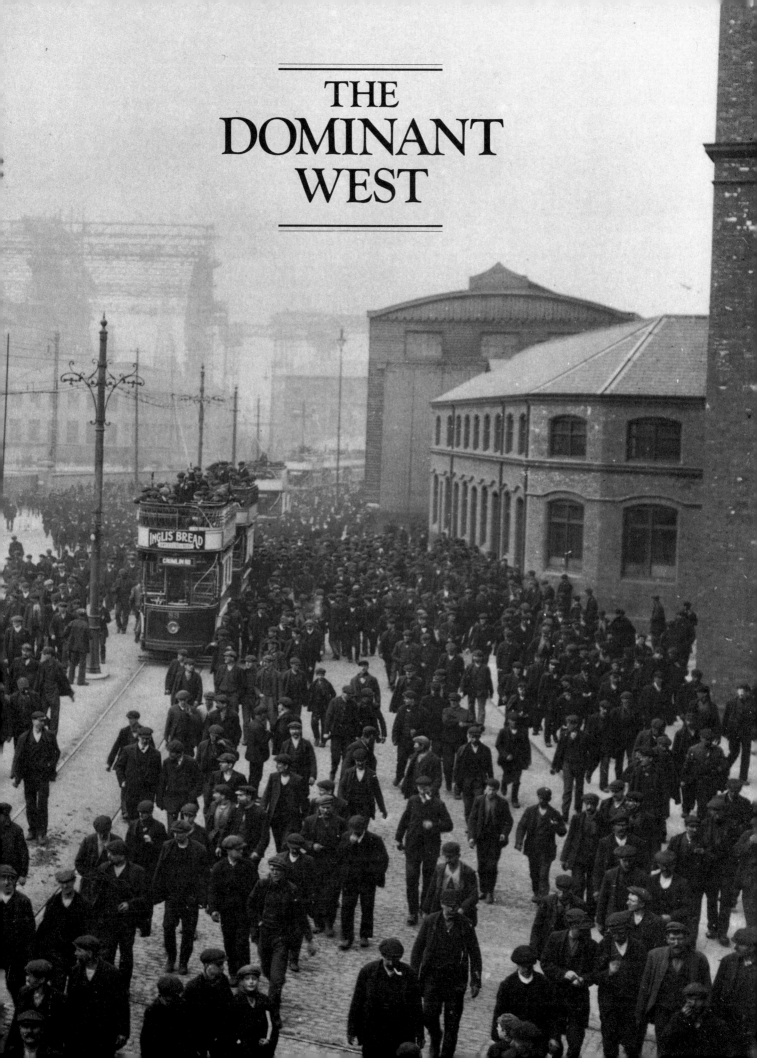

THE
DOMINANT
WEST

Time Chart

	1900	1901	1902	1903	1904	1905	1906
Industry	• Sep: Strike of 150,000 miners in the USA • 26 Oct: Belgium adopts old age pensions • American Federation of Labor (AFL) formed from 216 trade unions (USA)	• J.P. Morgan founds the United States Steel Corporation	• German steel company Krupp buys the Germania–Werft shipyard in Kiel (Ger)	• 3 Jan: Report of the Irish Land conference suggests revision of rental payments • Henry Ford founds the Ford Automobile Company (USA) • J.P. Morgan founds the International Mercantile and Marine Company shipping trust in New York (USA) • Foundation of the Telefunken wireless telegraphy company (Ger)	• C. Duisberg merges the chemical plants Bayer, Agfa and Badische Anilin to form I.G. Farben (Ger) • Foundation of the Daimler automobile plant near Stuttgart (Ger) • Foundation of the Rolls Royce automobile company (UK)	• Foundation of the International Agricultural Institute in Rome (It)	• Foundation of the Mercedes automobile company in Berlin (Ger) • Katanga Mining Union founded in the Belgian Congo
Technology	• 2 Jul: First trial flight of rigid airship *Star*, designed by F. Graf Zeppelin • First escalator demonstrated at the world exhibition in Paris	• 13 Dec: Marconi send the first radio telegram across the Atlantic Ocean • K.C. Gillette applies for a patent for his exchangeable razor blade shaver (USA)	• Aswan dam built by B. Baker is completed (Egy) • R.A. Fesseden develops the wireless telephone (USA) • A. Korn invents photo-telegraphy (Ger)	• 17 Dec: First controlled powered flight by the Wright brothers (USA) • L. and A. Lumière develop the first viable color photography (Fr) • Industrial artificial silk developed (USA)	• 4 May: Beginning of the construction of the Panama Canal • Invention of the electron valve by J.A. Fleming (UK) • Completion of the Trans-Siberian railroad (Russ)	• J.W. Rubel and C. Hermann develop offset printing • Fouche and Picard invent oxyacetylene welding (Fr) • Introduction of compressed air hammers in coal mining (Ger)	• L. Baekeland founds the synthetic resin industry (Bel) • A. Fisher constructs the first washing machine with a horizontal cylinder (USA)
Finance	• Mar: Gold dollar become the official currency of the USA • Establishment of the Hokkaido Takushoko Ginko, bank for financing the development of Hokkaido (Jap)	• J.P. Morgan merges the Carnegie Steel Corporation and the Federal Steel Corporation to the US Steel Corporation (USA) • Establishment of the Banco Hispano Americano and Banco de Vizcaya (Sp)	• Establishment of the Industrybank (Jap) • Establishment of the Banco Español de Credito (Sp)	• Mar: Fixing of a constant gold-silver parity (USA) • Jul: An international monetary conference in Berlin demands a constant currency parity between countries of the gold and the silver blocs • Bankers Trust Company established in New York	• Establishment of the Banque de l'Union Parisienne (Fr) • Establishment of the Bank of Italy by Giannini in San Francisco (USA) • Establishment of the Bank of the Ministry of Finance (China)	• Loan agreed for Russia on the condition that Russia supports France at the Morocco conference in Algeciras (Fr) • Manufacturers Trust Company established in New York (USA)	
Economic Policy	• Feb: Beginning of severe strikes in Vienna, Brussels and Bohemia	• Feb: Strike against the tax policy of the Catalonian government (Sp) • Jul: Beginning of a steelworkers strike in the USA • Dec: Demonstrations and riots by unemployed workers in Budapest (Aust-Hung)	• Jan: Establishment of the first Labor Office • Feb: Reduction of miners' working hours to nine per day • Apr: Consultations regarding the merging of all cartels and syndicates into a single economic association (Ger) • Oct: Strike of two-thirds of French miners	• Mar: Legislation for the regulation of childrens' labor enforced (Ger) • May: British Colonial minister J. Chamberlain begins campaigning for an imperial tariff association (UK) • Nov: Strike of Spanish miners, demanding their wages be paid weekly	• Jun: Establishment of the German Employers Association • Aug: End of disruption in the petrol industry at Boryslaw. Demand met for a reduction of working hours (Aust-Hung)	• Jan: Strike of miners in the Ruhr and in Belgium, demanding a reduction of working hours (Ger/Bel) • Mar: Introduction of the eight-hour day for miners under 18 (UK) • Aug: Severe strikes and disruption in Russia and Poland • Sep: Trade Union Congress demands the introduction of an eight-hour day and free trade (UK)	• Mar: Beginning of a severe strike movement in Germany • May: US government prohibits any further expansion of the Rockefeller Oil Trust by passing the Sherman Act
International		• Sep: Congress of the International Association for the legal protection of workers agrees on a package of workers' legislation for all countries • Foundation of the International Trade Union in Amsterdam	• Jan: Germany obtains a licence from Turkey to build a railway from Konia to Baghdad • Mar: Agreement between UK and Persia regarding the construction of a telegraph line • May: International Congress of Miners demands nationalization of all mines • 28 Jun: USA buys rights off French Panama Company	• Feb: Trade agreement between UK and Persia • Nov: Canada decides on a further increase of taxes on German imports • Dec: New trade agreement between Italy and Austria	• Jan: Trade agreement between the USA and China • Aug: International Congress of Miners demands the introduction of a fixed minimum wage • Germany signs commercial treaties with Belgium, Russia, Switzerland, Serbia and Austria-Hungary	• May: Meeting of the International Conference for the Protection of Laborers discusses night work for women	• Jul: Tariff war between Austria and Serbia • Night-work by women internationally forbidden
Misc.	• Boxer Rebellion in China suppressed	• Coronation of Edward VII on the death of Victoria (UK)	• 31 May: End of the Boer War	• 3 Nov: Panama made independent of Colombia	• Beginning of the Russo-Japanese war	• Oct: First revolution in Russia	• Foundation of the Labour party (UK)

1907	1908	1909	1910	1911	1912	1913	1914
• J.P. Morgan organizes a fund by order of the US treasury to support destitute companies during the economic crisis (USA) • Shell Oil Trust founded (UK) • Ball bearing plant founded in Göteborg (Swe)	• General Motors Company founded in Detroit (USA) • Ford develops assembly line for the mass production of the Model T (USA) • Zeppelin airship company established (Ger)	• Ford specializes its car production on the Model T (USA) • German Gelsenkirchener Bergwerks AG begins steel production in Luxembourg	• Rotary hoe first used • Establishment of the Rockefeller Foundation for the promotion of science (USA)	• Standard Oil Trust dissolved on the basis of antitrust legislation • Poor harvest in Russia. Famine in many parts of the country	• May: The world's largest ship, Imperator, launched (Ger) • Dec: 245 miners killed by an explosion in a coal mine in Hokkaido (Jap)	• I. Kreuger founds his match plant (Swe) • BASF builds an ammonia plant in Oppau (Ger)	• Jan: Introduction of minimum wages and profit-sharing at Ford (USA)
• Chemotherapy introduced by P. Ehrlich as a treatment for infectious diseases (Ger) • Lumière brothers invent color-scanner plate to improve color photography (Fr)	• Invention of the gyro-compass by H. Anschütz-Kaempfe • A. Wilm invents the alloy Duralmin (Ger)	• 24 Feb: First color moving picture shown in Brighton (UK) • 25 Jul: L. Blériot flies across English Channel in 27 minutes (Fr)	• G. Claude invents the fluorescent light tube (Fr) • B. Ljundström constructs the high-pressure steam turbine (Nor)	• E. Rutherford develops the theory of the atomic nucleus structure (UK)	• Krupp patents acid resistant chrome-nickel steel (Ger) • V. Kaplan begins development of a turbine for the exploitation of small waterfalls (Aust-Hung)	• 14 Aug: Opening of world's longest water pipe in Los Angeles (USA) • F. Bergius develops coal high pressure hydrogenation (Ger)	• Feb: Opening of the Tanganyika Railway from Dar es Salaam to Lake Tanganyika • Opening of the Panama Canal (USA)
• 21 Oct: Financial crisis in the USA, with the collapse of 31 national banks and 2 state banks • Swiss National Bank established as the central bank of Switzerland • Establishment of the Bank of the Ministry of Transport (China)	• The gold standard comes into force (Ger) • Establishment of the first savings banks in the USA • Appointment of the National Currency Commission to devise a new banking system (USA)	• Jun: Reichsbank notes become legal tender (Ger)	• Note-issuing monopoly for the Swiss National Bank • Merger of the Guarantee Trust Company, the Morton Trust Company and the Fifth Avenue Trust Company to form the First Bank (USA) • Establishment of the first industrial banks (USA)	• 9 Sep: Collapse at the Berlin stock exchange due to the Morocco crisis and German colonial policy • Nov: Circulation of bank notes fixed to 6.3 billion francs until 1925 (Fr) • Establishment of the Australian central bank	• J.P. Morgan acquires the majority share in the Guarantee Trust Company and in the Bankers Trust Company (USA) • Establishment of the Swiss Bank by the merger of two provincial banks • Sumitomo Bank and Yasuda Bank become stock companies (Jap)	• Dec: Twelve Federal Reserve Banks and one Federal Reserve Board established (USA) • Establishment of the National Credit Bank (Fr) • Establishment of the Bank of China	• Jul: Run on many central banks in Europe. Decrease in the gold reserves of the Bank of England from £38.6 to £28 billion • Aug: Closing of the stock exchanges and the suspension of the convertibility of many currencies with the outbreak of World War I
• Jan: Establishment of a colonial action committee, urging an intensive colonial policy • May: French sailors in Marseille proclaim a general strike for better working conditions	• Mar: Meeting of employers in Berlin agrees on collective wage agreements (Ger)	• Aug: Severe strike movement in Sweden • Dec: Complaint by the Standard Oil Company at the Supreme Court against the demanded suspension of its trust and against the anti-cartel legislation (USA)	• Jan: English miners strike for an eight-hour day (UK) • Apr: Measures taken by the Russian government for the economic development of Siberia, including the construction of a railway from Moscow to Irkutsk • Aug/Sep: Dockers strike in Germany and in the UK for higher wages • Oct: Strike of French railwaymen	• Jan: Miners' strikes in the Belgian coal district • Aug: Beginning of strikes by English railwaymen (UK)	• Mar: Miners' strike in the Ruhr ends in failure (Ger) • Apr: Gold miners' strike in Siberia suppressed by the army (Russ) • Apr: Law on minimum wages for miners put into force (UK)	• Aug: USA declare an economic boycott against Mexico	• May: Trade unions of miners, transport workers and railwaymen found a common committee for collective bargaining (UK) • Aug: All parties in the Reichstag agree on a large war credit for the government (Ger)
• Jun: Agreement between Japan and France on trading in China • Jul: Agreement between Japan and Russia on trading in China • Aug: China opens seven towns in Manchuria for international trade	• Feb: International navigation conference in London establishes passenger fares • Sep: International Conference for the Protection of Labor demands prohibition of night work for children	• May: Mutual consultations of German and English workers • Jul: Agreement between USA and Germany on the use of patents	• Feb: Agreement on the construction and management of the St Gotthard railway between Germany, Italy and Switzerland • Jul: Commercial treaty between Austria-Hungary and Serbia	• Japanese commercial treaties with the UK (3 Apr), France and Germany (28 Jun) • Dec: Agreement between the UK, Russia and France prohibiting the capture of seals			• Anglo-German and Franco-German agreement on the management of railways in the Ottoman Empire
• Formation of the Triple Entente of Russia, France and the UK	• Austria-Hungary annexes Bosnia-Herzegovina		• Japan annexes Korea • 1 Jul: Union of South Africa becomes a Dominion	• Chinese revolution initiated by the Young Chinese Movement	• Italy occupies the Dodecanese Islands (Turk) • First Balkan war. Turks virtually expelled from Europe	• Second Balkan war. Bulgaria cedes territory to Serbia, Greece and Romania	• 28 Jun: Assassination of Franz Ferdinand in Sarajevo (Serbia) initiates crisis leading in August to the outbreak of World War I

Datafile

The economic growth of industrial and industrializing countries accelerated from 1890 so much that the 25 years before World War I have been called a second industrial revolution. Among the causes for this, emphasis has been laid upon new technologies such as electricity and mass production which created new products like the motor car. But this period also witnessed the final maturity of long-established manufacturing techniques. Further, industrialization took root in an increasing number of countries, spreading out from its original cores in northwestern Europe and New England. Mass markets grew rapidly, particularly in the established industrial countries – Britain, the United States and Germany.

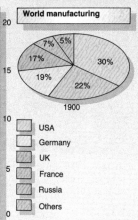

Imported capital

◀ Industrialization in Scandinavia generated a demand for capital which initially could not be met from local sources. Foreign capital therefore played a vital role over a short period in the emerging industrial economies of Sweden, Norway and Denmark in the 1890s and 1900s. This overseas capital introduced the electrochemical industry to Norway and was responsible for the development of iron ore mining in northern Sweden.

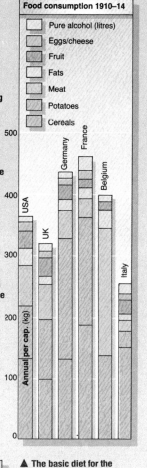

Food consumption 1910–14

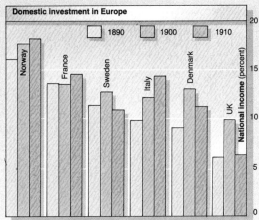

Domestic investment in Europe

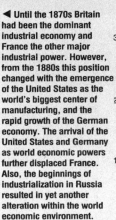

World manufacturing

◀ Until the 1870s Britain had been the dominant industrial economy and France the other major industrial power. However, from the 1880s this position changed with the emergence of the United States as the world's biggest center of manufacturing, and the rapid growth of the German economy. The arrival of the United States and Germany as world economic powers further displaced France. Also, the beginnings of industrialization in Russia resulted in yet another alteration within the world economic environment.

▲ Although data sources for investment before 1914 vary in quality and approach, it seems clear that newly industrializing regions and countries such as Scandinavia and Italy were characterized by relatively high levels of national income devoted to investment, as was France. By contrast, Britain's rate of investment was low.

▼▼ During the 1890s and 1900s Europeans formed a declining proportion of American immigrants, falling from over three-quarters of the total in 1890 to just over half by 1910. Britain and Scandinavia continued to be important, but to this "old" migration was added a "new" from Southern and Eastern Europe, especially Italy and Russia.

▲ The basic diet for the mass of the population consisted of starch, which was eaten in the form of grains or potatoes. In richer countries there was greater variety, provided by meats, fats and fruits. There were also substantial national variations, partly the result of differing geography, local availability and varying tastes.

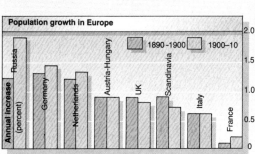

Population growth in Europe

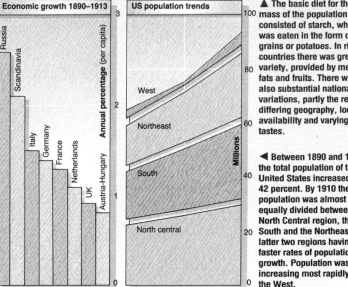

Economic growth 1890–1913

US population trends

◀ Between 1890 and 1910 the total population of the United States increased by 42 percent. By 1910 the population was almost equally divided between the North Central region, the South and the Northeast, the latter two regions having faster rates of population growth. Population was increasing most rapidly in the West.

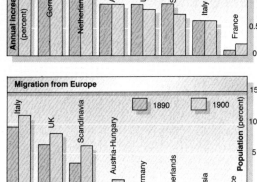

Migration from Europe

▲ The European economy as a whole was growing at an average rate of 1.5 percent per year at the turn of the century. Most of the newly industrializing countries, such as Italy, were expanding rapidly from a low initial base, whereas generally the larger established industrial nations were growing more slowly.

▶ Industrialization led to a decline in the proportion of the labor force engaged in agriculture, forestry and fishing. This shift of labor into manufacturing and service industries is a clear marker of economic growth. In Britain that process was substantially complete by 1900 but in Eastern and Southern Europe it was just beginning.

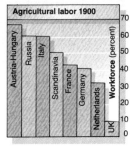

Agricultural labor 1900

INDUSTRIAL AND URBAN GROWTH

By the beginning of the 20th century there were two main geographical centers of industrialization in the world – northwest Europe and the northeastern United States. Within these areas modern economic growth was already well established, whereas in other regions such as Scandinavia, northern Italy, Russia and the northern central states of the United States, industrialization was just beginning to get under way. This geographical dispersion of the process of modernization coincided with an overall acceleration in the rate of material advance experienced by most industrial economies from the 1890s. The concepts and techniques that are now used for measuring economic growth, involving national income calculations, did not become current until the interwar period, but when using a modern measure such as Gross National Product (GNP) per capita at constant prices, it would appear that economic growth was taking place in Europe at a rate of around 1.5 percent per annum between the late 1880s and 1913. Such rates of growth are, however, only estimates, or even "guesstimates", since, unlike similar figures for later in the century, they are based upon a very wide range of contemporary data of varying qualities.

▼ The modern canning industry developed from the 1870s, but the mechanization of the preparation of fruits and vegetables only began at the turn of the century. Consequently the food processing and packing industries continued to employ substantial numbers of low-paid unskilled workers, often women and children, to prepare produce, in this instance beans.

The post-1890 period of renewed growth involved, as in earlier years, regional variations within Europe. Faster growth of both that group of countries which had experienced industrialization relatively later, such as Germany, and those countries and regions where industrialization was just beginning, such as Russia, Scandinavia and Italy, contrasted with countries that could be labeled as "early industrializers", such as Belgium, Switzerland and the United Kingdom, which grew at less than the European average. The United Kingdom continued to be the richest European country, but the richest by far of all the advanced industrial economies was the United States, which in 1913 had a real GNP per capita five times greater than the European average and 25 percent higher than that of the United Kingdom. This divergence was of long standing, having been apparent from the second quarter of the 19th century. The American rate of economic growth between 1890 and 1913, the period of resumption of faster growth, appears to have been around 1.8 percent per annum, greater than that of the major European industrial economies but not so rapid as in the newly industrializing countries like Scandinavia or Russia.

▼ Between 1880 and 1920, more than 23 million immigrants settled in the United States. This flow of people across the Atlantic from Europe in crowded ships was marked by considerable year-to-year fluctuations, with peaks in 1892, 1907 and 1914. These peaks coincided with periods of prosperity in America; the migrants were drawn by employment opportunities. Such attractions were made known in Europe through advertisements, coupled with offers of financial assistance, placed by American railroad and steamship companies together with managers of mills and factories.

Population growth and migration

Economic growth amongst the advanced industrial countries during the 25 years or so before 1914 was the product of many factors. It was assisted by population growth, a result of birth rates exceeding death rates. Birth rates had fallen in northwestern Europe from the mid-1870s but this new demographic trend did not become established amongst the populations of Eastern Europe until after 1900. A decline in infant mortality was largely responsible for the fall in the death rate and was most pronounced by 1913 in Scandinavia and Western Europe. In contrast, infant mortality rates remained high in Eastern Europe, with rates of over 200 per thousand continuing during the first decade of the 20th century in Russia and Austria-Hungary.

Unlike the rest of Europe, France had had, since the 1860s, an extremely low rate of population increase, which transformed it from one of the most densely settled countries in 1800 to one of the least by the eve of World War I. Moreover, the low birth rate gave France an aging population in advance of other European countries, which had substantial effects before 1914 both on the size of the French labor force and on French consumption patterns.

Rates of natural increase were modified by international migration. It has been estimated that between 1850 and 1914 more than forty million people left the Old World for the New, equivalent to 10 percent of Europe's population. By the 1900s, the movement of Europeans to the western hemisphere was largely a flow from the Mediter-

▲ From the 1880s immigrants to America came increasingly from Southern and Eastern Europe. By the late 1890s this "new" immigration made up more than half of the transatlantic flow and in 1910 over three-quarters of it. Within the "new" migration, Italians, like this mother with her children, predominated; nearly two million Italians moved to the United States between 1898 and 1907, in response to population pressure at home. However, Italians were so poor that they could only afford to migrate either during periods of domestic prosperity, such as the 1880s, or with financial assistance from those who had already made the arduous journey to America.

► Between 1880 and 1920 a third of the Jews of Eastern Europe migrated, 90 percent to the United States. Over one and a half million Jews arrived in America between 1900 and 1914, with a peak of 152,000 in 1906. They went partly in reaction to population pressure, and partly to avoid persecution in Russia. Most were young and skilled, and often whole families moved, the father travelling first. Russian Jews settled particularly in New York, Chicago and Philadelphia. New York's Lower East Side had 540,000 Jewish migrants, the crowded tenements containing workshops, basement synagogues, saloons and cafés.

ranean region and the Balkans, which acted as a safety valve to the population problem that bedeviled the peasant-based societies in these areas. As a result, the high rate of natural increase in Italy, at 16.4 per thousand, was transformed into a relatively slow rate of population growth of 0.65 percent per annum during the opening decade of the 20th century.

Generally migration, whether within an economy or international, involved movement from the countryside to the town. The agricultural labor force was a reserve army upon which urban manufacturing and service industries could draw as they expanded. Consequently the size of an economy's agricultural labor force represented a potential for economic growth as well as a measure of the extent of industrialization. The relative size of the agricultural labor force fell after 1890 in industrial and industrializing countries in Europe, principally as a result of two developments – national economic growth and international migration. These processes had gone farthest in the case of Britain, the first industrial nation, and consequently, the British economy was faced with a labor problem in the 1900s, since nearly all the gains in productivity arising from the movement of the labor force out of agriculture into industry had already accrued. In most other European countries this transfer of labor had still to take place in a major way. While this did represent a potential for future growth, it also meant that their manufacturing industries were faced with domestic markets of low consumption power, so that, as in the case of Sweden, their industries had to depend to some extent on export markets.

Labor, as a factor of production, was important not just in terms of numbers and its location within an economy, but also with regard to its quality – its skills and education. Increasingly

from 1890 workers in manufacturing were semiskilled or unskilled machine minders, rather than industrial artisans owning their own tools and both jealous and proud of their skills. At the same time, as science and applied technology came more to the fore in the closing decades of the 19th century, an educated workforce became more necessary.

By the 1900s primary education was becoming commonplace in Europe. Secondary education was still an innovation and was available to relatively small numbers, but Germany was establishing a lead. All countries had tertiary education systems and in many there were specific institutes designed to advance industrial technology. Many of the latter had their roots in the early part of the 19th century when they had been established with state support as a means to emulate Britain's industrial progress. Britain, however, continued to be a laggard in this matter and there remained within many branches of British manufacturing industry a continuing emphasis on hand skills and empiricism, which had served well initially, but by the 1900s was becoming increasingly outmoded.

In the United States, population was growing rapidly immediately before 1914, at rates comparable to the highest in Europe, those of Russia. As in Europe, birth and death rates were falling, the former from the 1840s. However, whereas most European countries were losing population as a result of international migration, the United States was a major migrant receiver. Generally international migrants were young, so that the median age of the American population in 1890 was 22, and still only 24 in 1910. The continuing influx of foreign labor contributed to the expansion of the economy. During the 25 years before 1914, there was an overall decline in the number of migrants from Europe and, within this total, there was a fall in the flow from northwestern

▼ By 1914 Germany had the largest electrical manufacturing industry in Europe. One of the biggest German firms was the Allgemeine Electricitäts-Gesellschaft of Emil Rathenau, whose Berlin workshops in the 1900s produced very large three-phase motors and transformers. Electricity was increasingly generated in this way to provide fixed motor power. Electrical power could now be directly applied to tools, so dispensing with inefficient power transmission mechanisms.

Europe, but a rise in the numbers coming from Russia and Italy. There was also internal migration from rural settlements to towns and the proportion of the labor force employed directly in agriculture declined from over 42 percent in 1890 to under 32 percent by 1910. As in Europe, the American labor force was now increasingly educated, at least to a primary level; in 1900 over three-quarters of the 5–17 age group were at school.

The growth of investment

Modern economic growth involved increased investment in producer goods. It also increasingly meant investment in more specific assets such as machinery and plant that produced only a limited range of products, was therefore more risky. Because different measures have to be used for

national income, it is particularly difficult to make precise comparisons between countries. However, while levels of investment had always varied over time, by 1900 the differing national fluctuations of what became known as the "trade cycle" were coming broadly into line as a result of economic integration brought about by the development of the world economy. Accordingly, by 1900 industrial countries were experiencing a common pattern of booms and slumps, not only in trade but also in investment.

In all the European countries for which reliable figures are available, the growth of investment was faster than the rate of population growth. The only exception was the United Kingdom in the 1900s, a reflection of British investment overseas rather than at home, and of the slowing down of the rate of British domestic economic growth dur-

Energy and Power

The further development and wider geographical diffusion of industrialization led to a rapidly growing use of energy. It has been estimated that world production of commercial sources of energy increased by nearly a thousand percent between 1860 and 1913. This growth in the generation and use of energy went hand in hand with the replacement of animate sources of power by inanimate sources. In the United States, for instance, animals had provided over three-quarters of such power in 1849, but by 1923 their share had fallen to barely three percent of an overall capacity, which had increased from 10 to 684 million horsepower, much of it concentrated in manufacturing, mines and quarries, railroads and shipping.

The main source of energy was coal; in 1913 coal was responsible, directly and indirectly, for nearly ninety percent of the world's energy output, with oil, gas and water providing the balance. World coal production increased from 132 million tons in 1860 to 314 million tonnes in 1880, and to 701 million tonnes by 1900. The United States was by far the biggest producer, followed by the United Kingdom and Germany, and to a lesser extent France and Belgium. Coal was used in metal smelting and refining and in steam generation, the latter particularly in coal-rich economies such as Britain and Germany. From the 1880s electricity gradually became important, generated from steam turbines or falling water. In America the amount of electricity used rose from four percent of all power in 1899 to nearly forty percent by 1914. In 1912 the output of electricity from central generating stations in the United States totaled 17,600 million kW hours. Britain produced only 2500 million kW from public supply power stations. Hydroelectricity grew in suitable countries; in 1910 Canada had a total water-power capacity of 0.73 million kW and Switzerland had one of 0.604 million kW.

► **Electrical generation still began with raising steam.**

ing the Edwardian period. Actually, in nearly all European countries the rate of domestic investment fell somewhat after 1900, but the British experience was nonetheless significantly different, though it is difficult to assess the extent to which the relatively low level of national income employed in domestic investment was a significant factor in the retardation of British economic growth from the 1890s.

As with labor, there were international flows of finance – savings – by which capital formation in receiving countries could be financed. Britain, France and Germany were the major exporters of capital, British savings being largely directed to countries outside Europe. The main European countries to draw upon such savings were those countries where industrialization was just beginning – Russia, Scandinavia and Italy (though in the case of Italy such international borrowings were exceeded by remittances sent home by migrants overseas). By 1914, Sweden too had become a capital exporter. The United States was a net capital importer, but these inflows merely augmented an already high internal rate of saving. Domestic investment grew at 3.5 percent a year between 1890 and 1910, though it slackened during the ensuing decade. In these terms American economic growth was similar in nature to German – the momentum of an earlier industrialization being sustained by continuing high investment – and consequently both countries stood apart from the United Kingdom where growth was faltering after 1890 and domestic investment was low, especially after 1900.

Technological change

Beyond increasing quantities of labor and capital, there were other processes that were important for economic growth. One was increasing returns to scale, both as individual producing units gre larger, and therefore more economical to run, and as production became more specialized. Another was improved efficiency in the allocation of resources, as with the transfer of labor from low-productivity employment to high-productivity. This so-called "structural change" also encompassed the elimination of monopolies and discrimination in the markets for both finished goods and factors of production–land, labor and capital. Lastly, there was technological progress.

The resumption of growth after 1890, in the advanced economies of Europe as well as the United States, has often been called a second industrial revolution, resulting from a new stream of innovations. This involved the harnessing of electricity and organic chemistry and the development of the internal combustion engine, and witnessed the growing production of a widening range of consumer durables such as the sewing machine, the typewriter, the bicycle and the motor car. Their production in turn required other developments which were also part of this new cluster of innovations, namely, precision manufacture and assembly-line mass production. Although these had begun during the mid-19th century, they were dependent for their fuller development upon the availability of mass-produced steel from the 1880s and special steel alloys from the 1890s, as well as on standardization gauges, which reduced costs of manufacture primarily through dispensing with expensive "fitting" by hand. At the same time there was also a wider use of already established technologies, as was the case with steam power, especially in Britain, Germany and the United States, economies with ready access to cheap coal. In Britain, the use of steam power rose by nearly ten times between 1870 and 1907.

There were, then, two currents of technological change at work – the final working out of an old

and the inception of a new. They came together in different economies at different times and in different ways, helping to generate disparate patterns of growth. Germany expanded on the basis of both old and new manufacturing techniques. In France, which had not really experienced the first industrial revolution, modern growth only began with the second, starting in the 1890s. American growth has been conceived of in terms of long phases, with one such beginning at the end of the 1880s and being sustained until 1929. Newly industrializing countries adopted old and new technologies almost simultaneously at the turn of the century, as happened with ball bearing manufacture in Sweden and the production of electrical equipment in the Hungarian half of the Dual Monarchy.

The hallmark of this second industrial revolution was a closer alliance between science and technology, and its power source came progressively to be electricity. The origins of its commercial application lay in the provision of lighting in the 1870s. In the 1880s and 1890s it was developed as a source of motor power, powering among other things the streetcar and the elevator. It offered particular advantages to those economies without sufficient sources of coal, such as France, Switzerland and Italy, but the development of hydroelectricity was often costly, requiring substantial investment in dams and long-distance

▲ The growth of railroad networks from the 1850s created a demand for standardized components, like these wagon and engine-driving wheels being made at the Krupp works, Essen, in 1900. Down the centre aisle workers are manhandling wheels on which metal tyres are being fitted by heat shrinking. On either side wheels are being trued by turning on large lathes, powered from overhead shafts via belting. For these movements an overhead crane is employed, while the whole layout of the shop allows an uninterrupted flow of work. The railroads' demands on engineering led Krupps to become a substantial enterprise as early as the 1870s, when it employed 16,000 workers; by 1912 its payroll numbered nearly 70 thousand workers, a fifth of the population of Essen. The firm also employed 13,000 in its own collieries.

► Handmade cans for food packing had appeared in the 1820s, but the food industry was not revolutionized until the 1880s. During the last two decades of the 19th century, machines like this one were developed to produce cans and to solder, automatically, the lid onto the body of the can. The growth of the canning industry led to substantial increases in the demand for tinplate and until the 1890s Britain was the major world supplier. In 1889 the United States took 327,000 tonnes of tinplate from the South Wales industry, 80 percent of British exports, but the United States then raised import duties sharply.

transmission networks to transfer the energy to industrial and urban centers. Nonetheless, such was the high cost of coal-based power in these economies that within a few years, the basic innovations came about through advances in hydroelectricity. The practicality of hydroelectricity, coupled with the long-distance transmission of current, was demonstrated in 1885 when electricity generated in Creil was consumed in Paris, nearly 100 kilometers (60 miles) away. Six years later hydroelectricity was transferred 179 kilometers (112 miles) from Lauffen to Frankfurt.

The manufacture of electrical equipment, for the generation and the application of energy, was dominated by the United States and Germany. In 1913 the output of their electrical manufacturing industries amounted to £73.8 million and £65 million respectively after 1900 British output expanded, reaching £30 million by 1914.

New production methods

The generation and consumption of electricity required steel and the manufacture of precision, interchangeable, machine parts. Other developments reduced wasteful friction: the ball bearing, invented in 1877 by William Brown of Birmingham, England, was used from 1886 by Daniel

Rudge in his bicycles. Ball bearings came to be found in nearly all the new consumer durables, the production of which expanded greatly at the turn of the century, and which, like the sewing machine, were the result of whole series of technical advances since the mid-19th century.

The technical demands of precision manufacture and standardized interchangeable parts had already existed in the production of small arms, locks, clocks and agricultural machinery, but now an ever higher degree of precision was required and was justified by market demand. Precision was achieved by the employment and further development of light machine tools such as the turret lathe, which had been invented in the United States in the 1840s, and the universal milling machine, again an American invention (1861). With the availability from the 1890s of special self-hardening tool steels, these machine tools became more widely used: for instance, milling machines were employed widely in bicycle production. Automobile engines of the 1890s and 1900s set even higher requirements in terms of work across a range of complication, delicacy and precision, which could only be achieved through the substitution of grinding for cutting and scraping. In the 1890s grinding wheels came to be made with new amalgams of abrasives, in particular carborundum in 1896, and were employed in new ways, as with plunge grinding, developed by the American Charles H. Norton. This was adopted before 1914 in the United States for automotive engineering, but not in Europe, although it was used in both Britain and Germany in the building of railroad locomotives.

As well as the diffusion of new machine tools in mechanical engineering, from the 1870s this branch of industry shared an interest with the primary metal-producing industries in cost control through improved work organization and plant layout. This "scientific management" viewed labor as an animate machine, capable of being made more efficient by the reduction of wasted or redundant effort. Although this system was most highly developed in America, European

▼ Germany became a powerful economic force as the center of the development of new technologies. Werner von Siemens was a founder of the electrical industry. In 1903 his firm merged with Schuckert, establishing a concern able to rival AEG.

▲ In the late 19th century precision engineering had reached the stage of being able to produce complicated devices such as the typewriter, made by German firms from 1900. But their assembly was expensive and only profitable if a mass market could be tapped. Firms turned to advertising and, in the limited German market, to manufacturing other products.

engineers were also interested. It reached its pre-1914 climax in Detroit in the new Ford factory, where production had to be streamlined to meet a high demand for the Model T car in the 1910s. The answer was found in the moving assembly line. The results were spectacular: the time taken to produce a car fell from 12 hours 8 minutes in 1913 to 1 hour 33 minutes in 1914, when throughput amounted to 1,000 vehicles a day.

The retailing revolution

The new products of the early years of the century were aimed at a mass market; their economics depended upon a high output to reduce the unit costs of their manufacture. However, despite this lowering of costs, food and housing remained the largest items in the family expenditure of lower income groups.

Wages were rising, especially in northwestern Europe and the northeast of the United States. This was a result of increased employment in manufacturing with its much higher productivity, unionization of the workforce and, in northwestern Europe, the decline in family size. Of equal importance was the fall in the cost of food in America and in Britain and Denmark, the two European countries which did not protect their domestic agriculture against imports. Food prices fell during the last quarter of the 19th century as a result of the growth in world supplies and the fall in intercontinental transport costs following the completion of national railway systems and improvements in oceanic shipping.

The importance of this decline in the cost of food as against manufactures (the prices of which

were also falling) can be gauged from expenditure patterns. The family of a British workman earning £78 a year in 1901, which was then considered to be "good weekly wages", spent 41 percent of this on food. But in Europe, where agriculture was protected, the ratio was higher. A family with an equivalent income in Belgium spent 61 percent of it on food, in Germany 57 percent and in France 56 percent. A comparable American figure is not available, but outlays on food comprised just over 25 percent of total household expenditure on consumption in the United States in 1909. Even in Britain, for all the drop in food prices, in the mid-1890s nearly one-third of the urban working classes still lived below the poverty line.

Developing transport systems linking new sources of supply led in America and Britain to the growth of chains of grocery stores owned by a single company. One of the first American multiple food store chains was the Great Atlantic

▲ Modern retailing began in the advanced economies of the West in the 1880s. Its major feature was the mass sale of standardized packaged goods, but producers also recognized the advantages of differentiating markets. Display was made easier by the availability of cheap plate glass used in windows and cabinets, and middle-class customers were served by uniformed armies of assistants. Some distributors, such as Maillards, set up chains of outlets in grand hotels, like this candy store in a hotel on Fifth Avenue, New York.

◄ The need to change distribution systems was forced by the expansion of supply. A particularly British feature was the development in industrial cities of cooperative retail stores. By the 1900s most were affiliated either to the Cooperative Wholesale Society or the Scottish Wholesale Society which, in turn, imported foodstuffs from abroad, including tea from their own plantations in Ceylon.

and Pacific Tea Company established in the mid-1850s, and an early European pioneer was the Aerated Bread Company in the London area. New major wholesalers pioneered branding, advertising and the use of a sales force, and firms such as Quaker Oats, Campbells, Heinz and Bordin developed extensive purchasing and sales networks of their own. With the spread of refrigeration in the mid-1880s, other American food processors moved into mass distribution. The fresh meat packers – Swift, Armour, Morris and Cudahy – and the brewers – Pabst, Schlitz and Anheuser Busch – were among the first in the field.

Britain was the closest to American trends, being an open wealthy market for the world supply of primary products. The "retailing revolution" in Britain came with the development of multiple shops to sell imported foodstuffs. It began with "colonial wares" such as tea, the international supply of which was expanding through plantation production. Thomas Lipton opened his first shop in Glasgow in 1872. By 1890 he had 70 shops in London alone and in 1898 the firm, with 245 shops and 3,800 agencies selling its packeted tea, was turned into a public company. Regional chains of grocery shops developed in France too, while in Belgium the firm of Delhaize Frères, established in 1871, had 565 branches by 1904.

Imported foodstuffs were not the only basis for the development of chains of multiple shops; others were developed in Britain to sell books and stationery (initially from railway station kiosks), footwear, ready-made clothing, and drugs and other pharmaceutical products. In Britain shoe-making became factory-based from the late 1880s and by the 1900s it generally involved American machinery. Clothing came to be made in factories at about the same time: the number of factories in Leeds increased during the decade after 1881 from seven to 54. Initially factories concentrated upon men's clothing; however, by the turn of the century millinery and dressmaking had come within the orbit of the factory. By 1900 there were 257 multiple retailers controlling 11,650 shops in the United Kingdom, while in America there were 60 different chains of stores.

Among other innovations, cooperative production and distribution became a feature of northern industrial Britain, while mail order business was developed in America: with efficient communications, this provided a method of reaching the dispersed communities of rural America. The business was begun in 1872 by A. Montgomery Ward in Chicago, who was followed two decades later by Sears, Roebuck & Co.

Middle-class shopping and consumption was transformed from the 1850s with the remodeling in Paris of Bon Marché in 1852 by Aristide Boucicaut. He decided to sell good quality apparel at reasonable and fixed prices through shop assistants whom he paid on commission. Sales were further maximized by advertisements. Modern department stores grew up in London and New York during the 1860s. In Germany they spread after the formation of the Empire – Tietz in 1879, Karstadt in 1881 and Althoff in 1885. The most rapid expansion of the American shops – Macy's of New York, Marshall Field of Chicago, and John Wanamaker of Philadelphia and New York – was at the turn of the century. Most such establishments aimed at the bourgeois market, but the working classes got their department stores in the form of bazaars. Woolworths pioneered this genre in both America and Britain and Marks & Spencer in England. In Britain there was also the Cooperative store, with its continually expanding range of goods.

... Under the influence of the large department stores and clothing bazaars' which gradually penetrated into the small towns from the cities ... a certain strong demand for cheaper dress and ready-made novelties was carried into the circle of working-class women in the last decade before the war.

W. ZIMMERMANN

William Lever and "Sunlight" Soap

A mass market in Britain began to develop through the steady rise in money wages from the mid-1860s and the fall in the cost of foodstuffs from the mid-1870s. This provided opportunities for businessmen alert to these trends, one of whom was William Hesketh Lever. As the son of a British wholesale grocer who joined the family firm in 1867, becoming a partner in 1872, Lever was well placed both to observe and respond to new trends in consumption patterns. Initially he expanded the range of goods in which his firm dealt and widened the geographical area that it served. But he also took an interest in American retailing, especially branding, backed by advertising and other forms of more aggressive sales promotion. Lever was more than an astute salesman. In 1885, again following American trends, he moved into manufacturing, so combining volume production with mass distribution. He acquired an existing soap works, and chose the name "Sunlight" for his new product. From 1889 Lever developed Port Sunlight, near Liverpool, not just as a manufacturing enterprise, but set within its own garden village, a reflection of both Lever's flair for grand affairs and his paternalistic style of management.

▲ Lever's success was recognized when he was created a baronet in 1911. He became Baron Leverhulme in 1917.

▶ Employing American-style methods of sales promotion and branding, Lever transformed the market for soap, which for mass sales until the 1880s had consisted of unbranded, unwrapped soap cakes, retailed like potatoes. His forceful approach caused a hostile reaction amongst other producers.

Urbanization

The beginnings of mass markets during the quarter of a century before 1914 came about not only through the gradual rise in working-class levels of income in some economies, but also as a result of the increasing concentration of people in growing towns and cities. By 1914 there were 51 cities on the continent of Europe with populations of over 250,000, together with a further 15 in the United Kingdom and 20 in the United States. In continental Europe the populations of these substantial cities grew so fast between 1890 and 1910 that they nearly doubled in size. The American experience was generally similar, though in Britain the pace of expansion was slower, because the country was already more urbanized. Even so, there was an average expansion in Britain of one-third over the same period. The outcome of this further urban development was that by 1910, nearly 23 percent of the American population resided in cities with populations of more than a quarter of a million. In Germany the proportion was 14.6 percent and in the United Kingdom 30.9 percent.

What was remarkable, however, was the continuing increase in the size of cities which were already very large, a trait noticeable in both advanced economies and those countries which were industrializing, like Russia. Between 1890 and 1910, the most rapidly expanding cities amongst this group on the continent of Europe were primarily either German – Essen, Hamburg, Düsseldorf, Nuremberg, Frankfurt-am-Main, Stuttgart, Leipzig, Dresden, Bremen and Hanover – or Russian – Lódź, Kiev, St Petersburg, Warsaw and Moscow. The only other European city in this group was Rotterdam, the population of

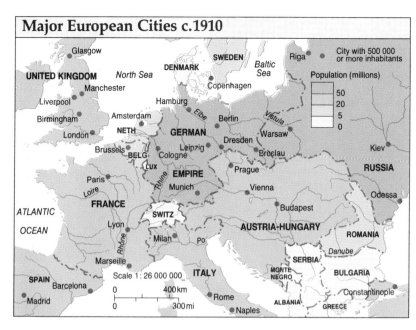

Major European Cities c.1910

which grew by 211 percent between 1890 and 1910. The forces for expansion were of varying kinds and not always the direct result of the development of manufacturing industry.

In Germany, Düsseldorf and Essen became large cities by 1910 as a result of the growth of industry – iron, steel, coal and engineering. But Frankfurt-am-Main and Leipzig were historic trading towns, long-standing sites of industrial fairs. During the 19th century Frankfurt became a modern commercial and financial center and toward the end of the century it acquired a local manufacturing base involving "new" industries such as electrical equipment manufacture.

▲ **Urbanization is a good guide to the spread of industrialization.** In early 20th-century Europe the population was increasingly moving to towns or cities. This was especially the case in northwestern Europe, the established industrial belt of the continent, which ran southeastwards from Glasgow to Paris, Lyons and Cologne. However, around this core of industrial cities, industrialization was spreading outwards, into Central Europe and in Mediterranean Europe.

◄ **Some towns, such as Hamburg, became giant cities** by the turn of the century not so much because of the growth of production, but rather as commercial service centers. Hamburg was the outlet for the products of Central Europe, in particular the industries of the middle Rhine and Bohemia, and was also the point of access for imports of raw materials from the rest of the world economy. Accordingly, manufacturing was largely restricted to supporting the activities of the port – shipbuilding and processing – and a large part of the population was involved in service trades, as merchants, bankers or clerks.

▶ **Britain retained world dominance in shipbuilding.** By 1913 the British mercantile marine had over eleven million tonnes of steam ships. With steam and sail combined, the United Kingdom accounted for a third of the world fleet in 1911; the German share was under ten percent, and the American less than three percent. During the five years before 1914 British shipyards built nearly two-thirds of the total tonnage launched.

Leipzig retained its importance as a trade fair city as well as a center of printing and publishing. In the north, Hamburg and Bremen developed processing industries and shipbuilding, while in southern Germany the further expansion of Stuttgart and Nuremberg at the turn of the century reflected the development of modern manufacturing methods in Württemberg and Bavaria.

Russian urbanization, and in particular the yet further growth of "giant" cities, was a reflection of the beginnings of industrialization. Like Lódź, St Petersburg was a cotton manufacturing center, but by 1900 it, together with the Moscow region, was also responsible for 20 percent of Russian iron and steel production. It also possessed some of the newer industries – electrical engineering, rubber, organic chemicals and the manufacture of motor cars – and by 1914 was also a major Russian financial center. Similarly, Moscow was by 1900 acquiring some of the characteristics of a mature industrial city. Important for metal refining and metal working, the city was also a center for textile production; its factory workforce increased from 67,000 to 100,000 during the 1890s.

The only "giant" British city which experienced continued rapid growth was Birmingham, which was a center for engineering and metalworking, producing by 1911 electrical products, tools, dies, munitions, bicycles and motor cars. But other cities grew too: Sheffield became a center of production of high-speed steels in the 1900s. Belfast, Hull and Newcastle thrived on shipbuilding and marine engineering – shipbuilding was the economy's most successful staple industry in international terms. Newcastle was a coal export port, while Hull's importance and continuing growth also derived from its processing industries; together with Grimsby, it grew with the development of steam trawl fishing. Bristol too expanded rapidly from a diversified economic base, with general engineering employing over ten thousand people by 1911, a port, and processing industries such as tobacco as well as brewing.

The process of the continued growth of some very large cities in the United States had characteristics in common with Germany, Russia and Britain. But it was the expansion of engineering in states like Ohio, Indiana, Illinois, Michigan and Wisconsin that led to the further growth in size of Detroit and Cleveland, as well as Chicago, and to a consequent change in their function from internal marketing centers to industrial conurbations. There were also some relatively small towns that mushroomed into very large cities by 1910, like Los Angeles, whose growth reflected the general rapid expansion of population in the American West, particularly California.

The further development of Cleveland and Detroit took place from a firm basis – they were Great Lakes ports which had expanded substantially as distributing centers following the completion of the Erie Canal in 1825. In Detroit the development of automobile manufacture sustained the city's growth. Cleveland had been a more substantial internal marketing center but, although enjoying good rail connections, the city's hinterland was essentially limited, and it remained best known as an oil processor. Chicago was

preeminent amongst the internal marketing centers of the United States. By 1880 it was the butcher, meat packer, grain distributor and lumber merchant of the United States. It also began to develop as an industrial center through the growth of a steel industry based upon the resources of the Lake Superior region, and it gained other industries which diversified its growing manufacturing base – shoe companies fleeing from organized labor in New England, German breweries, Jewish tailoring, and telephone factories which all drew in migrant labor.

New York, along with its satellite Newark, was the only eastern seaboard port city that continued to grow substantially at the turn of the century, nearly doubling in size between 1890 and 1910. The city's major function was as a port with an associated commercial and financial complex, but it also had a manufacturing function, embracing the clothing trade and tobacco processing, as well as printing, a shoe industry and glassmaking. Only Greater London was bigger in numbers.

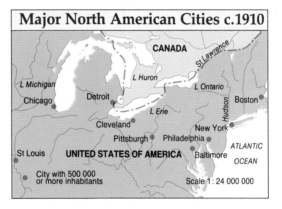

The American city is typical of the industrial world, whether it be in Germany, England, France, Belgium, or Italy. The city is a product of the nineteenth century; it is a by-product of steam, electricity, and transportation.

F. C. HOWE, EUROPEAN CITIES AT WORK

◀ At the end of the 19th century some towns and cities along the southern shores of the Great Lakes, which had been primarily marketing centers, were transformed into sizable industrial places with the growth of engineering. This new development attracted labor from Canada, from the black population in the South, and from the Old World. In Chicago in 1890, over 40 percent of the city's population were foreign-born, and in 1915 Chicago had the third largest urban Polish community in the world.

Urban transport systems

Cities in advanced economies during the 19th century were places of dense settlement, until urban systems of mass transport were developed. The omnibus, a French innovation, catered primarily for the middle-class residential districts; it was the horse tramway which provided public transport, cheap enough for at least some sections of the working classes. This had started as isolated lines in New York and New Orleans in the 1830s and by the 1870s had spread to many European cities. However, the market for such transport systems was restricted by the technology employed, the conditions under which they operated and that problem of all commuter systems – the daily fluctuation in load.

Steam proved generally to be suitable only for suburban and rural light railways and tramways, particularly in Europe. Electrical traction was explored from 1881, and was quickly adopted in the United States. In Europe the switch to electric traction involving the Sprague system of overhead wires was less rapid. Other methods were already working – battery and conduit – and above all, there was a European esthetic objection to the overhead wire, especially along grand boulevards and in public squares. Authorities in Berlin, Birmingham, Munich, Nancy, Paris and Vienna initially refused to have the skylines of their city centers disrupted by cat's cradles of wires. However, by 1914 the electric tram with the offensive overhead wire had become commonplace in European cities. Between 1886 and 1910 the number of tram passengers in Austria-Hungary, France, Germany and Great Britain increased from 920 million to 6.7 billion. German and French towns and cities got off to a quick start, but British electrification came a decade later. Glasgow proved to be a model, the city deciding in 1894 to operate its own system and electrifying it from 1899 with Westinghouse equipment; other British municipalities followed, and the Glasgow example of municipally operated electrified tramways soon spread to the rest of Europe, France excepted.

Even with the tram, city streets remained so congested that planners considered placing the urban railway either above or below ground level. American cities, beginning with New York in 1867, built elevated lines, as later did some European cities such as Berlin and Vienna, whereas in London an underground system was developed, beginning with the opening of the Metropolitan line in 1863. The construction of London's first true "tube" underground railway, the City & South London, began in 1886. Employing electric traction, it opened in 1890. Glasgow, Budapest, Paris, Berlin and Hamburg all developed underground systems. In the United States, elevated city lines were electrified, beginning with New York in 1895, and the development of electric subways also got under way. The first New York subway was opened in 1904. At the same time, a further threat to the tram's dominance was beginning to appear. In 1903 and 1904 motor buses started to convey London passengers; carbon compounds now began to replace ammonia as the pollutant of urban streets.

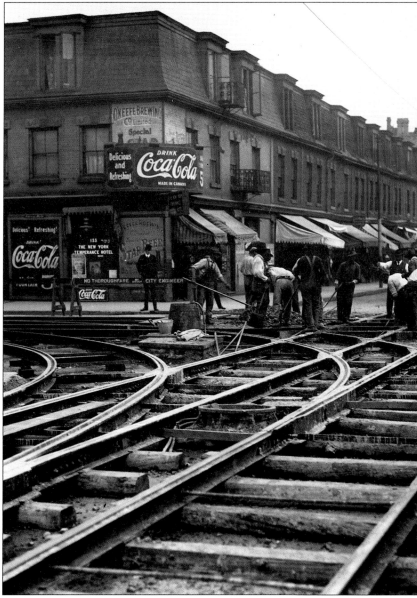

◀ The electric trolley car made possible the development of suburbs, permitting towns to spread outwards, but it also connected the countryside to the cities, increasing their importance as retail and commercial centers. Above all, the trolley transformed the journey to work for the ordinary man.

▶ Traffic jams acted as a spur to the development of the underground railway network in London. This was designed initially to connect the main railway termini, but it then spread outwards and grew into a commuter network.

▼ Building the new urban transport systems initially caused disruption. However, their construction represented sizable investment which accelerated economic growth and in particular encouraged the growth of the electrical manufacturing industry.

Industrial concentration

By the 1880s, large concentrations of industrial capital had emerged, especially in Germany and the United States, and by the 1900s some large companies were wielding monopoly power over their respective industries. The growth of firm size is a complex process. Technical and financial economies that arose from higher production capacities were important. These led to production economies of scale and also allowed firms to become more specialized. There emerged clearer differentiations of internal functions, such as management structures, the conduct of marketing, the growth of internal finance and the support of research and development, where it was cheaper to undertake such activities within a firm, rather than employing outside specialists. In particular, some "new" products required closer contact with the customer; German sewing machine and bicycle producers, for example, moved into both retailing and managing their own exports. As a result of such growth, output in some industries became concentrated in the hands of fewer firms. The increasing size of enterprises went hand in hand with the gradual disappearance of family-based firms and the consequent divorce of ownership from control. Salaried managers became a new industrial caste and, in at least some German industries, measured their success through the continuing growth of their respective firms, often undertaken by acquiring other enterprises.

Industrial concentration was carried further in the United States, Germany and to some extent in Britain by the formation of cartels, trusts and holding companies in industries such as sugar, oil and iron and steel, and by a spate of mergers. Following the Wall Street crash of 1893, American companies rationalized production by concentrating manufacturing in a limited number of plants, and coupled this to national marketing and distribution networks. Britain's efforts at rationalization were not so successful.

Vertical integration – whereby companies acquired their sources of raw materials and took over the firms that bought their semi-finished wares – also took place, especially in the American metals industries and in German chemicals. By 1905, big business had come to stay in the United States and Germany, and had gained a toehold in Britain.

International economic rivalry

The growth of American and German manufacturing from the 1880s led to the displacement of Britain as the "workshop of the world". Britain's share of the world market was sharply cut back during the 1890s, and Germany became her major competitor in Europe. American competition arose from the mid-1890s, but the bulk of American exports were still made up of raw materials, and so did not affect British trade. The rise of this competition did not become a matter of national concern until German and American products entered the domestic British market.

Germany had technological superiority in organic chemicals and electrical equipment, and the global spread of German exports was coupled with the growth of a German mercantile marine, now in a position to rival British companies. Imports of American machinery and manufactures rose eightfold between 1890 and 1899. American promoters were behind the programs for the electrification of the London underground, whilst American shipping acquisitions forced the British Government to provide subsidies and finance to the Cunard Co. to construct two fast mail ships, so as to secure the continuance of the British character of the firm. The Imperial Tobacco Company held off the attack by the American Tobacco Co. on the British market in 1902. These experiences led to British concern that weakening economic power might also mean waning political power, a concern which persisted through the first decade of the century, even after the jingoism of the Boer War period had subsided.

THE MODEL T FORD AND THE MASS MARKET

The man who designed the car for everyday life was Henry Ford. The son of a farming family of Irish and Flemish origin, Ford's reputation as an automobile engineer was established by his second car, built between 1897 and 1899 with the backing of local Detroit merchants. Whereas Ford at this stage wanted to build racers, his backers were interested in commercial vehicles; Ford left and his original company was established as the Cadillac Motor Co.

Ford in 1902 turned to the development of a car to be sold to the mass market. The Ford Motor Co. was formed in June 1903, when the mass-market Model A was put on public sale at a retail price of $850. The first small car that Ford produced in any quantity, involving standardized design, was the N of 1906–07, which sold initially at $600. In 1906–07 the company moved to Highland Park, which at first occupied 24 hectares (60 acres) but eventually spread to 92 hectares (230 acres), of which 21 hectares consisted of floor space. Here, from 1 October 1908, the Model T went into production. It was a standardized utility vehicle with interchangeable parts; Ford had been responsible for the basic concept, but the detailed design had been undertaken by two company engineers – C. Harold Wills and Joseph Galamb. Depending upon specification, complete cars were first sold at prices in the range $850 to $1000, but by August 1916 these had fallen to $345 to $360. It was the company's sole product until 1927, with output expanding rapidly until the early 1920s.

By 1913 there was a Ford car dealer in every American town with population greater than 2000. The T, always a basic car, was particularly attractive to the rural communities of the American mid-West and High Plains. Its volume production, reaching 2000 a day by 1916, was only achieved by the development of the moving production line at Highland Park between 1910 and 1914. This involved bringing the work to the labor force, and at waist height to reduce redundant effort. The concept of a continually moving track was introduced in the spring of 1913, initially for the assembly of the flywheel magneto coil.

Giovanni Agnelli, one of the founders of Fiat, returned to Turin in 1912 after a VIP tour of the Highland Park factory convinced that he had seen the future: "I have just returned from America where I wanted to see for myself the danger that is threatening – competition is becoming more and more difficult every day." Fiat decided to integrate the production process on the American pattern, and by the end of World War I the immense new Lingotto factory had begun to rise on the outskirts of Turin.

▶ The Model T was the car for rural America in the 1910s. During 1916–17, they were built at a rate of about 2000 a day and, by 1921, five million had been produced. Based on a common chassis and running gear, the car could be refashioned in many ways.

▲▶ When the Model T was launched in 1908 it was cheap. However with mass production it became even cheaper and within eight years the price of the basic model had fallen by 60 percent, despite wartime inflation in the United States.

The Ford Four Cylinder, Twenty Horse Power, Five Passenger Touring Car
$850.00 Fob. Detroit

Ford Motor Company
Detroit

Ford constructed cars from the late 1890s and this is his first — the 1896 car — which owed much to two other Detroit automobile enthusiasts C. B. King and O. E. Barthel.

Ford's success came from the economics of production engineering, arising from the interchangeability of parts, married with the assembly line. The latter had its origins in Chicago meat packing.

Manufacture in volume needed a flow system of production and the "line" had many applications. Here cakes on a conveyor belt are being iced at waist height.

From the 1880s "scientific management" aimed at making human labor more efficient through inducing it to behave like a machine. By the 1980s, robots, controlled by computers, were dispensing with human labor.

Datafile

Increasingly from the mid-19th century the advanced industrial economies came into greater and greater contact with the nonindustrial world. The temperate and tropical belts, formally colonized, provided raw materials, markets for some manufacturers, and places of settlement and investment. Until the 1880s the main contacts were with the temperate primary producers and the Orient. By 1900 the focus shifted to the tropical world, especially Africa.

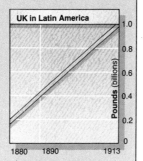

UK in Latin America

▲ By 1914 a quarter of British overseas lending consisted of investments in Latin America. Before 1890 the main areas of investment had been Argentina and Brazil, but after the turn of the century British investment encompassed the whole of the continent. It principally consisted of the finance of railroad construction.

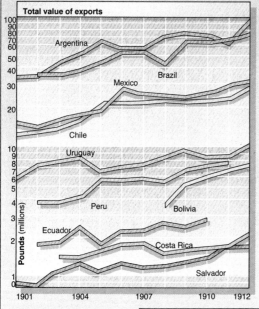

Total value of exports

◄ During the early 20th century Latin American exports grew substantially. The most important trading economies were the large, temperate, countries of Argentina and Brazil. Argentina supplied Britain with grains and from 1901 chilled beef, whereas Mexican trade was largely directed to the United States.

► Japanese overseas trade grew steadily from the early 1890s until 1914, when it expanded rapidly as a result of the war-induced boom, and especially the lack of European competition in Asian and Pacific markets. Until 1914 Japanese exports consisted largely of semi-manufactures, with a new trade in cotton yarn developing from the late 1890s. In 1914 raw silk, silk piece-goods, cotton yarn and cotton cloth comprised over 50 percent of exports, and they were to retain this dominance until the mid-1930s.

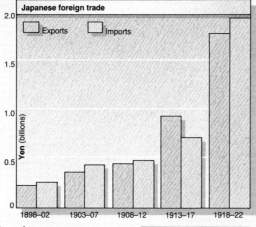

Japanese foreign trade

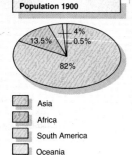

Population 1900

Asia
Africa
South America
Oceania

◄ Estimates of world population, and its distribution, at this period are difficult. Asia was the most populated continent of the nonindustrial world and has sizeable, crowded cities. In Africa, population may even have been declining slightly at the beginning of the 20th century.

► The pace of railroad construction in the industrial world slowed from 1900. By contrast, in the colonial world the turn of the century saw the establishment of primary routes.

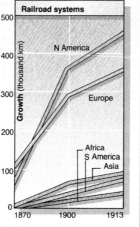

Railroad systems

In 1913 probably about two-thirds of the world's population lived outside the industrial and industrializing economies of Europe and the United States, though it is difficult to be precise because of inadequate and unreliable information. From the 1830s there was a growing divergence in average income per head between the populations of the industrial and industrializing countries on the one hand, and that of the rest of the world on the other, and by 1913 average incomes per head in developed countries were about three and a half times higher than those prevailing in the rest of the world. But within the "underdeveloped" world itself there were equally striking contrasts in material advance. In 1913 three temperate countries of recent European settlement – Australia, Canada and New Zealand – had average incomes per head higher than the average for all developed countries; in Australia and Canada average incomes indeed approached those of the most developed of the industrial economies. At the other end of the spectrum, average incomes per head in Latin American countries such as Argentina, Chile and Uruguay were only just over half of the average of developed countries, whereas in Asia they were only barely over a quarter.

COLONIES AND PRIMARY PRODUCERS

These wide and growing differences in average income were the product of many factors. One was the restricted geographical diffusion of industrialization – the main driving force behind the growth of incomes – before 1914; another was the unequal gains which arose from the trade between the industrial economies and the rest of the world. Third, and particularly with respect to the Dominions of the British Empire, were the advantages that accrued to the colonizing settlers from low ratios of population to natural resources. The increasing economic contact between the industrial economies and the rest of the world led in the latter to extensive, rather than intensive, economic development – the wider spread of commercial agriculture and the extraction of minerals. Although incomes rose as a consequence, the growth was not as rapid as that in Europe and North America.

European influences
Trade with the rest of the world, and in some cases investment and settlement, carried with them the diffusion of a European lifestyle. In certain areas, such as Latin America, there was already a foundation of European culture and social mores as a result of earlier Spanish and

▼ The temperate and tropical worlds became increasingly important to the advanced industrial economies as sources of raw materials and foodstuffs. New plantation systems were developed by Western capital and management, but frequently this involved transferring labor to work them. During the expansion of the Ceylon tea industry from the 1800s, Tamil labor from southern India was brought to the island to work the estates.

Portuguese colonization. This led to the development of large cities, usually ports, similar in architecture, layout, transport and other utility systems to Western cities such as London, Berlin, Paris and Madrid, through the influence of local middle-class groups who looked particularly to Europe for fashions and styles of living. By the 1880s European economic and social contact were also beginning to affect the tropical world and China, although European migration to these areas remained minimal.

From the 1860s the temperate lands in both the northern and southern hemispheres, together with India, were developed by European colonizers to provide the industrial economies of the world – in particular northwestern Europe – with foodstuffs and raw materials. The renewed momentum of growth of the industrial economies from the 1890s increased this demand, particularly for raw materials, and especially for basic ingredients of the new technologies of the late 19th and early 20th centuries, such as copper, rubber and bauxite. It was precisely these new economic demands which from the 1880s led to increased American and European involvement with those areas of the tropical world that would be able to supply their requirements.

Transport and trade

A growing marker of the impact of the advanced economies upon the rest of the world was the spread of the railroad, as its construction was largely initiated by American and European promoters and financed by American and European capital. Further, the track and rolling stock were usually supplied by either American or European firms, and the senior administrative staffs of the operating companies were generally American or European. In 1870 only 6.2 percent of the world's railroad lines lay outside the continents of Europe and North America. By 1900 that proportion had increased to over 18 percent and it rose to over 26 percent in 1913. Railroad construction during the years before 1914 expanded considerably in Central and South America, but the most dramatic increase was in Africa.

The volume of trade experienced by the tropical world as a whole increased threefold between 1883 and 1913. This was largely a result of increased exports from the tropics of cotton, oilseeds, cocoa, coffee, tobacco, bananas and rubber, with minerals making a contribution only after 1900. Alongside this production for export, the output of rice and other foodstuffs increased to supply the growing local labor forces involved in commercial export agriculture. The substantial post-1880 expansion of tropical exports led to rises in net national income per head, some countries and regions in particular experiencing very rapid export-led growth. Exports from West Africa grew by a factor of 5.48 between 1883 and 1913. Comparable expansion was experienced by Thailand, Ceylon, Central Africa and Indochina.

The growing railroad systems in the non-industrial world, both temperate and tropical, frequently radiated out from ports, some new, others well established. Hong Kong had been a barren island in 1841, but in 1900 41 percent of China's foreign trade was conducted through this British colony. The Treaty of Shimonoseki (1895) allowed foreigners to invest in, and operate, factories in Chinese treaty ports and in Hong Kong. This resulted in the development of textile and flour mills, cement works, tobacco processing, vegetable oil extraction and match manufacture.

By the 1860s the major merchants of Calcutta, together with the agents and managing agents of shipping and insurance companies, jute and cotton mills, other manufacturing companies, tea plantations, and coal and other mines were almost exclusively European. Further, as was to happen in Hong Kong from the 1890s, so in

▼ Cotton had been developed in Egypt as an export crop since the 1830s. By 1913 the area devoted to cotton cultivation was twice as great as in the mid-1890s, partly due to cotton now being included in the crop rotation every two years, as opposed to every three, and partly made possible by the greater supply of water made available for irrigation by the Delta barrage and the Aswan dam. Egyptian exports of cotton rose rapidly between the early 1890s and 1913. Britain took half of the crop exported, and Egypt's other main customers were the United States, Germany, France and Russia.

▲ Laying out estates drew upon land and labor, both relatively cheap resources in the underdeveloped countries. Not all of this development was the result of Western capital, however. In Ceylon, indigenous entrepreneurs played a major role. The 1911 census counted 93,000 owners, managers and "superior staff" on estates and plantations, of which only 1,600 were expatriate Europeans.

tivities of local, indigenous entrepreneurs. Coal, iron and textile machinery from Britain constituted 14 percent, 11 percent and 9.9 percent respectively of Brazilian imports during the opening years of the 20th century. There were comparable developments in the other major Latin American ports – Buenos Aires, the second port of the Americas, visited by 5137 vessels totaling 13.8 million tonnes in 1913, and Montevideo, with an international trade about half as great.

Amongst the Brazilian middle classes, especially during the mid-century, Paris was the ideal, but it was with Britain that Brazil had its greatest commercial dealings because of the dominance over the country's trade of British export-import interests. The desire of the Brazilian urban middle classes to copy European patterns of consumption required foodstuffs, furnishings and luxury goods. Urban improvement in Brazil moved in parallel with developments in Europe. Between 1862 and 1895 £2 million was invested in the sewage and water supply systems of Rio de Janeiro, and gas lighting companies were established in the late 1870s. By 1912 there were nine British-owned urban transport companies in Brazil. During the 1880s the British introduced sport. The first soccer match was played by the English in São Paulo in 1886; it was to become the national sport of most Brazilians.

Calcutta 30 years earlier European mercantile houses had begun to diversify their activities away from trade through acting as labor contractors for the railways, acting as agents for railway companies and insurance companies, owning ships and investing in jute mills, cotton spinning mills, tea plantations and coal mines. Where such enterprises were established by European mercantile houses as joint stock companies, they were frequently formed under British law and therefore registered in London.

As in Calcutta and Hong Kong, British mercantile houses in Brazilian ports from the 1870s spread their range of activities through investing in the development of local manufacturing capacity – textile plants, the shoe industry, and sugar and flour mills. The British-dominated Brazilian ports also became centers for the ac-

Formal and informal colonization

In spite of the rise in incomes amongst the primary producers from mid-century and within the tropical world from the 1880s, critics had grounds for stressing the negative aspects of the international activities of Western societies. The opening up of the markets of the less developed world to Western manufactures led to the decline

Malayan Rubber

The demand for rubber grew substantially after 1900, mainly as a result of the development of the automobile industry in the United States. This led to the growth of a commercial plantation industry, largely in Malaya, with the result that by 1914 exports from Malaya accounted for 38 percent of world trade in rubber. The industry began in the last quarter of the 19th century, when plants germinated at Kew Gardens in England from seed collected in South America were sent to Singapore. Trial tappings may have taken place earlier, but commercial exploitation did not begin until the mid-1890s when, with the rise in rubber prices due to the growth of the bicycle trade, the crop provided as an attractive alternative to coffee.

Initially rubber in Malaya was interplanted with earlier cash crops, such as coffee and coconuts, but the area of rubber stands in the Federated Malay States increased from 140 hectares (345 acres) in 1895 to 17,573 hectares (43,425 acres) by 1905. Commercial exports from Malaya began in 1904–05, joining supplies from Ceylon drawn from trees planted in the early 1890s, and this commercial plantation supply was well received, though wild "jungle" production, largely from South America, still dominated the market. The labor force largely consisted of Indian immigrants.

The development of mass production techniques in the American automobile industry resulted in phenomenal expansion in 1909–10, when the number of plantation companies floated reached a peak of 80. Prices rose to 12s 9d per ton in April 1910. By 1913 they had fallen to 2s 9d but plantation development continued, albeit at a slower, more circumspect, pace. Malayan exports became a regular flow from 1909, rising from 3,331 tonnes to 47,457 tonnes by 1914.

▼ The need for rubber grew as the demand for bicycles and cars increased, with the output of the American automobile industry rising rapidly. The supply of rubber was enlarged by plantations in Malaya and the East Indies and from 1900 the plantation product carried a higher market price than the wild Amazonian supply.

of local handicraft industries; and Western imports acted as a brake upon the local development of modern industry. Further, the expansion of commercial agriculture in the temperate and tropical "undeveloped" world disrupted traditional labor markets, whilst the "development" process was generally not only propelled but controlled by Western capital. Foreign mortgage companies financed the new farms and plantations, their products were processed and stored in Western warehousing and silo companies, their domestic transshipment was undertaken by foreign-controlled railroads, their export was conducted through foreign-controlled ports, financed by foreign merchant houses, banks and insurance companies and their international movement took place in foreign-owned ships.

Development, therefore, occurred under the auspices of a foreign, frequently British, import-export complex. The profits arising from it went largely overseas and although these, together with the proceeds of enhanced exports, amortised the foreign investment that had initiated them, locals, especially the growing urban masses, saw this process as a stream of "tribute" arising from the informal foreign control of their country. This was a populist feeling, often articulated by middle-class radical politicians in opposition to the ruling elites who generally dominated government and had a symbiotic relationship with foreign capital, from which they had materially benefited. Accordingly, economic development initiated by foreign capital often widened the social gulf and struck the sparks that would lead to economic nationalism.

Such "informal" Western control was a particular characteristic of American and European expansion in the temperate world, especially that of the British in southern Latin America. Western expansion in the tropics and the Far East occurred primarily from the 1880s in a political climate of the "new imperialism", which was characterized by contemporaries as showing a strong link between political and economic power. In addition to the formal colonization of some areas there was also informal economic colonization of traditional regimes which now had much faded auras of grandeur, as in the Ottoman Empire, the Persian Empire and China. China in particular was forcibly opened up from the mid-19th century through the treaty port system (that gave Europeans trading rights through particular ports) and the use by Europeans of extraterritorial rights. The Japanese, however, though interested in Western technology, consciously decided that their country was not to be subjected to the same process of competitive Western economic and political expansion and penetration.

▲ Diamonds were discovered at Kimberley in 1870 and by 1874 it was a cosmopolitan community of 50,000 people. In the early 1870s South Africa exported £1.6 million worth of diamonds annually. Kimberley created the migrant labor system; African workers were confined to the compound to stop illicit diamond dealing and prevent desertion.

▼ Gold mining at Witwatersrand grew from 1886. The Kimberley pattern of large-scale units provided the means for mechanical extraction.

Japanese industrialization

Japan was the only country outside Europe and North America to experience industrialization before 1914. Average income in Japan probably increased from being on a par with the Asian average in 1860 to exceeding it by 60 percent in 1913. This increase, while exceptional in Asian terms, was nevertheless not sufficient to keep up with the economically developed countries. The onset of modern Japanese economic growth had come with two shocks: the country's forced opening to the West in the mid-1850s through the imposition of free trade treaties, and an internal revolution which resulted in the accession of Emperor Meiji in 1868. The Emperor's government pursued two policies – *fukoku kyohei* (a rich country and strong army) and *shokusan kogyo* (increased production). These were conducted through the deliberate import of Western technology, with the government investing in infrastructure and manufacturing industry. For political reasons the government set its face against large imports of financial capital, so the beginnings were slow, the first signs of growth appearing in the mid-1880s; but it was propelled forward by increases in agricultural productivity and the rise from the 1900s of a "hybrid" manufacturing sector based upon small-scale industry but using the electric motor.

There was no change in agricultural organization, the Japanese countryside being characterized by small family farms. Agriculture continued to produce the same major products – rice, wheat, barley and the important industrial raw material, silk. Agricultural productivity rose as a result of a shift to arable production, the increasing application of fertilizer and improved irrigation techniques. Through the Land Tax the government was able to cream off the growing agricultural surplus and redistribute it to the emerging new industries. Increased agricultural productivity also allowed the transfer of labor from the countryside to the "hybrid" and modern manufacturing industries in the towns and ports. Finally, the peasant silk industry, along with tea, was a source of export products. The modern sector of the Japanese economy consisted above all of cotton textile production, which used domestic raw material supplies until the mid-1880s, when they were replaced by cheaper Indian imports.

By 1905 finished cotton and silk textile exports were replacing the traditional agricultural crops of tea and raw silk. The domestic modern industrial sector had by then reached a sufficient size for excise duties on consumption, income and business taxes, together with the customs duties, to replace the Land Tax as the fiscal engine of growth. Japan's labor force was now an urban proletariat, some of whom had received tertiary technical education. Investment in traditional techniques of production was declining and economic growth was becoming increasingly propelled by export demand, as the low level of income restricted the home market. During the years before 1914 the foundations of Japanese heavy industry were laid through the development of iron and steel, engineering and shipbuilding behind protective tariffs.

South American Exports c.1910

coffee
bananas
COSTA RICA
PANAMA
Caracas
Orinoco
VENEZUELA
BR GUIANA
Bogotá
DUTCH FR GUIANA
GUIANA
COLOMBIA
Japurá
cocoa
ivory
panama hats
Quito
ECUADOR
Ucayali
Amazon
Madeira
Araguaia
sugar
cotton
PERU
Lima
BRAZIL
coffee
rubber
maté
tobacco
cocoa
L Titicaca
La Paz
tin
rubber
silver
BOLIVIA
Paraguay
Rio de Janeiro
PARAGUAY
Asunción
Paraná
nitrates
copper
coal
CHILE
Colorado
URUGUAY
ATLANTIC OCEAN
wool
hides
meat
Santiago
Buenos Aires
Montevideo
PACIFIC
OCEAN
ARGENTINA
wheat
maize
linseed
hides

— Major trade route
→ Principal exports

Value of exports (million pounds)

	50
	10
	5
	0
	Data not available

Scale 1 : 54 000 000

▲ Latin America increasingly became an important source of raw materials and foodstuffs during the late 19th century. Coffee exports from Brazil led the way, but from the 1880s the opening up of the Argentinean pampas led to the shipment to Europe of grain and, with refrigeration, meat in the 1890s. In contrast Chile developed as a major supplier of nitrates, for the production of fertilizers and explosives, and of copper.

◀ By 1914 Japan was a major cotton producer, exporting substantial quantities. The origins of the 1914 industry lay in private mills, beginning in the early 1880s, of which the most important was the Osaka Boseki. It developed double-shift operations, involving night work, so that the mill was in production for 22 out of 24 hours a day. The labor force was largely made up of young female workers, drawn from the countryside, housed in purpose-built dormitories and subject to quasi-military discipline.

THE SPREAD OF RAIL TRANSPORT IN AFRICA

The "scramble for Africa" during the 1880s, when the European Powers rushed to plant their flags in every corner of the continent, had largely consisted of arbitrary boundary lines drawn on frequently inadequate maps in smoke-filled conference rooms in European capitals. But from the 1890s the African interior began to be penetrated by steel rails, often from newly laid-out ports. It was often the European and American railroad builders in Africa who first surveyed the land in detail, and their subsequent activity frequently involved a close public and formal alignment of state power with private capital. Germany, through state-backed corporations, built lines in Tanganyika from 1891, in Southwest Africa from 1897, in Kamerun from 1900, and in Togo from 1904. Italian construction got underway in Eritrea from 1887 and in Libya from 1911. The French built in Dakar and Niger from 1881, in Djibouti from 1897, in Dahomey from 1900 and in the Ivory Coast from 1904. However, the most substantial builders of railroads in Africa from the 1890s were the British.

The intentions of the railroad builders, like those of the imperialists themselves, mixed economic motives with strategic, and projects were financed which brought new lines to regions that were sometimes under the control of rival imperial powers. In eastern Africa the two main centers of British construction were the Sudan and Kenya. The Sudanese system was of military origin. In East Africa a railroad was built by the British from Mombasa to Lake Victoria, starting in 1895 and completed in December 1901 with an overall length of 954 kilometers (600 miles). Railroads had been laid in South Africa since 1860 and following the Boer War they were consolidated, with the lines in the Transvaal and Orange Free State becoming Central South African Railways. At the same time and during the Boer War period, new trunk lines were built in southern Africa, largely to provide communication with Northern and Southern Rhodesia.

The mixture of political and economic motives was manifested when the British imperialist Cecil Rhodes planned the Cape-to-Cairo railroad, which reached Bulawayo in 1897 with a branch to Salisbury in 1902, thereby providing a continuous route of 3392 kilometers (2100 miles) connecting Cape Town and Beira. But instead of aiming for the Rift Valley and the Nile as originally planned its builders took the railroad to the Wankie coalfield, reached in 1903. The lure of minerals then diverted the route even further from the original plan to the copper-rich area of the southern Congo border in 1909. By 1910 it had arrived at Elizabethville in the Belgian Congo. Here it linked with the railroad that ran inland from Benguela to the Katanga copperbelt, for which the British held the mining concession. British trade with central and southern Africa between the 1880s and the period 1911–15 increased by a factor of 3.3, whereas total British trade over the same period grew by less than two times.

Coal ■
Copper ▲
Diamonds ◆
Gold ●
Railroad —
Boundary c.1914 —·—

Scale 1 : 28 000 000

0   800km
0   600mi

► By 1900 Africa had been almost entirely divided up into colonies of the European Powers. This had begun in the 1830s with the French colonization of Algeria, but accelerated from the 1880s with "the scramble for Africa". The physical opening up of Africa by Westerners largely took the form of railroad building, frequently related to the exploitation of known mineral deposits.

▼ Western involvement with Africa was frequently portrayed romantically yet the symbolism, even in advertisements, reflected European concepts of dominance and superiority.

Gulf of Guinea

▼ Building tracks across a poorly explored continent posed considerable engineering difficulties, as a result of both the geology of the continent — it was a tableland — and its vegetation — the jungle. However in the tropics the local supply of hardwoods eased the construction of bridges.

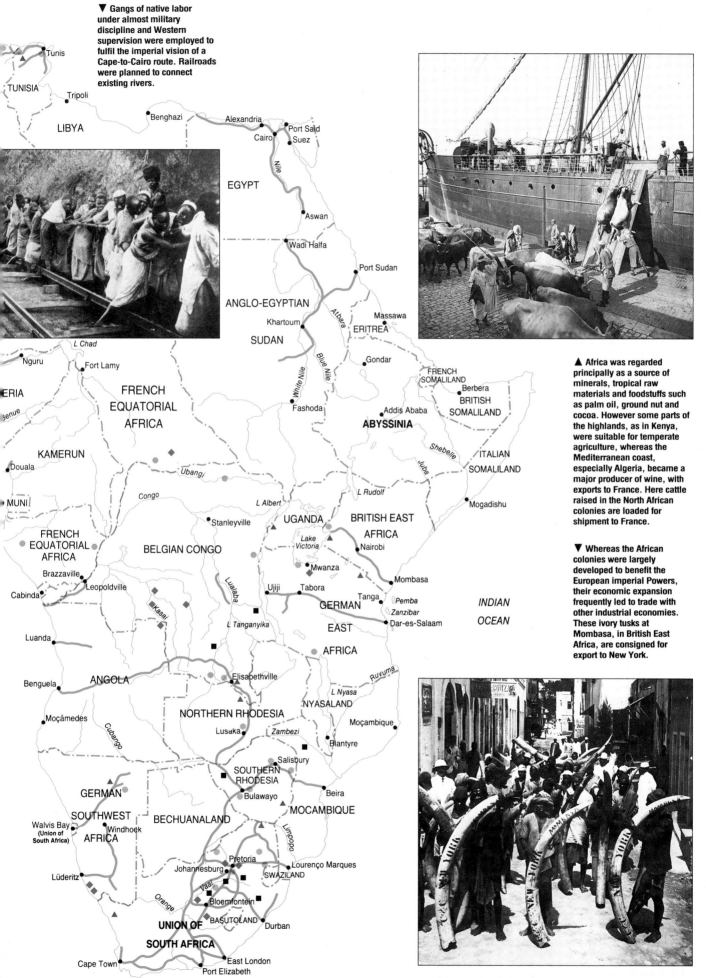

▼ Gangs of native labor under almost military discipline and Western supervision were employed to fulfil the imperial vision of a Cape-to-Cairo route. Railroads were planned to connect existing rivers.

▲ Africa was regarded principally as a source of minerals, tropical raw materials and foodstuffs such as palm oil, ground nut and cocoa. However some parts of the highlands, as in Kenya, were suitable for temperate agriculture, whereas the Mediterranean coast, especially Algeria, became a major producer of wine, with exports to France. Here cattle raised in the North African colonies are loaded for shipment to France.

▼ Whereas the African colonies were largely developed to benefit the European imperial Powers, their economic expansion frequently led to trade with other industrial economies. These ivory tusks at Mombasa, in British East Africa, are consigned for export to New York.

71

Datafile

By 1900 the world in many substantial respects had become an integrated economic community. One of the main factors responsible for this coalescence was the increasing speed of communications arising from the growth of telegraph networks, the further expansions of the system of oceanic cables and, in the advanced world, the growing use of the telephone. Distance still remained a problem, but continents were now straddled by railways and oceans crisscrossed by steamship lines. This produced a global market place, although dominated by the advanced industrial economies. Consumers in industrial cities could buy the produce of the whole world, while the advanced industrial economies were exporting manufactures to the Third World. International trade did knit the world together, but such strands of interdependence were now augmented by flows of labor and capital. However, as with visible trade, the migration of capital and labor overseas was largely a process which reinforced the economic power of the advanced economies.

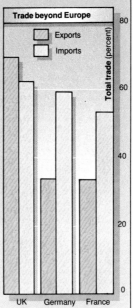

Trade beyond Europe

- Exports
- Imports

▲ There was sharp contrast in the trading patterns of the main European industrial economies. Both France and Germany were more dependent upon intra-European trade than Britain. Only 30 percent of British exports went to other European economies in 1913, only half as much as from France and Germany.

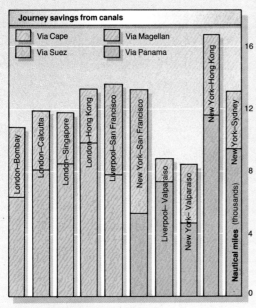

Journey savings from canals

- Via Cape
- Via Suez
- Via Magellan
- Via Panama

◀ The opening of the Suez and Panama canals in 1869 and 1914 respectively had a considerable effect upon intercontinental oceanic routes, by reducing voyages that had previously involved either rounding the Cape of Good Hope or the more perilous journey around the Horn. However, the canals could only be used by steam vessels.

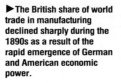

Overseas investment

1913

- UK
- France
- Germany
- Europe
- USA
- Others

◀ From the mid-1850s the British economy developed as the world's banker, supplying long-term finance, particularly for the construction of railways overseas. French and German capital exports were largely directed to the outer periphery of Europe. American finance began to be of global importance from the 1880s.

▶ The British share of world trade in manufacturing declined sharply during the 1890s as a result of the rapid emergence of German and American economic power.

- UK
- Germany
- France
- Others

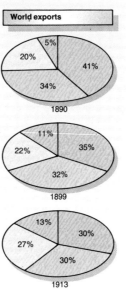

World exports

1890

1899

1913

The outstanding characteristic of economic affairs during the 19th century had been the emergence of a world economy. This was a result initially of the further development of trade, of swelling numbers of migrants, and lastly, from the 1850s, of the international migration of capital, above all from Britain to the United States, Australia and New Zealand, and Canada. These processes were eased by the fall in international transport costs and the increased speed of international communications. Until the mid-1880s the sailing ship remained the main mover of bulk cargoes. Mass-produced steel, together with major improvements in machine tool capabilities, finally tipped the balance in favor of steam from the late 1880s. High-pressure steam, when put in harness with triple-expansion engines, and nurtured by the development of a worldwide chain of coaling stations, made possible the operation of the steam tramp (cargo ship) of the last decades of the 19th century. The commercial operation of the steam tramp, nonetheless, depended upon a global communication system of intercontinental cables, through which owners and managing agents could readily give sailing orders to masters. The first Atlantic submarine cable was successfully laid in 1866.

In the growing complexity of world economic intercourse, trade and finance now moved from

ECONOMIC INTERDEPENDENCE

bilateral to multilateral relationships, whereby international balances were settled indirectly through transactions with "third" countries. Such a pattern of settlements, which became firmly established during the third quarter of the 19th century, did facilitate the further growth of international dealings, but also made the world economy more vulnerable to shocks. The growing integration of world economic activity provided the industrial and industrializing economies with new sources of food and raw materials and new markets for exports of manufactures. Areas of European temperate settlement also became important suppliers to the Old World of additional food, as well as being the new homes of increasing numbers of Europeans.

European trade
European foreign trade, excluding Russia, increased enormously between 1830 and 1914. In 1913 European trade was dominated by the three major industrial economies – Germany, France and the United Kingdom. These economies had collectively a share of two-thirds of total European exports and conducted over three-quarters of intra-European trade. Britain was less dependent upon intra-European trade as opposed to world trade than were Germany and France. From the 1870s a new pattern of trade started to develop.

▼ Exports from the tropical world grew substantially at the turn of the century. Nigeria's export trade expanded from £1.8 million in 1900 to £6.1 million by 1914, on the basis of palm products – which accounted for nearly 70 percent – tin, groundnuts and cocoa. Their development frequently involved slave or near slave labor.

An ever larger share consisted of the exchange of equivalent manufactures between the industrial economies in place of the exchange of manufactures for raw materials and foodstuffs. British imports of manufactures were nearly 19 percent by 1913. At first these largely consisted of fine textiles for the middle classes, but they were joined by organic dyestuffs and scientific instruments from Germany and motor cars, electrical machinery and iron and steel from the United States. Textiles, especially cottons, were a particular characteristic of British manufactured exports; the export trade of Germany and the United States was characterized by a greater importance of iron and steel. Although both Britain and Germany were advanced industrial economies before 1914, both also exported primary goods. Britain was a major world supplier of coal, and from 1900 Germany was an important provider of beet sugar to the rest of Europe.

French exports throughout the 19th century consisted primarily of high quality textiles – silks, cottons and woollens – for the richer markets of Europe and the United States, though Japanese competition for silks in America began in the 1890s. The French North African colonies became a significant market for French cotton cloth by 1913. French exports of other goods, such as chemicals and motor vehicles, were also growing.

Changing markets

Europe's growing interconnection with the rest of the world as a result of trade was most evident in the changing sources of imports of raw materials and foodstuffs. For example, by 1913 only three percent of British imports of cereals came from Europe, as North America, India and Argentina were now the main suppliers. However, following the removal of colonial preferences the share of British sugar imports from the Empire fell; by 1913, Europe supplied over half. Similarly, Baltic timber gained at North America's expense, supplying over eighty percent of British wood imports by the eve of World War I. French and German imports of wool switched to Australia and Argentina by 1913. After 1869, the raw material for the French silk manufacturing industry came from China, and by 1913 Brazil was the source of two-thirds of German coffee imports, whereas North Africa supplied over half of French imports of wine.

The growth of American exports turned the American visible trade account – that concerned with tangible goods – into continual surplus from the mid-1890s. The most significant factor was the increase in the relative share of semi-finished and finished manufactures, so much so that by 1914 they constituted half of the total value of American exports. Europe remained America's most important market, but with a declining share; rising markets were Canada, Asia and Latin America. Fewer manufactured goods were now imported, and imports mainly they con-sisted of those basic materials that were unavailable within the domestic economy for geological and climatic reasons – tropical fibers such as jute, coffee, tropical fruits and olive and coconut oils, together with rubber, nickel and tin.

European overseas investment

There was substantial migration from Europe overseas, especially to the United States, but later to southern Latin America, particularly Argentina. And to the increasing flow of goods and migrants, there was added from the mid-1850s exports of finance capital from some of the advanced economies. London was the premier financial center of the world economy, but New York's international importance was growing substantially, although it did not yet rival the older centers of Paris or Berlin.

Until the 1880s overseas investment had largely consisted of loans to governments, together with finance for railroad construction: over 40 percent of overseas securities bought by British investors between 1865 and 1914 were destined to finance railroad companies abroad. British overseas investment in this period was largely concentrated on the temperate regions of recent settlement – the United States, southern Latin America, Canada, Australia and New Zealand. About forty percent of this investment could be termed "direct", as it involved managerial control. Much of this was undertaken by "free-standing firms" – British companies, registered under British company law, and with a British office, but operating

French Investment in Russia

Russian industrialization from the 1890s was
financed substantially through the import of
foreign capital. French residents were the main
suppliers, holding in 1914 a third of all Russian
bonds and a seventh of all Russian shares.
French investors in the 1890s were disillusioned
with the low yield available on most domestic
securities; Russian shares offered higher
dividends, and the rewards that could be
obtained were already being demonstrated in the
development of the Dnieper region by Belgian
capital and German investment in Russian
Poland and the Urals. Further encouragement
came from the stabilization of the rouble and the
lure of orders arising from the state-managed
expansion of the railroad system. However,
foreign companies operating within Russia were
subject to higher taxes than local concerns, so the
possibilities of establishing "freestanding" French
companies within Russia were restricted.
Therefore French investment took place initially
through the pioneering Belgian concerns and
then through the medium of Russian domestic
companies.

French capital contributed to the formation
of the southern Russian industrial complex,
bringing about vertical integration and the
consequent creation of large plants employing
technologies superior to those then current in
French domestic industry. After 1900 there was
increased French investment in the Russian
banking system and a rising emphasis on
financial holdings in the growing oil industry,
usually in the form of shares of either Russian
or English companies.

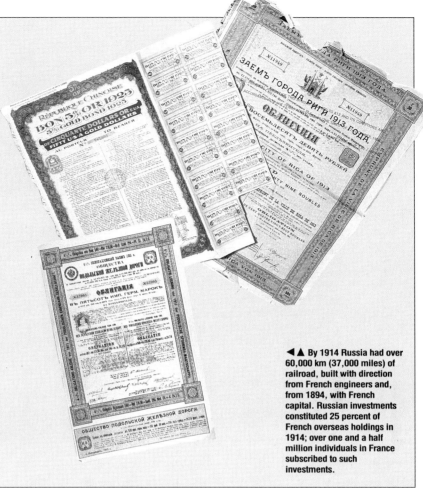

◀▲ By 1914 Russia had over
60,000 km (37,000 miles) of
railroad, built with direction
from French engineers and,
from 1894, with French
capital. Russian investments
constituted 25 percent of
French overseas holdings in
1914; over one and a half
million individuals in France
subscribed to such
investments.

an enterprise in a foreign country. For instance,
in many such railroad companies the London
board of directors was largely concerned with
financial control, while overseas there was a
second, local, board, responsible for operation of
the line. Such a dual management structure, with
clear divisions of function, seems also to have
been common in the cases of mining and plantation companies.

French and German foreign investment was for
the most part undertaken within Europe, mirror-
ing the greater importance for these economies of
intra-European dealings. However, from the
1890s, and especially after 1900, French and German foreign investment became more global in
scope, now being undertaken increasingly in the
United States, Latin America, Africa and China.
Political alliances played a part in this, as in the
case of the French lending to Russia from the
1890s, which was very important in Russian industrial development.

It has been held that multinational companies
were particularly characteristic of American
foreign investment from the 1880s, but in fact
British enterprise led in this field. At least 119
British manufacturing firms between 1870 and
1939 undertook direct investment overseas. Early
British multinationals were largely involved in
engineering, chemicals, food, textiles and metallurgy. Before 1900 most of the foreign activity of
British multinationals was in overseas sales
offices, but by 1914 it involved overseas production facilities.

◀ Japanese banks began to expand overseas from 1878, when the Dai Ichi Bank opened a branch office in Korea. Its business was taken over in 1909 by the Bank of Korea, renamed the Bank of Chosen in 1911. The Yokohama Specie bank opened branch offices in Manchuria from 1900. Again reflecting the widening of Japan's international interests, the Toyo Takushoku K. K. (Far East Colonial Co.) was established in 1908, as a development bank for Korea.

Debtors and creditors

The growth and increasing intricacy of international dealings led to a change in the underlying pattern of financial settlements. Until the 1890s such patterns consisted of isolated systems, linked only through Britain. Consequently liquidity pressure – a shortage of funds – in one such system could only be transmitted to another via Britain. From the 1890s, however, the whole global system became fully integrated, often bypassing Britain entirely. There were several reasons for this change. One was the rising return stream of substantial annual payments of interest by Britain's foreign debtors. Another was the growing importance of French, and also German, capital exports from the 1890s and their consequent return flows of interest payments. Yet another was the spread of industrialization in Europe and the growth of demand, on the part of industrial nations other than Britain, for primary products from non-European sources. Lastly, from the 1890s the demand for manufactures amongst countries that were part of the British Empire came increasingly to be met by American and European concerns. The overall effect of all these developments was that by 1914 industrial Europe, together with the United States, had substantial deficits with the primary producing countries, but were creditors of Britain, which in turn was a creditor of the primary producing world.

Many foreign banks had offices in London and many foreign countries kept sterling balances there. London supplied the liquidity for the increasing scale of international dealings through the provision of trade credit, long-term overseas lending and Britain's continuing import surplus. The United Kingdom before 1914 was an ideal international creditor because of her free trade policy, which allowed debtors to accumulate sterling through exports to Britain. Further, cyclical falls in British long-term lending could be offset by parallel increases in the British import surplus, as happened during the 1890s.

The gold standard and reserve currencies

Confidence in sterling as a stockholding and trading currency was increased during the last quarter of the 19th century by the fall in the gold price of silver, the other monetary metal, which was used substantially in Europe, Latin America and the East. From 1868 until the 1890s the adoption of a bimetallic monetary standard was internationally considered, and the Bank of England went as far as balloting its directors, but finally decided to have no truck with the proposal to establish a firm monetary link between gold and silver. (India, which was on a silver standard, was regarded as a separate problem.) The attitude of London's institutions was influential in leading most of the major economies to adopt the gold standard by the 1890s. Germany did so in 1871 and in 1878 the mints of the European Latin Monetary Union were closed to silver, with the

▼ The central sorting office in the post office of Toronto, Canada. The post remained the most important medium for communications even after the development of the international cable network. Indeed cables were confirmed by letter, a practice that persisted into the 20th century.

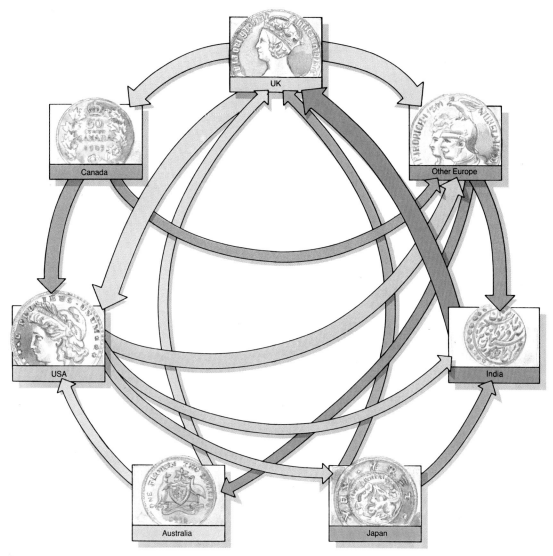

◄ The growing integration of the world economy was particularly marked by the complexity of financial flows which mirrored the movements of goods and capital. From the 1870s world trade became increasingly multinational, with payment deficits and surpluses balanced through dealings with many countries. This diagram broadly indicates the flow of financial settlements between various regions of the world in the years before 1914. Thus Britain's international deficits with North America and Europe were offset by surpluses with India and Australia, which in turn had surpluses with Europe and the United States.

result that Belgium and Switzerland moved onto the gold standard; in 1900 the United States did likewise.

In theory, the gold standard was a mechanism for keeping prices internationally in line. It was based on three factors. First, currencies were allotted gold values, thereby establishing international exchange rates, and currencies were backed by holdings of gold; second, the free movement of gold was permitted between countries; and, third, a country's domestic money supply was more or less automatically linked to the international movement of gold. It was assumed that the money supply of a country losing gold would contract, thereby bringing about a fall in its domestic prices, which in turn would make its internationally traded goods more competitive, raise exports and reduce imports, leading to an inflow of gold. In practice, the institutional structure of the international gold standard was extremely diverse. Only Britain, Germany and the United States were on a full gold standard. Further, the so-called "rules of the standard" were frequently disregarded as international flows of gold were restricted by the operations of certain central banks. In fact it would seem that before 1900 the world was actually using a sterling standard, with a number of countries backing their currencies not by gold holdings, but by holdings

of sterling-denominated securities. Adjustment to international payments problems was generally smooth; in the last resort international payment balances – deficits or surpluses – were accommodated through differential changes in the nations' rates of economic growth.

From the 1890s, while sterling remained the world currency, both the French franc and the German mark came to be held by other countries as reserve currencies. Official monetary reserves in the form of financial securities of other countries had advantages over gold in providing income in the form of interest, and because of their lower transport and transactions costs. But such holdings were also a result of dependency arising from debtor-creditor relationships: they were to become much more common after 1918.

International weights and measures
The role of the Bank of England in the international gold standard was made possible because London was the main gold market for the world, as well as the seat of several major commodity markets. By the late 19th century, Chicago and New York also had important commodity markets. Gradually the bases of measurement came to be standardized in such international commodity dealings, but some trades clung to traditional measures, such as the "long ton". By

The chief streams of British capital flowed into Canada, the United States, and Argentina. Mexico, Brazil, Chile, and other countries in South America also benefited by more or less large British investments. A small flood of British capital poured into South Africa, while Egypt and the colonies on the east and west coasts of Africa were not neglected. India and the Far East vied with Russia and Australia in their endeavours to obtain British capital.

C. K. HOBSON, THE EXPORT OF CAPITAL (1914)

1900 there were two general measurement systems – British imperial and metric. The imperial system prevailed in the English-speaking world, though even there variations occurred, such as the American pint containing only 16 fluid ounces, as opposed to 20 in the British "imperial" system. Similarly, nautical miles were by no means equivalent to an English land mile. On a wider international basis there was a halting adoption of the metric system. Its basic unit of measurement for length was the meter, accepted by the French National Assembly in 1790 and defined as "one ten-millonth of the quarter meridian from the North Pole to the Equator, passing through Paris". owever, the use of the standard meter and its weight equivalent, the kilogram, was not made mandatory even in France until 1840. Wider adoption came but slowly, assisted by the international exhibitions of 1851 (London) and 1855 (Paris). A conference in Paris in 1870 prepared the way for the establishment in 1875 of an International Bureau of Weights and Measures, and 18 countries, including the United States, signed the "Treaty of the Meter".

Improvements in communications
International economic and social intercourse was also improved by agreements over communications. The Universal Postal Union had its origins in a meeting held in Paris in 1863, and in 1874, 22 states signed the Berne Convention which established a uniform postal tariff, together with a formula for disbursing revenue between the countries through which an international postal communication passed. There were parallel international agreements over telegraphy; 20 European states signed the Paris Convention of 1865, and a decade later the International Telegraph Union was formed.

Much postal traffic was carried by the railroad and the expansion of the railroad system led to the spread of the telegraph network, as well as to the introduction of standardized time. Greenwich Mean Time became the British standard in 1880, although Dublin continued to be 25 minutes behind GMT until 1916. Other countries similarly established comparable local standards, with Paris being the astronomical center in France, Pulkovo in Russia and Washington in the United States. The standardization of world time arose not only from the needs of railroad travelers but also out of the requirements of maritime navigation and the pressure exerted by international scientific congresses.

Scientific cooperation
Standardization involved national pride and international rivalry; it often arose out of a lengthy two-stage process, led by the generation of a scientific consensus and followed by international diplomacy. Formal international scientific meetings began to increase in numbers from the 1850s; the first international health conference took place in Paris in 1851 and the first international physiological conference in 1889. Meetings were often twinned with exhibitions: alongside the Paris International Exhibition of 1900 there were scientific congresses covering mathematics, physics, meteorology, chemistry, botany, geology and psychology, as well as branches of the applied sciences. This increase in formal meetings of the scientific community went hand in hand with closer alliances between national bodies.

Copyright protection and international law
The concerns of science were but one aspect covered by the 25,000 international agreements concluded by 1917. The drawing up of such agreements became more difficult when ideas became property and had earning power. This

▲ Alexander Graham Bell invented the telephone in 1876 and assigned his patents to a company known from 1880 as American Bell Telephone. This acquired the Western Electric Co. in 1882 and established the American Telephone and Telegraph Co. in 1885 to provide long-distance services. By 1893 there were 266,000 Bell telephones in service in the United States, mainly in the business centers of the main cities. Bell's patent rights lapsed in 1893, which led to the rapid emergence of competitors. By 1907 there were over six million telephones in the United States, of which more than three million were Bell.

◄ The Bell system was acquired in 1907 by a New York banking group headed by George F. Baker and J. P. Morgan. Under the management of Theodore Vail, Bell now changed policy, buying up the independent companies and agreeing to supply equipment to non-Bell concerns.

was less the case with copyright, for which reciprocal treaties had been signed since 1797. An International Copyright Union was established by the Berne Convention of 1886 and was further developed by the Berlin Convention of 1908 and the Protocol of 1914. The United States stood apart, although American legislation in 1909 gave copyright to domiciled foreign authors and to authors resident in nations with which the United States had reciprocal treaties.

There were comparable developments in the case of patents, but the Convention of the International Union for the Protection of Industrial Property of 1883, signed by 39 countries, did not override national laws. Consequently, even within the British Empire an inventor still had to file 40 patent applications.

International law grew largely in the same manner as English common law – through the invocation of practice and precedent as authorities for current decisions. This was how the thousands of international tribunals in existence by 1914 generally operated. Greater codification came at the end of the 19th century in the fields of the conduct of war and labor conditions. The Hague Conferences of 1899 and 1906 established a Permanent Court of Arbitration, as well as rules for the treatment of prisoners of war. Articles 4 to 20 of the First Hague Convention laid down that prisoners of war should be well treated – in terms of being fed, housed and clothed on the same basis as the troops of the captor government. While in captivity prisoners could be made to work, but not for military purposes, and under reasonable conditions. Further, prisoners were not to be punished for trying to escape. The Declaration of London in 1909 laid down rules for naval warfare, particularly the conduct of blockades and the treatment of prize and neutral vessels.

These concerns were paralleled by a growing consensus over the need for international action regarding the regulation of working conditions. In 1900 the International Association for Labor Legislation was established in Paris and the two subsequent Berne Conferences of 1905 and 1906 resulted in the signing of conventions for the protection of labor, particularly the prohibition of night work for women and the use of less toxic chemicals where possible, for example advocating white phosphorus in match manufacture. These actions gained increasing international respect, for example in Japan, but the work of the Berne Conference of 1913 was frustrated by the outbreak of war in August 1914.

▲ The use of the telephone grew more slowly in Europe than in the United States. In 1914 Denmark led Europe with 45 telephones per thousand inhabitants; in Germany there were 21, in Britain 17 and in France eight. There had been only 1,370 telephone subscribers in Britain in 1888, when a small but growing trunk network had been established. However, the system was not very efficient or effective, especially the privately run exchanges. The trunk network was progressively taken over by the Post Office from 1892, and municipally run local telephone systems developed from 1899. In the same year the Post Office began to replace private companies, beginning in London.

Tackling Disease

The eradication of communicable diseases became possible from the 1880s as a result of three broad lines of scientific advance. In 1870 Louis Pasteur began to put forward the germ theory, on the basis of studies of the action of microbes upon silk worms; Joseph Lister was meanwhile developing aseptic techniques; and in 1876, Robert Koch established a definite connection between illness and the presence of a microbe, a discovery which led to the subsequent development of the science of bacteriology. These developments brought about the general acceptance that disease was spread by contagion, as opposed to "bad air". The human body was now recognized as the host for many diseases, spread either by direct contact or by food handled by a disease carrier. It was also realized that certain fatal illnesses, like malaria, are transmitted by biting insects.

Major epidemics led to greater insights. A team of American Army surgeons was formed in 1900 after an outbreak of yellow fever. After research carried out in Cuba, they discovered that the disease was transmitted by the mosquito. The remedy was mosquito control, which began in Havana, and the techniques

which were developed were applied in Panama to enable the construction of the Panama Canal. At the same time, studies in India and elsewhere established the role of the mosquito in the spread of first bird and then human malaria. Once more insect control, with swamp drainage, spraying and protective screens for housing, became the method of eradicating the disease, together with the use of quinine as a cure for sufferers.

By the early 20th century it was recognized that the eight most serious tropical diseases – cholera, amebic dysentery, bacillary dysentery, hookworm, malaria, plague, typhus and yellow fever – were all controllable by improvements in sanitation, mosquito control or vaccination. In the temperate world fatalities from diphtheria, scarlet fever, smallpox and typhoid fever had become uncommon; while those from tuberculosis had been greatly reduced. With the retreat of these diseases, cities in advanced countries had become considerably healthier, and the death rate fell rapidly from the 1870s onwards. But even in the Western world, there remained the problems of influenza, pneumonia and syphilis.

INVENTORS AND INVENTIONS

In the 19th century Thomas Edison had demonstrated the potential of "inventions factories", with his pioneering laboratories at Menlo Park. Large companies like General Electric and Du Pont followed suit. Invention became more and more the province of such companies, who could provide the resources needed to make fundamental breakthroughs, and put teams of scientists to work on a problem. Yet vital discoveries were still made by lone geniuses. Ample funding alone did not make inventions, as the United States War Department found when it funded S.P. Langley's attempts to build an aircraft. Langley's "Aerodrome" failed to fly in 1903, the same year as the Wright brothers achieved powered flight.

As science and technology grew ever more specialized, the chances of a lone inventor making an entirely new discovery grew less and less. Making the right invention at the right time and at the right price was no longer enough. Quality control and marketing became more and more important ingredients for success. Even though lone inventors could succeed for a time, large corporations might soon outclass them once a market had been established. This was what happened to John Logie Baird, whose mechanical television system proved technically inadequate, and was replaced by electronic systems developed by RCA and EMI.

However, if an inventor hit on the right technological fix, and held key patents to protect the invention, it was possible to lay the foundation of a new company, and repeat the successes of Marconi and Edison. In 1937 the American John Chester Carlson patented the principle of the photocopier, and out of his work grew the Xerox Corporation. Part of Carlson's success was that he made contact with a firm that was looking for a new product, and was willing to put in the resources to transform Carlson's ideas into the Xerox photocopier. Similarly, Edwin Land developed the Polaroid camera in the 1940s, and founded the Polaroid corporation.

Key patents, however, were of little use unless a market existed, or could be created for the innovation. The rise of the electronics industry created new opportunities for inventors. The key breakthrough, the transistor, was produced by John Bardeen, Walter Brattain and William Shockley at Bell Laboratories in 1947. Shockley's development led to miniaturized electronic components, and to the microchip. Availability of specialized chips made it possible to create new products based on the chips produced by the large corporations.

Such inventors succeeded in exploiting markets the large corporations had overlooked. In the 1970s one such market was the home computer. A number of small home computer companies grew up in California's "Silicon Valley". Perhaps the best known was Apple Computers, founded by Stephen Wozniak and Steven Jobs. Starting from a garage workshop, Apple dominated the home computer market and grew into a multinational company.

◄ Some inventions have become ubiquitous, yet their inventors are virtually forgotten. The zipper fastener was originally patented in 1893 by American Whitcomb L. Judson, though the modern fastener was not developed until 1913, by the Swede Gideon Sundback. Mass production began during World War I.

▼ Otto Lilienthal, of Germany, made pioneering studies of gliders in the 1890s, building a hill from which to test his devices. He made more than 2,000 flights, and died in 1896 when his glider crashed. His work resulted in much basic aeronautical knowledge.

►► The British inventor Clive Sinclair made his fortune in the 1970s from cheap electronic devices sold through mail order. His attempt to branch out into a battery-powered tricycle brought disaster.

▼ The patent for Carlson's xerox dry photographic copier. The paper is wrapped around a charged drum and the image focused onto it. Where light falls, the image is conducted away. Toning powder adheres only to the charged particles.

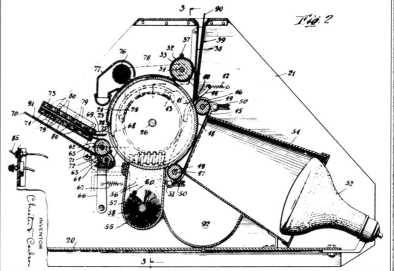

► The American inventor Thomas Edison made many pioneering discoveries of his own, and developed the concept of the research laboratory at Menlo Park, in New Jersey. Here he and his assistant (on the ladder) study the filament of a lightbulb.

◄▼In the 1970s the Briton Stephen Salter developed a "duck", a device to convert the energy in ocean waves, into electricty. Pilot schemes were not scaled up to production levels through lack of institutional interest.

THE EMERGENT MASSES

Time Chart

	1900	1901	1902	1903	1904	1905	1906	1907
Rural life	• Irrigated cropland totals 100 million acres worldwide, up from 20 million in 1880	• By May, 1.25 million have died in famine in India. British report blames over-population	• National Reclamation Act encourages family farms (USA) • Dec: Protectionist tariff enforced in Germany, restoring higher duty on imported agricultural products	• Russian harvest fails, creating a famine which claims the lives of millions	• First caterpillar tractor produced in California (USA)	• 1 Feb: US President Roosevelt creates a Bureau of Forestry within the US Department of Agriculture • Foundation of the International Agricultural Institute in Rome	• Prime minister Pyotr Stolypin reforms the *mir* system by distributing communal land among the peasantry (Russ) • China pledges to suppress cultivation and consumption of opium over ten years	• Four million people starving in China due to famine caused by heavy rains and crop failure • 20 million starving, Russia's worst ever famine
Industry and labor	• Feb: Formation of Labour Representative Committee (UK) • Sep: Fifth Congress of the Socialist International in Paris • Dec: National Civic Federation formed in the USA, for the arbitration of labor disputes • American Federation of Labor (AF of L) is formed from 216 trade unions • Only 3.5% of the US workforce is unionized	• Jul: Beginning of a steelworkers' strike in USA • Dec: Unemployed workers demonstrate and riot in Budapest (Aust-Hung) • Foundation in Amsterdam of the International Trade Union • Taff Vale Ruling: House of Lords rules that unions can be sued (UK)	• Jan–Feb: Strikes of Mediterranean Railway employees demanding recognition of their union • 7 Apr: Foundation of the Texas Oil Company (Texaco) (USA) • 12 May–13 Oct: United Mine Workers strike demanding a nine-hour day and wage increase (USA) • Oct: Two-thirds of French miners are out on strike	• Apr: Week-long general strike in the Netherlands, put down by the military • Nov: Spanish miners strike, demanding their wages be paid weekly • Legislation for the regulation of children's labor in the USA and Germany • 50,000 Chinese coolies are imported into the Transvaal, but prove to be disorderly so are repatriated in 1907 (SA)	• 27 Apr: Australia elects a minority Labor government • Aug: End of disruption in the petrol industry at Boryslaw (Aust-Hung) with the demand met for a reduction of working hours	• Sep: Trades Union Congress makes provisions for free trade and an eight-hour day (UK) • Foundation of the Bethlehem Steel Company (USA) • China boycotts US goods as a protest against the latter's restrictive immigration policies • Strike of miners in the Ruhr and Belgium, demanding a reduction of working hours (Ger/Bel)	• Mar: Series of severe strikes begins in Germany • Dec: Trade Disputes Act reverses the 1901 ruling in the Taff Vale case (UK) • Labour Representative Committee becomes the Parliamentary Labour Party (UK) • Upton sinclair's *The Jungle* exposes the terrible conditions in the meat packing industry (USA)	• May: Sailors in Marseille proclaim a general strike for improved working conditions (Fr) • Formation of the Confédération Générale des Vignerons, an organization of vineyard workers, after a decline in wine prices in 1906 caused an epidemic of strikes and unrest (until 191?) (Fr)
Government and people	• Mar: French legislation limits working day for women and children to eleven hours • May: First trial of proportional representation, in Belgium • Jul: Canada forbids the immigration of paupers and criminals	• Sep: Congress of the International Association for the Legal Protection of Workers agrees on a package of workers' legislation for all countries • 21 Dec: Women vote for the first time in Norwegian local elections	• 1 Feb: Working day for women and children reduced from 11 to 10.5 hours (Fr) • 5 Feb: Miners' working day is fixed at nine hours (Fr) • Dec: Education Act places elementary and secondary education under the control of county councils	• 14 Feb: US Congress votes to create a Department of Commerce and Labor • 22 Mar: Coal Commission suggests shorter hours and higher pay (USA) • Aug: International Miners' Conference calls for minimum wage and eight-hour day	• National Child Labor Committee created by reformers to promote protective legislation (USA) • Interdepartmental Committee on Physical Deterioration reports on bad living conditions and ill-health in British slums	• May: Meeting of the International Conference for the Protection of Laborers discusses night work for women • Eight-hour day introduced for all miners under 18 years (UK)	• May: US government prohibits any further expansion of the Rockefeller Oil Trust by passing the Sherman Act • School Meals Act provides free meals for children (UK) • US Pure Food and Drug Act prohibits misbranding of and tampering with foods	• Feb: US Congress legislates to limit entry of Japanese laborers after immigration peaks at 1.29 million • 15 Mar: First woman elected to parliament in Finland • May: First meeting of the Women's Labour League chaired by Ramsay MacDonald (UK)
Religion	• Aug–Apr 1901: Anti-Jewish riots in Odessa (Russ) • Shintoism is reinstated in Japan to counter Buddhist influences	• Feb: Spain is swept by anti-Jesuit riots • Apr: Pope Leo XIII condemns the European trend toward state regulation of the Catholic Church	• Harvard professor William James writes *Varieties of Religious Experience*, an attempt to reconcile science and religion (USA)	• 18 Mar: French government refuses all applications to teach from religious orders • Aug: Accession of Pope Pius X on the death of Leo XIII • Unification of the black churches in South Africa to form the Ethiopian Church		• 8 Nov: Pogroms are initiated by the "Black Hundreds" terrorists in Odessa. By 1909, 50,000 Jews have been killed (Russ) • 9 Dec: French law decrees the separation of Church and State, a move condemned by Pius X	• American Jewish Commission founded to protect the rights of Jews and fight prejudice • Publication of Albert Schweitzer's *The Quest for the Historical Jesus* (Ger)	• 8 Sep: Pius X issues papal encyclical *Pascendi gregis*, condemning liberal modernists who recently were calling for a revision of Church policy and dogma to square them with modern scientific scholarship (It)
Events and trends	• Dec: British deaths in the Boer War reach 11,000 • Freud publishes *The Interpretation of Dreams*, a work which revolutionizes understanding of the human unconscious (Aust-Hung) • Kodak introduces the Box Brownie camera, thus popularizing photography (USA)	• 11 Dec: Marconi transmits the first transatlantic wireless signal • European population exceeds 400 million • First Nobel Prizes awarded in Sweden • Oldsmobile, the first mass-produced gasoline-driven car, is introduced (USA)	• 15 Feb: Berlin underground railroad (U-bahn) opens • 4 Mar: Foundation of the American Automobile Association • Dec: Completion of the first Aswan Dam (Egy) • Publication of J.A. Hobson's *Imperialism*, a work whose ideas later become part of Leninist ideology (UK)	• Aug: Sixth Zionist conference in Basel (Swi) rejects a British proposal for a Jewish homeland in Uganda • 10 Oct: Foundation of the Women's Social and Political Union by Emmeline Pankhurst (UK) • "Typhoid Mary" is discovered to be the carrier of the disease during an epidemic in New York (USA)	• Mar: Publication of color photographs in London's *Daily Illustrated Mirror* (UK) • 27 Oct: Opening of the New York Subway • Thomas Sullivan pioneers the teabag (USA)	• 4 Apr: Earthquake in Lahore, India, claims over 10,000 lives • English suffragettes step up their campaign with hunger strikes and acts of violence • Publication of Max Weber's *The Protestant Ethic and the Spirit of Capitalism*, arguing that Luther and Calvin are among the wellsprings of modern capitalism (Ger)	• 19 Apr: Severe earthquake in San Francisco kills 1,000 people and destroys much of the city (USA) • Roman Catholic clergyman John Ryan condemns insufficient wage systems in *A Living Wage* (USA)	• Bubonic plague kills 1.3 million in India • Lord Baden Powell founds the Boy Scout Movement (UK) • Mohandas Gandhi begins a campaign of passive resistance (*satyagraha*) to the Asiatic registration bill of 22 Mar (Ind) • Mothers' Day first celebrated, in the US
Politics	• Jun–Aug: Boxer Uprising against the foreign presence in China is put down by an international task force	• 22 Jan: Death of Queen Victoria and accession of Edward VII (UK) • 6 Sep: Theodore Roosevelt becomes president after the assassination of McKinley (USA)	• 31 May: Boer rebels surrender to the British in South Africa • 28 Jun: USA pays $40 million for the Panama Canal	• 18 Nov: Signing of the Panama Canal Treaty • Bolsheviks led by Lenin split from the Mensheviks at the London Congress of the Russian Social Democratic Party	• 8 Feb: Beginning of the Russo-Japanese War	• 9 Jan: First revolution in Russia begins on Bloody Sunday • 5 Sep: Treaty of Portsmouth ends Russo-Japanese War after the Russian defeat	• Rehabilitation of Alfred Dreyfus after it is proved that the charges of treason brought against him in 1894 were false (Fr)	• 10 Jun: Franco-Japanese Treaty ensures open door economic access to China

| --- | --- | --- | --- | --- | --- | --- |
0% of horsepower on glish and Welsh farms provided by horses Rural population of USA s to 50% of total	• First kibbutz started at Degania Aleph (Pal) • US lumber production reaches its peak	• Mexican social revolution is led by Madero against President Diaz who had allowed Indian and mestizo land to be taken by whites • R. Biffen breeds Little Jos, a wheat suitable for British climate and resistant to the yellow rust fungus	• Famine reduces 30 million Russians to starvation, even though 13.7 million tonnes of Russian grain is exported	• New Homestead Act reduces residence requirement from five to three years (USA) • Department of Justice orders the dissolution of the International Harvester Trust (USA)		• Revelation that British farmers produce less than 25% of the nation's grain needs • George Washington Carver reveals experiment results showing how peanuts and sweet potatoes can replenish soil fertility (USA)
8 Feb: Plan for the riction of Japanese or emigration to the A mooted by Japan, to le disputes between the countries ep: International nference for the tection of Labor nands prohibition of nt-work for children upreme Court risons three AF of L ders for violating an nction against a boycott A)	• Apr–May: Paris postal workers on strike over demands to unionize and to affiliate with the Confédération Générale du Travail (Fr) • Aug: One-month general strike in Sweden over economic conditions • Three-month strike by 20,000 garment workers (USA)	• Jan: British miners strike for an eight-hour day • Aug–Sep: Dockers strike for higher wages (Ger/UK) • Oct: Strike of French railroadmen nearly leads to a general strike	• Jan: Miners' strike in the Belgian coal district • 15 May: Supreme Court breaks up Rockefeller's Standard Oil Company (USA) • Aug: British railroadmen go on strike • Olivetti Company founded (It)	• Jan: General strike in Lisbon over dissatisfaction with the new regime • Mar: Miners' strike in the Ruhr ends in failure • Apr: Army suppresses goldminers' strike in Siberia (Russ) • May–Jun: Transport strike in London causes a sympathetic strike by 100,000 dockers (UK) • Textile workers' strike in Lawrence, Massachusetts, demonstrates the power of the International Workers of the World (IWW) (USA)	• 14–24 Apr: 100,000 miners strike in Belgium demanding a revision of the franchise laws (achieved May 1919) • Department of Labor is created by the Wilson administration in response to AF of L pressure (USA) • United Federation of Labor and of the Social Democratic Party founded in New Zealand, providing for the interests of industrial workers	• Jan: General strike initiated by South African gold and diamond miners and railroadmen • Jan: Ford Motor Co introduces profit-sharing and higher wages to avoid threatened labor trouble (USA) • May: Trade unions of miners, transport workers and railroadmen found a common committee for collective bargaining (UK) • 15 Oct: Clayton Anti-Trust Act strengthens government stand against combinations (USA)
valid and Old Age sions Act passed in stralia	• Apr: Lloyd George introduces the "People's Budget" with new taxes to fund welfare provision (UK) • May: Old Age Pensions Act provides for noncontributory pension of five shillings per week for those over 70 years (UK) • Federal old age pensions awarded to those over 65 and resident in Australia for over 25 years	• Apr: First majority Labor government in Australia continues the program of heavy taxation and allowing "desirable" white immigrants to settle the Northern Territory • Old age pensions introduced in France • China abolishes slavery	• 30 Apr: Constitutional court establishes female suffrage in Portugal • Dec: Lloyd George's National Insurance Act provides unemployment insurance for 2.25 million workers (UK)	• 29 Mar: Minimum wage enforced after a strike of 1,500,000 miners (UK) • Massachusetts institutes a minimum wage law for women and children (USA) • Russia adopts workmen's insurance • French Code du Travail issued	• 25 Feb: US introduces federal income tax via the Sixteenth Amendment • Apr: Suffragette leader Emmeline Pankhurst is sentenced to three years imprisonment (UK) • 29 Jun: Norwegian parliament grants women equal electoral rights with men	• Jan: General Hertzog founds the Nationalist Party in South Africa, which becomes a platform for Boer separatism • 26 May: UK House of Commons passes the Irish Home Rule Bill for the third time, bypassing the Lords by way of the 1911 Parliament Act (enforced 1920)
ompletion of the Hejaz lroad to the holy places Mecca and Medina after nt years (Ott Emp)			• 19 Apr: Provisional government in Portugal separates Church and State		• 13 Jan: Pope bans films from churches and forbids films of a religious nature • Rudolf Steiner founds the first Goetheanum, for the teaching of anthroposophy, at Dornach (Swi) • B'nai B'rith founds the Anti-Defamation League to fight antisemitism (USA)	• May: Reports of extreme cruelties by Serbians against Albanian muslims • Aug: Death of Pope Pius X, succeeded by Benedict XV
reation of the Federal eau of Investigation I) (USA) ug: Ford introduces the del T automobile he Times newspaper of don is acquired by count Northcliffe who publishes the London ly Mail and the Daily ror (UK)	• Jun: National Negro Committee founded in New York, becoming the National Association for the Advancement of Colored People (NAACP) in 1910 (USA) • Selfridge, the first large department store in Britain, founded by US businessman H.G. Selfridge, opens in London (UK) • Girl Guides established in the UK	• Boy Scouts and Campfire Girls of America are founded • Pathé Gazette pioneers the film newsreel (USA/UK) • Fathers' Day first celebrated, in Spokane, Washington DC (USA)	• 17 Apr: New York's Ellis Island records a record influx of 11,745 immigrants in a single day (USA) • 16 Dec: Roald Amundsen raises the Norwegian flag over the South Pole, two months ahead of Robert F. Scott • Founding of Union or Death (The Black Hand), an anti-Austrian propagandist society, in Serbia	• 15 Apr: Sinking of the S.S. Titanic on her maiden voyage across the Atlantic Ocean; 1,513 lives are lost • Journal Pravda begins to voice the ideas of Russia's underground Communist Party • Benito Mussolini becomes chief editor of the Italian Socialist Party newspaper Avanti • Mar: Girl Scouts of America founded	• Marcus Garvey founds the Universal Negro Improvement Association (Jam) • Dr Henry Plotz discovers a typhoid vaccine (USA)	• Oct: George Eastman announces the invention of the color photo process (USA) • US feminist Margaret Sanger introduces the term "birth control" in The Woman Rebel and exiles herself to England to avoid prosecution
		• 31 May: Union of South Africa becomes a Commonwealth dominion under Louis Botha • 22 Aug: Japan annexes Korea and renames it Chosen	• 10 Aug: Parliament Act restricts House of Lords veto power (UK) • 10 Oct: Revolution begins in China leading to the end of the Manchu dynasty	• 12 Feb: Abdication of boy-emperor Pu Yi, and a provisional government takes control in China (15 Feb) • 18 Oct: Outbreak of First Balkan War	• 4 Mar: Woodrow Wilson becomes 28th US president (until 1921)	• 28 Jun: Assassination in Sarajevo (Bosnia) of Archduke Franz Ferdinand of Austria creates war crisis • 1–3 Aug: Germany declares war on Russia and France, and invades Belgium

Datafile

The systematic study of society began in the 19th century partly in response to anxiety among ruling groups about the social impact of industrialization and urbanization. The breakdown of "social order" was widely feared. By the beginning of the 20th century the "second industrial revolution", based on electricity and chemicals, was under way. Big corporations were becoming established, and industrial work was beginning to be subject to new methods of control under "scientific management". Yet most people, even in the advanced industrial nations, were still peasant farmers, agricultural workers or employees in small enterprises. "Industrial society" was not yet fully formed.

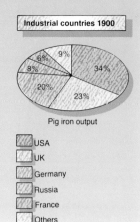

Industrial countries 1900

Pig iron output

USA

UK

Germany

Russia

France

Others

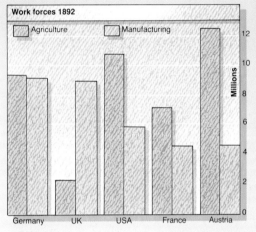

Work forces 1892

Agriculture   Manufacturing

Germany   UK   USA   France   Austria

▲ By 1900 industrial leadership, reflected here in the relative output of a basic industrial product, had passed to the United States. The world economy, however, still depended on British financial and shipping services, and was based on sterling.

◄ Only in the United Kingdom was there an "industrial society" in which more were employed in manufacturing than in agriculture. But the United States produced more with fewer manufacturing workers.

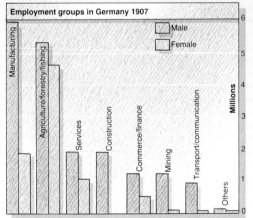

Employment groups in Germany 1907

Male
Female

Manufacturing · Agriculture/forestry/fishing · Services · Construction · Commerce/finance · Mining · Transport/communication · Others

◄ By 1907 among German men manufacturing had overtaken agriculture as the chief source of employment. But the proportion of the whole work force employed in manufacturing was only to increase from 29 to 33 percent by 1939. Meanwhile the services sectors (including finance, commerce and transport) increased from 22 to 32 percent. Where agriculture has declined worldwide in the 20th century, "services" has usually become the predominant employment sector – not manufacturing.

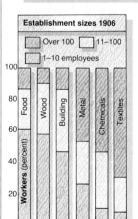

Establishment sizes 1906

Over 100   11–100
1–10 employees

Food · Wood · Building · Metal · Chemicals · Textiles

Workers (percent)

◄ In 1906 59 percent of all industrial workers in France were still employed in establishments with less than ten employees. But the proportion in big factories was much higher in the modern industries based on machine production.

► Europe's rural areas encompassed a wide range of economies, as is suggested by this information for prewar France. Local agricultural practice could influence social structures, producing distinctive local areas or *pays*.

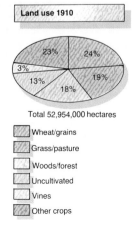

Land use 1910

Total 52,954,000 hectares

Wheat/grains
Grass/pasture
Woods/forest
Uncultivated
Vines
Other crops

At the beginning of the 20th century parts of northwest Europe and North America were caught up in profound social change as a consequence of industrialization – the process in which the productivity of human labor is raised through the harnessing of power and the application of science to improve production methods. Industrialization was organized by capitalists: private owners of wealth who invested it to earn profits and who employed the labor of others. For these employees, industrialization meant that they lived in big cities (rather than villages or small towns), worked in factories or offices (rather than in agriculture), and that the pace of work was determined by machinery (rather than individual capacity).

Industrialization and employment

How far had capitalist industrialization proceeded by the beginning of the 20th century? The first and for a time the only industrial society was that of Britain, where industrialization had first gathered pace toward the end of the 18th century. But by 1900 Britain's industrial supremacy had given way in the face of competition from the United States and from Germany. By 1913 the United States accounted for about one-third of the world's manufacturing output, equal to the shares of Germany, Britain and France combined. But even in these, the advanced industrial nations of the world, the extent to which societies had become dependent on industry was limited. A contemporary British statistician, Michael Mulhall, wrote as follows, referring to what he called "the nations of Christendom": "One half of the world is engaged in agricultural pursuits, one fourth in manufactures, one-tenth in trade and transport and the remainder [15 percent] in professions, public service and other useful occupations". It is true that by 1914 less than half of the labor force was employed in agriculture in Britain, France, Germany, the Low Countries and the United States, but in France the proportion so engaged remained 43 percent and in Germany 35 percent. Only in Britain was it as low as 8 percent.

In spite of the rapid growth in the number and size of cities which had taken place in the 19th century, there was no country apart from Britain where the total urban population exceeded that of the rural areas. Not until 1920, indeed, did the urban population of the United States outstrip that of the rural areas.

Outside the west the most important industrializing state was Imperial Russia. There industrialization was being telescoped into a few decades by drawing on foreign technology, skills and investment. Between 1909 and 1913 alone industrial output rose by 54 percent and the factory work force increased by 30 percent.

NEW WORLDS OF WORK

The world of manufacturing itself, however, remained in some ways remarkably unchanged from the conditions previously found in craft workshops, even in the advanced industrial nations. It has been said of American industry at the beginning of the century that "the factory remained a congeries of craftsmen's shops rather than an integrated plant". In London the 8,500 factories using power employed an average of only 41 workers each. Large-scale industrial enterprises were in fact more prominent as a proportion of new industry in Russia, though this suggests a misleading impression of advance given that it reflects the labor intensity and lower productivity of Russian industry.

Before the Industrial Revolution industrial work had largely consisted of "manufacturing", literally understood as "the process of making by hand" and thereby subject to dependence upon skills of individuals. In factory production work

▼ A production line at one of Henry Ford's automobile plants c. 1913, where "the pace was inexorable, the pressure for ever-better production insistent".

consisted of a system of "machinofacture", in which the pace of work was dictated by machines and was thereby more under the control of employers or owners. Yet by 1900 the transition from manufacture to machinofacture had not in fact proceeded very far.

Social order and change in the countryside

In the late 19th century, partly in response to fears about the breakdown of "social order", the study of human social institutions – sociology – had become established as an academic discipline. Its first practitioners, notably the Frenchman Emile Durkheim (1858–1917), considered that many of the social problems of their time had been caused by the spread of industry and the expansion of cities. The pioneering academic sociologists sought to interpret these changes. Durkheim suggested that there had been a change in the basis of the social order: from "mechanical solidarity"

to "organic solidarity". In traditional rural societies people did the same kind of work and generally had the same kinds of experiences and identities but in societies where there was a great range of specialized jobs, people were related to each other by each performing a necessary inter-related task. By implication, even if the range of occupations increased and people became more individual, a stable social order could be maintained because of people's economic inter-dependence.

Durkheim's theory seems to have presupposed that the process of industrialization was more complete than it actually was around 1900. In fact most of the world's people, even in the advanced industrial nations, remained agricultural workers, many of them still peasants – owners or tenant cultivators of small landholdings and some other assets which they worked with their own labor and with that of their household members. Moreover, some agriculture was proving to be

more flexible and adaptable than anyone had expected.

In the mid 19th century the radical German social thinker Karl Marx had suggested that the growth of large units of production in industry would be associated with a similar development in agriculture and that small-scale producers would be forced out. But again, another idea about likely social and economic changes proved incorrect. Several developments gave peasant agriculture a new lease of life: the establishment of peasant cooperatives; the gradual extension of political rights to peasants; protection of agricultural markets; increased education; and cheap transport. They expanded the potential for such activities as intensive small-scale livestock rearing, dairying and horticulture. Indeed, the long slump in international grain prices, from 1874 to 1896, hit the largest farms hardest and benefited the smallholders. Large farms had depended on wage laborers, who only did what they were told

▲ Smallholding peasants, seen here at a market in France, still made up much of the work force over most of Europe. The establishment of the wholesaler and distiller seen in the background, however, reflects the penetration of commerce into agriculture. The expansion of the railroad network had begun to break down isolated rural communities.

(and no more) and who would slacken their effort when no one was watching. The price depression dented the profitability of such farms and caused a reduction in the proportion of agricultural workers employed on them. By contrast, as a contemporary Russian economist, A.V. Chayanov, argued influentially, labor on the small peasant family farm was more motivated and flexible, and also responsive to changing conditions. In the late 19th and early 20th century peasant agriculture was sometimes becoming increasingly successful commercially.

The creation of big business
Even though capitalist industry had not taken over societies in the way in which many thinkers thought it must do, capitalism itself had by 1900 entered a new phase. Sometimes called "monopoly capitalism", it was a phase characterized by competition between a small number of rival large-scale firms rather than between individual small capitalists, and by imperialist rivalry between capitalist countries. The economic

depression after 1870 had given rise to protectionism and to a quest for new markets. There were also needs for new products, such as oil and rubber, and an expanding mass demand for tropical foodstuffs like bananas among the increasing numbers of people who lived by purchases in the market and were no longer dependent on self-provisioning.

The search for markets and for commodities, or sometimes political compulsion alone, drove the expansion of colonial empires. All these trends had considerable impact on the kind of employment available in many countries and on the organization of industry and business.

In the early 20th century new industries of the so-called "second industrial revolution" were emerging in the major industrial countries that were to dominate the century – oil and petrochemicals, electrical equipment, radio and communications, vehicles and many other forms of metal manufacture, synthetic materials, etc. Many of these industries could only be developed with major initial capital investment or, after the initial

New farm implements were being bought and they were costly. In the end it would perhaps be an economy but how could one be certain...? The most ignorant, that is to say the majority, evidently relied on the experience of the more prosperous and better educated. They copied them full of wonder at their knowledge and began to think that...it would be a good thing to be able to think things over, pen in hand.

R. THAUBAULT

Life in European Villages

In 1900 the majority of Europe's population lived in rural societies, usually in villages which had an average population of about 500. Strongly contrasting ideas about village life still persist. On the one hand there is an attractive picture of villages as "communities" regulated by values which supply physical and emotional security. On the other rural life is seen as backward and even rather brutish. Marx, for example, spoke of its "idiocy", and an observer of Russia in 1917 wrote that villagers "wallowed like pigs in the pestilential atmosphere, blended of the excretory putrescences exhaled from men and animals".

It is generally thought that traditional rural society, with all the virtues of the community, was in decline by the beginning of the century, due to the impact of schools, railroads and military conscription. Military service accustomed young peasants to urban values and tastes. Peasant families learned the uses of literacy and the transport revolution accelerated rural-urban migration. In 1861 11 percent of Frenchmen lived outside their native department; by 1918 25 percent. Bicycles extended the mobility of young men and allowed them to spend their evenings in cafes and bars in town. Modern sports replaced older village pastimes; folk-dancing began to be ousted by dancing by couples of waltzes and polkas; and folk songs were collected by folklorists to save them from extinction. But the historian of the French peasantry, Eugen Weber, believes that on balance the changes taking place were progressive as education encouraged greater independence from the old rural elite and standards of diet and health began to improve.

It is, however, possible to exaggerate the decline of the "traditional" society. In some ways the changes around 1900 made the countryside *more* rural, for urban competition hit precisely those groups in rural society who had previously provided the contacts between the peasantry and the world of the towns. Even by mid-century social mobility in the countryside was still often restricted. A study of one French village shows that three-quarters of the residents in 1946 had

been born in the village or less than 20km (12.5 mi) away, and that of the 4,000 children born there since 1821 only 50 had finished secondary school. The standard of living remained modest. Three-quarters of the villagers' income was spent on food and their staples were bread and soup.

The image of the self-regulating village community has been extremely powerful in ideas about social development and change, and it is sometimes sought to be renewed through progams of "community development". In practice, however, village societies are often deeply divided by differences of interests.

▲ A village council in Russia, where communal land ownership and organization of farming still survived. It is said that "The commune was a sort of democracy, but a democracy of minority – male heads of household (like those seen here) under whose interests were subsumed the interests of the majority".

development, by attaining great economies of scale. Production rapidly became very concentrated and in some cases companies developed into monopolies. Thus, the tendency to seek control of national markets was considerably enhanced in comparison with the 19th century. In the United States the process of concentration was associated with particular individuals, the "robber barons", and with their business empires which often dominated particular industries: Andrew Carnegie, Henry Ford, Cornelius Vanderbilt, J.P. Morgan etc. John D. Rockefeller made prodigious monopoly profits from the fledgling oil industry.

Great size of firm implied that the enormous mass of shareholders could no longer play any serious role in directing a company. Ownership and management separated. The majority of shareholders became passive "rentiers" or "coupon clippers", with no role in the company except privileged access to a share of profits (and even that was determined by those who managed the company). Giant companies were controlled by those with the largest block of shares, often

financial institutions, banks and insurance companies, with professional managers (who only became "owners" by virtue of being given the company's shares as part of a salary payment). Firms thus often assumed a life and stability independent of the personal fortunes of particular businessmen. They also presented a quite different image from what had gone before. The old competitive markets with a mass of firms scrambling for advantage gave way to large-scale managerial and bureaucratic hierarchies, from the Individual to the Corporation, from the ethics of the jungle to those of status.

The growth in the size of firms was paralleled by the increasing importance of the State. As businesses grew larger and became more sophisticated the demand for educated labor increased enormously. "White collar" workers were becoming increasingly important and a mass phenomenon (unlike the few clerical staff a half century earlier). A mass educational system and universal literacy were becoming necessary, and with it other underpinnings of rising labor productivity – health and welfare schemes.

▲▼ Clerical black coats (like these at Cadbury's in England), were a badge of respectability. Working conditions were improved by inventions such as the electric fan (below), though office jobs became routinized like industrial production.

New organization of work

The depression of the 1870s and 1880s revealed to many industrialists the inadequacy of their control over labor in the workplace. In America this was observed by the pioneer of "scientific management", F.W. Taylor. He wrote that "in most of the shops in this country, the shop [is] really run by the workmen and not by the bosses". Though prices fell during the depression, workers were able to maintain the level of money wages, so that labor costs rose and profits were squeezed. In response employers developed what was known as the "drive system" of production, involving mechanization and decreased reliance on skilled labor, and closer supervision by foremen.

The application of electrical power contributed to the development of the drive system. The machine tools industry was transformed by the introduction of automatic lathes and riveting machines, reducing the level of skills necessary in the manufacture of ships and machines, and encouraging a more rapid pace of work.

The key symbol of the new technology – combining both new methods of organization and new technologies – was the continually moving assembly line. It was introduced by the American automobile manufacturer Henry Ford in 1913. He employed nearly 14,000 people at his plants in Detroit, and from this time the majority were semiskilled workers using electric-powered equipment to repeat simple operations within a complex manufacturing process. In the words of the sociologist Hugh Beynon, "The machines were the masters and the men had to keep pace with them" – a pattern of work depicted movingly in Charlie Chaplin's film *Modern Times* (1936).

The efforts of employers in the United States to increase their control over labor were met with resistance, reflected in increasing labor unrest toward the end of the 19th century. Then, however, the rise of big corporations saw the introduction of policies to undercut worker opposition. These included the establishment of centralized personnel departments, cooperation with and sometimes cooptation of craft unions and manipulation of ethnic differences among workers.

The last was assisted by fresh waves of immigration. For the most part the immigrants (mainly from the backward regions of eastern and southern Europe) were prepared to take on the most disagreeable jobs and to endure long hours and ruthless exploitation. Mechanization and the simultaneous expansion of the supply of cheap labor undermined craft skills and served to reduce more and more jobs to the level of the semi-skilled. After 1900 the proportion of the industrial labor force made up by such operatives increased and the ratio of their wages to those of skilled workers declined, while the numbers of supervisory workers increased in proportion to those engaged in production.

The growth of industrial bureaucracy, as of public bureaucracy, was assisted by such recent innovations as the typewriter and the adding machine. In offices too work became more routinized, faster paced and noisier.

Bureaucracy

Karl Marx argued that industrial capitalism is the fundamental determinant of modern social change. The German sociologist Max Weber (1864–1920), however, thought that the development of capitalism is itself an effect of a deeper process, which he referred to as that of "rationalization". This means the reorganization of social and economic life according to principles of efficiency, on the basis of technical knowledge. The application of these principles to administration creates bureaucracy which, Weber said, "means fundamentally the exercise of control on the basis of knowledge". Bureaucracies have a clear hierarchy of authority to coordinate decision making; they have written rules of procedure; and they are staffed by salaried officials (as above) who should make a clear separation between their official tasks and their private lives. They should act according to the rules of the organization so that its functioning is made independent of their individual characteristics. Weber's belief that bureaucracy is the best way of organizing large numbers of people has been borne out by the growth in importance of the white-collar workers who staff bureaucracies.

Of course you know I thought I was somebody when I got a job because jobs under an employer were just a thing almost unheard of...They were just engaged and their own craft and suchlike, but get work outside of the home and under an employer and just at a specified job – you thought yourself somebody then.

PETER HENRY
GOODS CHECKER

▼ A dormitory of a Russian factory, c. 1900. Conditions in Russia's large-scale industries were typical of those to be found in most industrializing countries. Factories were overcrowded and stifling; workers were closely supervised; accidents were frequent. The working week was six days, the working day over 11 hours. Forty percent of workers lived in factory dormitories, the remainder packed into rented rooms or apartments. Relief from a monotonous and hard existence was provided by religious holidays, by playing cards and by bouts of heavy drinking.

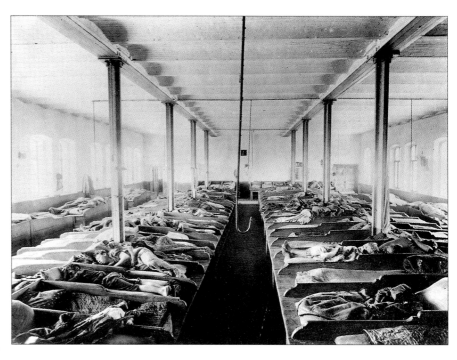

ART AND RELIGION

Antonio Gaudí, Spanish architect of the fantastic and still unfinished Church of the Holy Family (Sagrada Familia) in Barcelona, once said, "my client is not in a hurry". Religion has, indeed, given many artists in the 20th century a meditative space in which to fulfil their ideas. Equally it has given some of them a fierce endeavor. The French painter Georges Rouault's ambition was to paint a Christ that would convert anyone to Christianity at sight.

These two artists signaled the preoccupation with religious questions and themes which has been so marked a feature of this century, despite its being frequently characterized as "godless" by believers and unbelievers alike. To go outside the Western world, to Africa, India, the Far East and Latin America, is to realize that the idea of the world as "godless" was always a European presumption. But even in the West, if the artists can be taken as indicative of the times, the 20th century has been, if not God-fearing or faithful, then certainly God-concerned, even where the concern has been for loss of faith. This has shown itself not only at the obvious level where architects like Le Corbusier and Gaudí have built chapels and churches; artists like Matisse and Chagall have decorated them; composers like Britten have written masses; and writers like Mauriac, Bernanos, Greene, Joyce, Eliot and Rilke have considered the matter of faith from many angles. There has also been an openness to religious questions across the frontiers of the great faiths: composers like Messiaen and artists like Mark Tobey have used not just the forms but the spirit of non-Western religious traditions in their work. Conversely, the Hindu Jamini Roy and Jew Marc Chagall – among others – have responded vividly to Christian imagery.

Equally fruitful, from the point of view of painting, has been a concern with contemplative themes. This involved an unspecific search for religious truth, especially in the work of Abstract Expressionists like Mark Rothko and Barnett Newman. The search after faith is part of faith itself. The degree of unspecificity is not a sign that the search has been abandoned, but that it has not been articulated in one of the world's dominant creeds. And the search for a living faith is continued, not concluded, in religion.

With the rise of skepticism and doubt in the past 150 years, there has been an ebbing away of religious certainty, which for many has left a gap in human understanding. A surprising number of people have sought to use art as a means of filling that gap, though art – a human creation – can never fully replace religious truth – the object of contemplation itself.

▼ *18 Cantos* (1963) by Barnett Newman, one of the many almost impersonal works of flat color broken by sharp, thin strips, in which the artist sought a truth beyond individuality.

▶▶ Stained-glass windows by Chagall for the Hadassah Medical Center, in Jerusalem. The subject is Napthali, one of the 12 tribes of Israel. His glowing vision made a religious celebration that reached across religious divides.

▶▲ *Face of Christ* (1937–38) by Georges Rouault. The heavy outlines, glowing colors and simple composition of many of his works derived from his apprenticeship in stained glass. Rouault's other main theme was sinful humanity.

◄▼ Architectural sketch by Francisco Valls (left) and sculptural detail (main image) of the Church of the Holy Family by Antonio Gaudí, began in Barcelona in 1882 and still incomplete. It is a triumphant statement of traditional Catholic faith in an age of doubt.

Datafile

The prewar period saw the consolidation in Europe (though not in America) of mass political parties based on the working class as well as of a range of organized interest groups, including trade unions. The development of these institutions was matched by increasing state intervention in education, health care and social welfare. The middle class, meanwhile, distinguished by access to secondary education, developed a new leisure ethic.

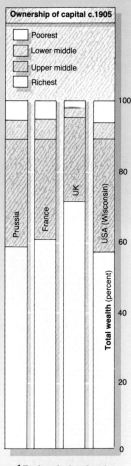

Ownership of capital c.1905

- Poorest
- Lower middle
- Upper middle
- Richest

Prussia / France / UK / USA (Wisconsin)

Total wealth (percent)

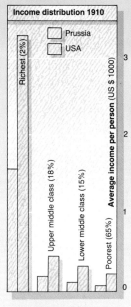

Income distribution 1910

- Prussia
- USA

Richest (2%)
Upper middle class (18%)
Lower middle class (15%)
Poorest (65%)

Average income per person (US $ 1000)

▶ **There was sharp inequality in wealth, measured here by the money value of property. In the UK the richest 2 percent owned nearly three times as much as the rest of society. These disparities were reflected in the life style of the plutocratic "leisure class", which also permeated the middle classes.**

◀ **Average incomes were higher in the USA than in Prussia, but not notably more equally distributed. America offered opportunity for European immigrants but not necessarily upward social mobility. The "rags-to-riches" thesis of economic and social advancement has been found wanting in historical studies of American cities.**

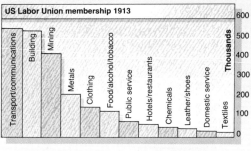

US Labor Union membership 1913

Transport/communications, Building, Mining, Metals, Clothing, Food/alcohol/tobacco, Public service, Hotels/restaurants, Chemicals, Leather/shoes, Domestic service, Textiles

Thousands

◀ **Trade unionism faced more determined resistance in the USA than in Europe but by 1913 the American Federation of Labor (a loose federation of national unions made up especially of skilled workers) had more than 2 million members. Unionism was especially strong in transport, mining and construction.**

Social structure 1897

Russian Poland
3%
24%
73%

European Russia
5%
11%
84%

- Peasants
- Burghers
- Others

(nobles/high officials/clergy/merchants/foreigners)

◀ **The western parts of the Russian Empire, including Poland, were more commercialized and industrialized than the Russian heartland. This lent force to Russian nationalist movements. The more diversified social structure of Poland is reflected here in the higher proportion of townsmen or "burghers".**

▶ **Governments now took on many more functions, becoming more involved in economic management, providing infrastructure, education and welfare services. They thus needed more information and to monitor and police the population more closely. Consequently public bureaucracies expanded rapidly.**

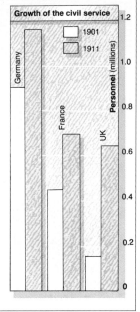

Growth of the civil service

- 1901
- 1911

Germany / France / UK

Personnel (millions)

If capitalist industrialization – based on the 18th-century Industrial Revolution – is one of the great forces which has shaped 20th-century society another is the struggle for democracy, which was powerfully influenced by that other revolution of the late 18th century, the French Revolution. Both the French Revolution and the Industrial Revolution were animated by the same currents of individualism and rationalism in 18th-century European thought. Although there is no inherent or necessary connection between industrialization and the development of a political system in which "the people" rule (the basic meaning of democracy), it was generally believed among thinkers and most statesmen in the early 20th century that industrialization had to be accompanied by the involvement of the mass of the people in political life.

There were still great variations in patterns of social and economic life, which the French geographers of the time sought to explain in terms of the concept of *pays* – referring to distinctive regional cultures at quite a small scale. But there was also a strong trend of standardization, encouraged by the growth of factory organization and of cities, by the beginnings of mass consumption (marked, for example, by the success of F.W. Woolworth's "five and ten cent stores" of which there were over 1,000 in the United States by 1911), and by the spread of primary education. Industrialization and its administration required the expansion of literacy and basic education, and the numbers of schools, pupils and teachers multiplied even in the more backward parts of Europe. The general level of education was higher in the United States, though even there in 1910 more than 90 percent of children still only received an elementary education lasting on average for just six years.

These standardizing forces seemed to some, in the words of the 19th-century French statesman Alexis de Tocqueville, "to be rendering people into a uniform mass, alike in their thoughts and attitudes". The relationships between, first, this "mass" and the elites, marked in the early part of the century by a widening economic gap, and, second, between the masses and the state were a matter of major concern. Some feared the threat the masses seemed to pose to the established order, others the extent to which standardization represented a threat to individual liberty. Yet the trend of democratization – of widening franchises with the relaxation of property and educational qualifications for voting rights, and even of the extension of the franchise to women (pioneered on the margins of the western world in Wyoming (USA), New Zealand and South Australia in the 1890s) – was generally accepted outside Spain and eastern Europe. Even so, by 1914 electorates were

MASSES AND ELITES

still usually restricted to between 30 and 40 percent of the adult population. The persistence of autocracy in Russia was regarded elsewhere as a matter of shame, and in other countries, in spite of their fears, rulers did not seriously contemplate a return to authoritarian rule.

Imperial Russia remained a vast multinational peasant society dominated and held together by an absolute monarchy, an all-pervasive state bureaucracy, a relatively small commercial-industrial sector, a large standing army of mainly peasant conscripts, the Russian Orthodox Church and a privileged landed nobility. The established church and the nobility were for the most part servants and guardians of the state. They derived their power and position from a long history of obsequious service to the czarist autocracy. As with its Soviet successor, but unlike most western states, the authority and legitimacy of the Imperial Russian state were based upon a strong and monolithic official ideology, known as that of "Orthodoxy, Autocracy and Nationality", which was deliberately critical of democratic liberalism.

▼ The solidarity of their communities helped to make miners the vanguard of the labor movement. In mining villages the "pub" was a center of community and it was here that Welsh coal miners discussed the progress of a national strike in 1912.

Workers, the labor movement and mass culture
The British historian Eric Hobsbawm argues that "Democracy created rather than followed political consciousness amongst workers and peasants"; the expansion of democracy in the late 19th and early 20th centuries brought about the political mobilization of the masses by and for electoral competition. By 1900 the growth of the mass party-cum-movement, based on the working class and involving a complex of local branches and associations, marked the development of civil society in place of the fragmented, localized and personalized loyalties of the past.

Who were the masses who were organized by the new parties? The "working class" – those dependent upon work for wages – was far from homogeneous, though there were some massive groups including notably the miners (who numbered 800,000 in Germany and more than a million in Britain in 1907). Important differences in the organization of production persisted between large-scale factories and small workshops, and workers were divided by differences

of skill and in the nature of the work they did, as well as by ethnic differences of nationality, language and religion; for example, the powerful Western Federation of Miners in the United States was divided by antagonisms between skilled Methodists from Cornwall and less skilled Catholics of Irish origin. There was also an increasingly significant intermediate stratum of the old small property-owning class of artisans, craftsmen and small shopkeepers, and the new middle class of nonmanual and white-collar workers-for-wages. The growth of this lower middle class perhaps helped to define "working class" identity.

In spite of the differences among them, manual wage workers were receptive to socialist ideas. Their recognition of themselves as a collectivity was assisted by the widening gap in wealth and incomes between workers and owners of capital. The latter now came to be identified, as

employers had not been before, with "the privileged", the old target of radical political attack. Awareness of class identity was reinforced by the residential segregation of workers and others in the expanding cities. There were towns like Bochum in Germany, or Middlesbrough in northeast England, built around heavy industry, in which most of the population was of manual workers who might rarely meet people from other backgrounds. In the great cities working-class areas like Wedding in Berlin or West Ham in London grew up, their dwellings clearly distinguished from those of the new middle-class quarters or suburbs.

A further element in the formation of the working class was increasing state intervention. For workers' struggles for the regulation of the length of the working day, and of conditions in the workplace, to be effective required the intervention of the state. But this then in turn called forth

▶▶ **The Carnegie company built this steel town at Homestead, Pennsylvania, USA. For the European immigrants in the work force, industrial work meant the acceptance of factory discipline; but this was usually preferable to their previous servile dependence. Real wages rose slightly to 1914, and the working week was reduced from 66 to 55 hours.**

▶ **The front page of a special German paper for May Day 1900 celebrated the advance of the labor movement.**

▼ **The powers of American unions, meanwhile, were eroded by the courts. Strikes were bitterly fought, leading here (in Philadelphia, Pennsylvania, in 1910) to street violence.**

an increasingly organized response by workers. As Hobsbawm puts it, "the state unified the class", and no other class had such consistent need for state action.

The modern labor movement had begun to take shape in Europe and North America in the 1880s, assisted by the relaxation of laws limiting strikes and the formation of unions, notably in Britain (where unions acquired a legal status not seriously challenged until the 1980s), and to a lesser extent in France and Germany. The Federal Government of the United States, by contrast, remained more willing to intervene on the bosses' side, and employers there were able to use court injunctions to break strikes up until the 1930s. In the industrial states of Europe direct action was not illegal as it had been before (though there were continuing struggles, as over the right to picket); this, together with increasing literacy and, until the 1900s, increasing workers' incomes, encouraged the growth of the labor movement.

In the 1890s a new kind of industrial unionism arose, showing much less hesitation about strike action than was the case with the older craft unions. The industry-based unions grew up among miners and transport workers, especially dockworkers. Coal-miners became the group of workers most likely to conduct repeated, massive strikes, encouraged by their sheer numbers, the conditions of their work and the cohesiveness of the communities in which they lived.

By the first decade of the 20th century union membership was massive. In Britain unions had more than 3 million members, those in Germany 1.5 million and in France about 1 million. Industry-wide strikes took place in mining and in transport; national general strikes occurred in some countries (in Belgium, Holland and Sweden), and in Britain at least nationwide collective agreements were quite common.

In the United States trade unionism made more faltering progress because of government support for employers, ethnic divisions among workers, and the tenacity of the American Dream – that no one needed to remain a hired worker. Workers themselves thus supported capitalist values. Yet the American Federation of Labor (the AF of L) was formed in 1881, mainly by skilled workers. It was dominated by the moderate Samuel Gompers from 1886 until his death in 1924, and his pragmatism, rejection of socialist influences and of the idea of a separate labor party did much to secure the acceptability of the AF of L in a political environment which was very hostile to labor organization.

The development of the drive system of management meant that unionism lost ground in the 1900s, but by 1914 the AF of L had more than 2 million members. This was in spite of the challenge posed by the revolutionary movement of the International Workers of the World (known as "the Wobblies"), which had been founded in Chicago in 1905 and intended to unite all wage-earners in class war against capitalism. Never a large organization, the IWW still provoked fears and singular hostility amongst employers, to which it quite soon succumbed leaving a rich legacy only in American folklore.

Diet and Social Differences

In all societies food is a sensitive indicator of differences of wealth and status. In England at the beginning of the 20th century a well-known high-society hostess wrote: "No dinner should consist of more than eight dishes: soup, fish, *entrée*, joint, game, sweet, *hors d'oeuvre* and perhaps an ice, but each dish should be perfect of its kind". In the British city of York, according to the 1901 survey of poverty in the city made by the industrialist and social researcher Seebohm Rowntree, average consumption among the poor represented on average 2,069 calories per day. This was less than some experts believe to be necessary for good health among working adults, and comparable with intakes of dietary energy observed in large parts of the "Third World" today. Similarly in rural Russia early in the century, "In the diet of poor households the basic position is occupied by bread, potatoes and other cheap foodstuffs while in the diet of rich households wheaten bread is more important and so are meat and fat, milk, confectionery and so on". But the diets of the poor were improving in the industrial countries. Surveys showed that, in England at least, even rural laborers were able to spend more on meat than on bread.

Later, in the years after World War I in the West, consumption of fruit, vegetables and eggs in particular increased while that of bread declined. But still the main meal in poorer working families in Britain was supper, "consisting of strong tea, bread and margarine, tinned salmon or sardines – if this could be afforded – or otherwise fish and meat pastes". Yet by 1927 slimming had become fashionable among the better-off, and concerns about "healthy eating" took off. The medical journal *The Lancet*, for example, introduced the idea of the importance of "roughage" in a healthy diet. There immediately appeared "roughage" breakfast foods such as bran to supply this need. Toward the end of the century in the rich countries diet and health became a major preoccupation, reflected in the increased consumption of foods such as pasta and poultry, but alongside the popularity too of "fast" or "junk" food.

The growth of the civil state

In industrial Europe meanwhile, the increasing strength of the labor movement – reflected in an unprecedented wave of labor agitation and strikes between 1905 and 1914 and in the electoral advances of labor and socialist parties – drew forth a different response from governments. Following the German chancellor Bismarck's example, when in the 1880s he introduced social insurance to undercut support for socialism, European governments deployed what has been called "the strategy of the soft embrace"; they initiated programs of social welfare and reform. Austria, Denmark and Italy introduced programs modeled on the German example before 1900. In Britain old age pensions, public labor exchanges, health and unemployment insurance were all introduced between 1906 and 1914. Old age pensions were introduced in France in 1911. In the USA no such legislation existed by 1914 and even child labor remained uncontrolled by Federal law, in spite of the reforming intentions of the Progressive politicians. It is too early yet to speak of the "welfare state" in Europe, for the coverage of legislation like the National Insurance Act of 1911 in Britain was still restricted, and the amount of income redistributed very little. But the social reforms of the early 20th century mark a major departure from the liberal values of the previous century and a shift toward collectivism, prompting concerns amongst some politicians and philosophers about the erosion of individual liberty. They involved too, growth in the size of public bureaucracies. In Britain, for example, government employees increased threefold between 1891 and 1911.

The very success of the labor movement and of disciplined class parties in western Europe in wresting concessions from governments and rulers in fact helped to undermine revolutionary aspirations. The future was increasingly seen in terms of successful working-class collectivism within the structures of industrial capitalism rather than in those of revolutionary change. Ruling classes discovered that democracy was compatible with the stability of industrial capitalism. The success of their efforts at incorporating the masses by means of political and social reforms and by appeals to patriotism, the thrills of empire, and a "tradition" that was deliberately created – as in the institution of new festivals like the Fourteenth of July in France – was finally demonstrated in the way workers volunteered to fight each other after August 1914.

The democratization of political life in industrializing societies gave rise not only to the consolidation of working-class identity but also to nationalism. The word itself only acquired currency toward the end of the 19th century, when it seems that the imaginary community of "the nation" could fill the gap left by the weakening of ties of kinship, community and religion, and the depersonalization of social relations. Democracy, especially elections, gave opportunity for groups to mobilize as Czechs, or Germans, or Italians, and attempts were made by left- and right-wing politicians alike to combine their appeals with those of nationalism. States sought to use

▲ Public baths where children might be bathed, like these in London, helped to improve urban living standards. But research by Seebohm Rowntree in the English cathedral city of York in 1901 showed that 30 percent lived in poverty. In the United States at this time about 40 percent of wage-earning families lived below the official poverty line.

◀ Payment of old-age pensions started in Britain in 1909, 20 years after their introduction in Germany. The British scheme was paid for from taxation and thus represented a departure from principles of self-help, but it still involved a means test. In France the unions protested that pensions which began at age 65 would come too late.

This was the heyday of vaudeville and music hall, and of popular music and humor which by gently mocking class divisions accommodated rather than threatened them.

The existence of these activities was an expression of the new ethics of the workplace, which created a clear distinction between "work" and "leisure". Workers increasingly sought fulfilment outside work itself. Organized religion largely failed to provide a framework for their lives, and the strength of organized religion lay elsewhere. Even in America, in spite of investment in church building, and increasing church membership, active church-going became increasingly middle class.

Elites and middle classes
Who were the rulers of the industrializing societies of the West? Though monarchies survived in most of Europe, the 19th century is sometimes described as "the bourgeois century" because of the new ascendancy of capitalist owners of industry, business and finance. But historians now differ in their views as to the eclipse or the persistence of the power of the old landed aristocracies.

It is clear that the formerly dominant values ascribing high status as a right of birth and social position had given way before those associated with the market, and that social power was closely correlated with wealth. Equally there is no doubt that members of the "big bourgeoisie" sought to take on aristocratic standards. Self-made American millionaires, for example, married into European noble families. It is probably best to think of the ruling classes of the European industrial nations as being formed by landed noblemen who had often developed commercial and industrial interests, and by the industrial and financial bourgeoisie whose politics and attitudes were susceptible to aristocratic influences.

They were relieved of anxiety. They were suddenly rich. Independent for life! At first when they went down to the Post Office to draw it [their first pension], tears of gratitude would run down the cheeks of some, and they would say as they picked up their money, "God bless that Lord George!"

FLORA THOMPSON

▼ Expanded access to elementary education, standardized under state control, assisted in the foundations of nationalism. Here a German teacher leads cheers for the Kaiser in the first week of World War I. German primary schools encouraged hard work, obedience and piety, not critical thought, in order to create the perfect *Untertan* (subject).

the idea of "the nation" as ideological cement – a process both made necessary and facilitated by the spread of elementary education. This in turn helped to make language into a primary condition of nationality as the official language of the state and the medium of instruction marked out social groups as they had not been before. It was the period in which, according to one seminal history, "peasants turned into Frenchmen". National identities competed with and complemented the sense of class consciousness and both, similarly, might combine with consciousness of religious community as among Poles and Irish Catholics.

Consciousness of class was thus only one kind of identity fostered by industrialization and the spread of democracy. But workers' sense of belonging to a separate social world is shown too in the formation of a distinct culture, characterized by distinctive clothing – the ubiquitous peaked cap became a badge of working class membership; by involvement in particular sports and recreations – football and gardening (listed, with "country walks", as their favorite leisure pursuit by German workers in a survey before World War I); and by choice of entertainments.

At the upper end of society there were the phenomenally wealthy, pilloried by contemporaries as "the plutocracy" and described by the American economist Thorstein Veblen (in a book published in 1899) as "the Leisure Class". They were distinguished by their conspicuous consumption and conspicuous leisure. There was then a range of people clearly distinguished at the ends of, on the one side, smaller industrialists and businessmen, or high-ranking civil servants and professionals, and at the other the "old" "petty bourgeoisie" of tradesmen and artisans, but who were not very clearly differentiated from each other between these extremes. Much of their behavior came to be concerned with establishing social boundaries, marking out differences. Literacy and increasing individual self-consciousness tended to diffuse bourgeois values, and the criteria for membership of the bourgeoisie (availability of time for leisure, filled with distinctive activities, notably sports like racing or yachting, or the somewhat more popular golf and tennis, and formal education beyond the elementary level, which clearly showed the ability for adolescents to postpone earning a living) permeated the middling ranks of society. The big bourgeoisie had to keep itself open, also, to new recruits and needed to conciliate the middle classes. Further down the social hierarchy the members of the new lower middle class of white-collar workers and the "middle" middle class of managers sought to distinguish themselves from the working class, sometimes by the adoption of reactionary politics. It was often among them, as among "the little men" of the old small property-owning petty bourgeoisie, that nationalism took a particularly strong hold, and with it antisemitism and virulent dogmas of racial supremacy.

Social structures in Russia and Eastern Europe

In the West social structure and class configurations determined the nature of the state; in Russia, the autocratic state determined the nature of the social hierarchy and social relations and prescribed the functions, obligations and prerogatives of each legally defined "social estate" (*soslovie*). Everyone was registered as belonging to a particular social estate at birth – to the nobility, the clergy, the peasantry, etc – and normally remained there till death, although there was some upward mobility through state-service or through entrepreneurial success recognized by the state. This formal hierarchy was, however, slowly giving way to a more variegated and autonomous class structure.

Advancing commercialization and occupational specialization in the economy were accompanied by a gradual increase in class consciousness, culminating in a socially divisive flowering of class-based organizations in the 1890s and 1900s. These interlocked explosively with the simultaneous emergence of significant autonomist and separatist movements among ethnic minorities: Poles, Finns, Jews, Latvians, Estonians, Lithuanians, Georgians, Armenians, Azeris and Volga Tatars. Parts of the Russian Empire's western borderlands, especially the

◄ Cleaning the silver was a job for servants even in lower middle-class families. In a provincial British city 29 percent of families belonged to the "servant keeping class". Domestic service was the major occupation open to women. But numbers of female servants trailed urban growth and in France even began to decline in the 1890s.

They [servants] accept social inequalities as one of the consequences of human existence and they firmly believe that it is above all by faithful duty that they can improve the general lot.
SERVANTS' TRADE UNION NEWSPAPER, 1907

▲ By 1900 the expanding European middle classes had begun to relax. A leisure ethic replaced the earlier emphasis on hard work. Idling in a fashionable restaurant (here at Vichy in France) was among their pursuits. But these also included cycling, new styles of dancing and organized sports. Devotion to religion declined – in response one pastor even suggested drive-in sevices for cyclists! Attitudes toward sex were loosened and the whole notion of what a woman should look like – slender and a little athletic – evolved as part of the leisured life style.

Baltic provinces and Poland, were more commercialized and/or industrialized than the Russian heartland. Capitalism accelerated the emergence of increasingly assertive "national bourgeoisies", as well as peasantries and proletariats among the ethnic minorities and intensified the social disruption and distress that normally accompany rural commercialization and the early stages of industrialization. It also ended the nationalities' parochialism, raised national and class consciousness, and fostered mass support for nationalist and class-based movements. These class and ethnic divisions, further inflamed by religious tensions, were the major ingredients in the seething caldron which boiled over in the 1905 revolution, aptly described by Lenin as the "dress rehearsal" for 1917.

The peasantry as a class
From the 1860s to 1914, from Ireland to the Urals, peasants were emerging as a conscious class with specific interests and aspirations. At first these were often articulated on the peasants' behalf by bourgeois politicians or members of the intelligentsia who sometimes wanted to use peasants for their own ends, but other social changes awakened peasants to the need to articulate

their interests and organize themselves: the long-delayed dissolution of serfdom in Russia and Eastern Europe (1840s to 1880s); the slowly increasing availability of rural schooling; growing contact with the expanding ranks of village teachers, doctors and local government officials, and with the rural industrial proletariat (railroadmen and miners); the eye-opening experiences provided by more universal military service and occasional employment in towns; the opening of the peasants' world and widening of their horizons by national market integration and railroad networks. By 1905–07 there were major peasant-based mass movements in Ireland, France, Denmark, Sweden, Finland, Latvia, Estonia, Lithuania, Georgia, Poland, the Ukraine, Russia and Romania. The great Romanian peasant revolt of 1907 was partly inspired by peasant revolts in the Russian Empire in 1905–06. Moreoover, during 1906–14 there was a spectacular growth of peasant cooperatives, consciously modelled on the trail-blazing Danish cooperatives of the 1880s–90s. Peasantist movements were also reaping the harvest of the 19th-century romantic, folkloristic, philological, "Völkisch" and Slavophil "rediscoveries" or "reinventions" of vernacular peasant cultures.

CHILDHOOD

Today childhood is seen ideally as a protective time, during which children should have the chance to flourish and learn within the security of a united and loving family. This does not hold true for all children, and has not always been the case. Before World War I in Europe, childhood for many ended abruptly at 12 when children could legally begin work. Many earned their keep even younger. It was only the children of the rich who could enjoy workfree lives devoted to a combination of education and play. While working-class children entered premature adulthood through labor, childhood was often curtailed, even for the better-off, by authoritarian parents who instilled strict codes of conduct in their "little adults" and taught them to control their emotions.

Following the war, women became more intimately involved with their children. They were offered a glut of "expert" advice on "mothercraft", ranging from the strict regime of four-hourly feeds for babies, promoted in the 1930s by the British pediatrician Frederick Truby King, to the atmosphere of indulgent affection encouraged by the 1950s American child-expert Benjamin Spock. Today many Western parents elect "natural childbirth", though supported by the technological professionalism of hospital births which has done much to reduce the dangers to mother and child alike. There is also greater informality between children and adults, with fathers playing a greater role. Increased rates of divorce and single-parent families mean family forms are more varied, but all tend to be child-centered.

For many, grinding poverty means that the birth of a child represents if not a new contributor to the family work force then yet another mouth to feed. The consequences can be dire. City centers throughout the world abound with street children who live by their wits, begging, ragpicking, washing cars or engaging in petty crime. Most vulnerable among them are the child prostitutes and "rent boys", victims of pimps and pedophiles alike.

Despite poverty and deprivation, many Third World children work alongside family members in the home, fields or workplace. In some instances this may give rise to strong bonds of affection and a sense of identity and security, learning skills and values that equip them for life. This can be contrasted with children in the West, who often face increased competition and parental expectations of achievement which can lead to psychological stress and sometimes a sense that love is conditional on their performance.

▲ ▶ Better-off children in pre-1914 Europe were raised to be "seen-and-not-heard". Boys were sent to boarding schools at the age of seven or eight. Girls were taught beauty and deportment and encouraged in genteel accomplishments such as music and needlework.

▶ In wealthier homes at the turn of the century, parents were distant figures. Children were brought up by nannies who took them from the nursery, bathed and dressed in their best clothes, to their parents for an hour or so a day. Children formed close bonds with their nannies.

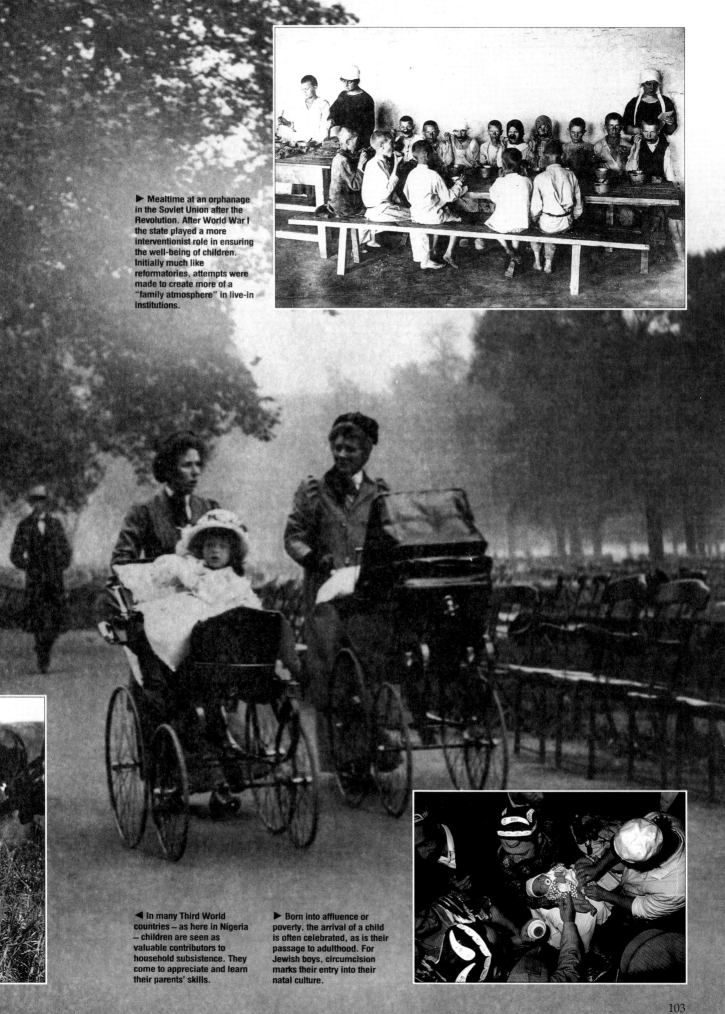

► Mealtime at an orphanage in the Soviet Union after the Revolution. After World War I the state played a more interventionist role in ensuring the well-being of children. Initially much like reformatories, attempts were made to create more of a "family atmosphere" in live-in institutions.

◄ In many Third World countries – as here in Nigeria – children are seen as valuable contributors to household subsistence. They come to appreciate and learn their parents' skills.

► Born into affluence or poverty, the arrival of a child is often celebrated, as is their passage to adulthood. For Jewish boys, circumcision marks their entry into their natal culture.

Datafile

There was widespread anxiety around 1900 about the collapse of "social order". Industrialization and urbanization were thought to be destroying the family and the communities which had supposedly characterized rural society. In practice working people developed new communities in the cities, based on novel organizations rather than on recreation of the old. Contrary to popular belief, small "nuclear" families had been the norm before the Industrial Revolution; both patriarchy – male dominance in the family – and parental control over children were still strong. The dissociation of work and family life was beginning to change the expectations men and women had of each other.

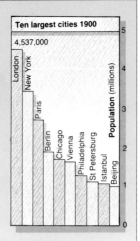

Ten largest cities 1900

4,537,000

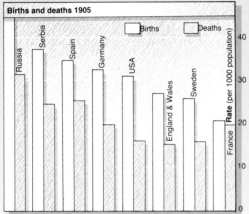

Births and deaths 1905

▲ **European city growth in the last part of the 19th century resulted particularly from the natural growth of their populations consequent upon the fall of the death rate; American cities grew because immigrants settled in them. The great cities were found also in the old civilizations of Ottoman Turkey and China, while the expansion of colonial capitalism created disproportionately large urban centers. Melbourne, Buenos Aires and Calcutta were all bigger than Amsterdam, Milan, and Munich.**

▲ **Death rates had been quite sharply reduced in the industrialized countries. Birth rates remained high for a time and so populations grew rapidly. France led the way in reducing birth rates (perhaps because peasants wished to prevent the division of landholding between numerous heirs), and had experienced the so-called "demographic transition" to low birth and death rates and a stable population. Generally in western Europe population growth had slowed; not so in the east and south.**

▼▶ **Population growth in western Europe had been rapid by historical standards. But its distinctive pattern of later marriage and a high proportion of bachelors and spinsters, seen here (below) in data for Belgium and Sweden, meant that growth was more modest than it has been in the contemporary Third World. The effects of a tendency for earlier marriage in the early 20th century were offset by increasing practice of birth control, partly reflected in the reduction in household size in the USA (right).**

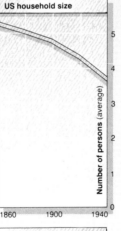

US household size

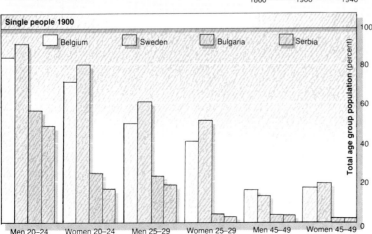

Single people 1900

At the beginning of the 20th century there was already a firmly established belief that the family was in decline and decay as a result of the growth of industrial society. Members of the middle classes and conservative commentators of that time expressed particular concern about the family life of the urban working classes. They blamed the perceived deterioration of the qualities of life and sentiments experienced within the family for declining standards in society at large. The spread of women's labor in the cities, the growth of organized youth and women's movements and the political mobilization of women and children by the new political forces on the Left – all of which removed women and young people from the orbit of the family – were seen by the ruling classes as a byproduct of the destruction of family life by industrialization.

Despite a shared concern at both ends of the political spectrum for its integrity and stability, the family became the focus of conflict between rival ideologies. The ruling classes saw the stable family as a major bulwark against the radicalization of industrial workers and believed that socialists, feminists and other radicals were destroying marriage and family life by undermining the patriarchal assumptions of the dominant culture of bourgeois society. The promotion of emancipatory aspirations, which threatened established norms of male authority within the family, was thus a constant source of anxiety to those who sought to uphold social stability by maintaining the "traditional" blessings of hearth and home. Such concern is illustrated by the fact that by the end of the 19th century a theory about "ideal family types", (developed especially by the French sociologist F. Le Play, 1806–82) firmly upheld the so-called "stable" large patriarchal peasant family of preindustrial times as a model of authority for the whole of society, while declaring the "new" smaller urban family to be the "unstable" product of industrialization.

Family life in the cities

The *modern* nuclear family was in fact not so much the product of structural changes within the domestic group in industrializing societies as the notion of the large preindustrial family would suggest. It is now generally accepted that throughout most of western Europe and the United States, and even among the Russian peasantry, the *conjugal* (rather than "extended") family, consisting of husband, wife and four or five children, with servants, lodgers or apprentices where appropriate, has been the common family form since at least the 16th century. It has even been suggested that the existence of the so-called *modern* nuclear family prior to the Industrial Revolution made the social transition to a new

THE FAMILY UNDER THREAT?

way of life far easier for people as they gathered their children and packed up their belongings to seek a new livelihood in the cities. What they had to leave behind – old and diverse community values of neighborhood and friendship, or family relationships – they tended to reconstruct in their new environment or they adapted old values to new needs. Nowhere else was the tenacious struggle to preserve traditions greater than in the family. Thus the cities offered a varied picture of rural people come to town, all with their own strongly local customs, family traditions and rituals.

During the times of large-scale migration it was common for whole communities to plan together their exodus to a nearby city or to seek a new life by emigrating to North or South America. The majority were peasants and all of them had their own particular national or regional identity. In the cities, or in the new country, a new and often more urgent dependency on relatives or neighbors, especially in hard times, made people seek out the support of those they had known before

▼ A British family. In Europe not only authoritarian familial ideals, but also preindustrial notions of honor, social standards and moral codes set the tone for society's attitudes toward the family – an ideology that proved extremely hostile to women's emancipation in particular.

the misery of unemployment, poverty or illness began to threaten their sheer existence, rather than rely on poverty relief or charity.

With the tremendous housing shortage in the new industrial cities, relatives helped each other to find lodgings and work, and working-class women who were forced to contribute toward a family income reestablished support networks of childminding, or caring for the sick and the old. The street began to replace the market center or the village common for gossip and meetings among women on their way to do their shopping or while they idled for a while watching their children play. Men, on the other hand, increasingly drifted into a separate male world of leisure; the sports ground and the tavern, or the music hall – places where respectable women were rarely seen, and if so then usually only to claim the pay-packet before it had turned into beer or spirits.

Among the emigrants in America, close-knit Italian communities, for example, recreated a "little Italy" in their new surroundings. Old history

Life in American Ethnic Neighborhoods

By 1910 one-third of the population of the 12 largest American cities was foreign born. Different groups of immigrants tended to be concentrated in particular industries, for example the Italians in construction and textiles. Whatever the industry, they undertook the more disagreeable jobs and worked long hours in poor, often hazardous conditions. To find work non-English speakers tended to rely on compatriots who had preceded them. These established men who acted as intermediaries became "work-bosses" – *padrones* among the Italians; they were paid commissions by the men to whom they gave jobs. Not all *padrones* cheated, but enough did to give the system a bad name.

By the beginning of the century peasants from southern and eastern Europe formed the overwhelming majority of immigrants. Their adjustment to urban, industrial life was eased by the tendency of different groups to occupy particular neighborhoods within the congested slums in which they mostly lived. Here, despite appearances, they did not so much recreate the

communities from which they had come as establish them afresh. An Italian immigrant and community leader, Constantine Panunzio, said of the colony in Boston in which he lived that though it was "in no way a typical American community neither did it resemble Italy". The sociologist Robert E. Park wrote in 1920 that "In America the peasant discards his habits and acquires ideas. In America, above all, the immigrant organizes". Characteristic of Italian communities were mutual-benefit societies, Italian-language newspapers, Italian theater, opera and marionette shows, the celebration of religious festivals involving elaborate processions and an allegiance to Catholicism that was combined, however, with strong resistance to Irish domination of the Church in America. Mutual-benefit societies, of which there were for example 150 in Manhattan alone in 1900, required small but regular financial contributions from their members and provided notably for medical and funeral expenses. But the importance of the societies went beyond the merely instrumental, for the fraternities they

▲ An immigrant Jew. By 1910 New York had more Jews than the whole of western Europe. Unlike other immigrants they usually came in families and brought a high level of skill.

Ethnic Areas in Chicago

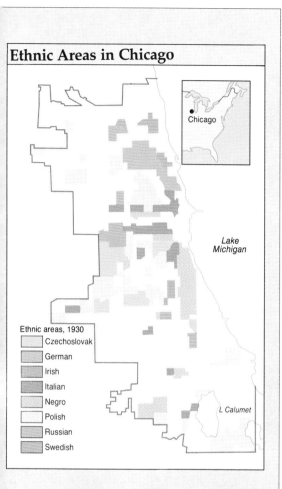

Chicago

Lake
Michigan

L Calumet

Ethnic areas, 1930

Czechoslovak
German
Irish
Italian
Negro
Polish
Russian
Swedish

◀ **An Italian family in New York's teeming Lower East Side. Immigrants craved Old World dishes partly because they could now afford them. The production or import from Italy of olive oil, spaghetti and salami became important for the immigrants' well-being.**

▲ **City neighborhoods in Chicago. The immigrants' desire to retain their identities and their search for emotional security led different groups to occupy distinct residential areas, creating a mosaic of ethnic neighborhoods, like this one in Chicago, 1930.**

established filled a social and psychological void for those uprooted from familiar surroundings and ways of life. One society described itself as an organization that "unites us and gives us strength, and will make us more acceptable in the eyes of the American people". The ethnic press also served as a bridge between life in the European village and that in the American city, providing leadership and voicing group demands and complaints. The Italian newspapers were not like those of Europe but were "addressed to the common man" (Park) and much more popular in language. The Italian theater, too, acquired a distinctive "Italian-American" style and idiom.

Exploited though they may have been, the immigrants enjoyed more abundant and varied food than they had known before. Part of what has become known internationally as "Italian food" – notably pizza – is rather an Italian-American creation. Saints parades were to Italian immigrants, in the words of an American social workers, "what a returned heroes parade is to us – a bond, a reminder, and the thrill of the uncommonplace". Over time these community organizations gave way to American counterparts, but they were vital in the early stages of immigrant adjustment.

and old values were maintained with pride and new ones were only gradually adopted when circumstances dictated. Paternal power remained unimpaired, and family loyalty carefully controlled any expansion into a so-called American culture. Confessional differences similarly marked out subcultural boundaries both in the "New World" and in Europe. In Germany, for example, the Catholic Church built for its members a kind of "ghetto-existence" within which authoritarian values and family rituals were carefully kept alive and the new values of industrial living decried.

In theory the authoritarian structure of the patriarchal household changed as soon as a family no longer possessed its own means of production (such as land or a family workshop), especially among the new working classes where property obligations or expectations to inherit a small shop or a farm no longer regulated the relations between father and son or daughter. While among the property-owning classes the old obligations to the family continued to regulate marriage arrangements, and channeled sons into suitable professions to enable them to take over the family business, the authority of the wage-earning head of household in theory remained intact only for as long as his dependents were reliant on his income. But family ties among workers often remained strong, born out of their insecure and unstable dependence on the market and their employers. Lack of housing meant that many of the working youth remained at home as lodgers while beginning to pursue their own life and leisure, separate from that of their fathers. Yet fathers still tended to initiate their sons into the world of men and factories, seeking positions for them, not infrequently transferring on to employers that aspect of parental control which once the master had had over the apprentice. The system of apprenticeship itself continued alongside the new relationship between worker and employer. The increasing stress on a more formal education, and longer years of schooling – designed to prepare sons (and only a small number of daughters) for an independent life in the world outside – also created new financial dependence on the head of household, delaying or postponing the time when youngsters would leave the parental home often far beyond the ages at which children once became apprentices or farmhands.

For others in the rural areas or the small market towns, those remaining on their farms or those who continued well into the 20th century to run their small craft enterprises, their shops or a small business, change was slow and uneven. For them marriage remained an economic institution and both husband and wife continued to work for their mutual support. Seemingly untouched by the debates over women's rights and by feminist issues (so much part of the urban Protestant middle-class scene of the late 19th and early 20th century), women continued in the traditional division of labor, serving behind the counter or even doing the book-keeping, milking the cows, growing vegetables and taking care of children, their menfolk's clothes and their stomachs.

However, there too patterns and the period of

Hold fast, this is most necessary in America. Forget your past, your customs, and your ideals. Select a goal and pursue it with all your might. No matter what happens to you, hold on. A final virtue is needed in America – called cheek...Do not say, "I cannot; I do not know."

HANDBOOK FOR IMMIGRANTS

▲ **"Urgent warning to girls emigrating! Don't accept any position abroad without first making close inquiries! If in need or danger apply to the captain of this ship" – a poster of The German National Committee for the International Campaign against the White Slave Trade. Between 1899 and 1910 males aged between 14 and 44 accounted for nearly 75 percent of the emigrants to the new world. The consequent small numbers of women traveling alone gave rise to fears for their moral safety.**

parental control did change as more and more of the young – both sons and daughters – left the farms, daughters often to take up domestic service, the principal occupation open to women of the lower classes until World War I, and sons to work in the factories. While many girls from poor agricultural areas went to cities such as Paris, London or Berlin to follow the increasing demand for domestic labor among the middle classes, others tended to move into towns not far away and parents kept a watchful eye over possible exploitation of their labor or person by their employers, illustrating a fairly mutual distrust between the two classes.

With compulsory education, girls too began to form their own circles of friends outside the home, dream of a different life and seek companionship among peers to a far greater extent than they had been able to in the 19th century. They read the new novels and magazines and gradually new expectations of love and marriage formed as they prepared themselves for their future roles as wives and mothers. Once married, however, the 19th-century pattern of family life repeated itself with the familiar stress on the essential quality on which women's moral worth depended, on "self-denial" or the "renunciation of self", embodied in its most perfect form in maternal love.

Middle-class social norms which idealized women's *natural* profession as mothers, ideally to the exclusion of paid employment outside the home, stood in stark contrast to the material needs of the vast majority of working-class women; their household budgets dictated that most of them needed to contribute income at

▲ A French miner being washed by his wife, c. 1900. In France, where there was no tradition of women working underground in coal mines and little other employment in mining areas, women concentrated on their menfolk and homes. A degree of living style, ornaments and photographs on the wall give some sense of settled existence, but it could easily be shattered by a mine disaster, such as that at Courrières in 1906 when 1,100 men were killed.

some stage of their lives. By 1900 family commitments, but more fundamentally the idealization of the family as the female domain, had clearly influenced patterns of women's employment. On the whole women were confined to more marginal activities in or associated with the household. Only a small number of women had qualified as professionals by the turn of the century, most of them as teachers (compare, however, the 4,500 women physicians in America in the 1890s with 93 in France in 1903), more so as semiprofessionals in health and child care. The majority of lower-class women worked as domestic servants or in laundries, hotels, restaurants or shops, in the textile or clothing industry, or in food processing. Although it became fairly usual for single girls in the lower classes to earn part of their upkeep, women's wages rarely reached a level that might have kept a woman alone. Up to 70 percent or more of single women were fully occupied by the early 1900s, but most left work on marriage, especially in the cities. In Berlin, for example, only 11 percent of married women were fully employed in 1907, compared with 26 percent for the whole of Germany or 45 percent of all widows.

It was among the middle classes that the official idealization of family life appeared perhaps even more contradictory. Late or loveless marriages or marriage contracts dependent on property had created a massive demand for the sexual services of prostitutes. This service was generally drawn from the family circles of the poor and was often better paid than the more legitimate forms of employment open to women. Already in the 1870s such "double morality" had sparked off crusades among feminists against the legalization of prostitution. Yet official concern over the moral threat of urban prostitution (seen to constitute one of the main social problems of city life alongside illegitimacy and alcohol abuse), which brought disease and humiliation on thousands of women, was leveled at the need to regulate this vice through legislation rather than at addressing its more fundamental causes. While middle-class wives had been elevated onto a pedestal of irreproachable purity by the 19th-century bourgeois male, their sexuality repressed or stifled in the family context, it was notably middle-class men who argued that prostitution was an efficient safety valve and therefore should not be abolished. The outcry against the so-called sexual liberation after World War I follows closely in the footsteps of such a model of official morality, and of course of the 19th-century role model of women as wives and mothers.

Women's closely defined sphere of activity within the home as it emerged in the 19th century was the result of a gradual transformation of the roles of both men and women. By 1900 the transition toward a *new* role division was complete. The new sexual division of labor was not determined by the needs of the family as a unit of production but rather by "natural" character traits ascribed to men and women. Attributing to women distinctive moral qualities led to a reevaluation of women's domestic roles and raised their status within the family. But it also

offered a new rationale for subordination within the context of industrialization by suggesting that these qualities of "innocence of spirit and purity of heart" could only blossom in the right setting – the home. As women's nature was viewed as being governed more by feeling than reason, making women more receptive and yielding, loving and caring and selfless than men, they were also ideally equipped for the care of the home and husband, the sick and old, the rearing of children and their socialization, acting as moral guardians of the home and of society at large.

Woman's destiny for a domestic role was further underscored by the lesser points of her irrational and passive nature which made her naturally dependent on the male who was seen as more of a thinking creature, bold and certain of purpose. Lack of analytical powers and ambition were also seen as naturally excluding women from the public world of business and politics. Portrayed as evil and corrupt, this was a world in which women needed the protection of the male,

◄ Pediatrics and new child-care methods were well established by the 1890s. Prenatal care and the instruction of pregnant women to reduce birth defects and problem deliveries were introduced around 1900. New knowledge in obstetrics and gynecology greatly reduced the number of women dying in childbirth. Here a nurse is instructing young mothers in London in 1908.

▼ Until mechanical labor-saving household appliances were developed, the physical load of the housewife was considerable. Even the use of this new mangle required strength.

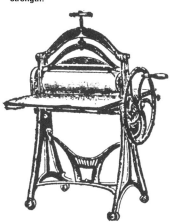

▼ Some industrial workers, especially coalminers, lived somewhat outside urban experience. Here miners' wives in an English mining village talk in the lane at the backs of their small houses. Industrial housing was often badly built.

▲ France pioneered the manufacture of cosmetics and French women used makeup long before it was accepted in polite society elsewhere. In other countries the open use of cosmetics by women "to impose or seduce into matrimony… by scents or paints" was generally looked upon with disfavor. Not until after World War I did such opinions disappear.

▼ A lady in the Ottoman sultan's harem, 1906. Harems were common in Muslim countries in the early decades of the 20th century. In some large households each wife had her own set of rooms and servants, in others three or four wives lived together and children were brought up as one family. In Turkey polygamy became illegal in 1926, in India (by the Hindu Marriage Act) not until 1955.

of the state and society. The understanding of women's need for protection in a morally corrupt world, despite their unique power as regenerators of society, was to have far-reaching and ambivalent consequences for their position in the public sphere throughout the 20th century. Thus protective policies for women and their roles as wives and mothers, rather than truly emancipatory ones, were to regulate their participation in the labor market, while the idea of their natural role continued to define educational opportunities, their work or professional prospects.

Increasing concern over the declining birthrate after 1900 added a new dimension to the interest in maintaining not only an ideology of separate spheres or the notion of female dependence, it also raised motherhood to a new level of social recognition. It received an aura of "professionalism" with new stress on child care and children's needs through the impact of science and psychology. As increasingly pronatal political concerns were now added to the moral imperatives of motherhood, the case for women's equality naturally had to be shelved. Even the developments in the women's movements bear out a fairly general trend toward accepting marriage and motherhood as women's primary role, a strengthening of domestic life and a sharpening of the two separate spheres of activity for men and women.

This polarization of sexual stereotypes was not simply the product of a revolution in the sphere of formal ideas, or of a new interest in the individual and his and her "natural" rights. It was an important byproduct of the dissociation of work and family life and thus a direct result of the changing economic structure of the industrializing world. The commitment to life-long marriage, the maintenance of family stability, a secure and affectionate context of home life and careful upbringing of children with reciprocal feelings of love and care became those maxims which were to govern family life once its function as an economic institution began to disappear, and the very basis of marriage and the nature of dependency of family members on each other began to change.

The Origins and Rise of Feminism

Women have always protested against their oppression. In the 18th century, when philosophers rejected old sources of truth (God) and offered a new secular model of family relationships, the nature and role of women received new attention. Feminism in a literary form was born. All the themes writers then introduced were to recur in feminist propaganda a century later. The word feminism itself appeared first in French in the early 19th century.

Organized feminism began by addressing itself to women's economic dependency and resulting exploitation. The two major objectives of moderate feminism around 1850–60 were the right for married women to own property and the admission of unmarried women to the professions. There followed demands for better educational opportunities (access to secondary schools and universities) which were necessary for the pursuit of a profession or the maintenance of middle-class status.

In Russia feminism emerged in the 1860s among the intelligentsia of the provincial nobility or the merchant class. The concentration of Russian feminists on educational rather than economic objectives reflects this background.

The most important social development underlying the rise of feminism in the West was the growth of the middle classes, and the

increasingly more prominent role they played in social and political life. Feminists virtually everywhere shared their liberal, Protestant-based values of independence, self-sufficiency, careers open to talents and equality before the law. This alliance with liberalism remained central to the politics of feminism. By the 1930s the general decline of liberal beliefs and values also sealed the fate of liberal feminism. When feminism reemerged in the 1960s–70s it had a new voice. A combination of socialism and sexual liberation clearly distinguished the ideology of the Women's Liberation movement from that of its predecessor.

The rise of socialism and of communist movements in the late 19th century was to have profound and often unexpected consequences for liberal feminism. By the end of the century the socialist women's movements formed the major and almost the only alternative forms of women's movements to that developed by middle-class feminists in the 19th century. The largest socialist women's movement was in Germany. Under the leadership of Clara Zetkin (1854–1933) it pioneered many advanced policies on female equality. Above all it represented the plight of working-class women who had often been overlooked in the feminists' struggle to emancipate the female sex.

▲ This running race for American young women on a company outing in 1908 reflects their greater personal freedom, strengthened by education and employment opportunities – including the professions. Feminists' demands from the 1850s focused on the disparity between men's and women's education which effectively barred women from professional jobs.

◀ Representatives of a German women's academic league, 1914. The power of authoritarian political systems to stunt the growth of reform movements such as feminism is clearly illustrated in Germany. The admission of women to universities after 1900 was not due to pressure exerted by the women's movements, but rather to reluctant concessions following the examples of other industrial nations.

EDUCATION

During the 19th century, education was given a vital role in creating a prosperous and united nation-state. By 1900 many European states had taken responsibility for providing a national educational system that was compulsory for all, at least in the elementary stages.

Schools of the early 20th century were usually very formal. Children sat in their desks in ranks under strict discipline, often enforced by physical violence. There was the feeling that knowledge and skills, national pride and moral values, had to be forced into reluctant minds. This view of education persisted into the 1920s and 1930s and beyond. It acquired a new form and intensity under the communist and fascist dictatorships of the interwar years when children were indoctrinated into becoming model citizens in the service of an overpowering state.

There was already a reaction against such views in the early 1900s. In the United States the educationalist John Dewey (1859–1952) saw the child as an individual with his or her own worth. In his view, the purpose of education was to draw out what was already there rather than force it into a new mold. In Italy Maria Montessori saw the ideal school as an environment where each child was encouraged to develop his or her own freedom. She echoed Dewey's idea that the teacher should be a fellow-worker with the child rather than an authority figure. Although the number of truly progressive schools remained few their influence was strong. By the 1950s many schools in the Western world had become less formal and more child-centered.

As society became increasingly complex and technologically advanced the demands made on the education system grew in other ways. While traditionally education had served to support the ruling elites of society, now there had to be a massive expansion of higher education to provide the intellectual and scientific elite needed to keep society running. Because society was changing so rapidly, continual updating through adult education for people of all sorts was needed and flexibility in acquiring new skills became as highly prized as knowledge itself. Opportunities for women in education also grew rapidly as traditional barriers between the sexes were broken down.

A high level of education brought power, access to elite jobs and thus status. Though this was the case universally, nowhere was this more obvious than in the newly independent countries of Asia and Africa. The small minority who progressed beyond secondary education found their efforts richly rewarded. However, elementary education was often formal and academic, with little emphasis on the skills needed for survival and development at village level. It is not surprising that a major development in the poorer world has been to provide education programs in basic skills such as literacy, nutrition and hygiene which can be taken to children and adults alike.

◄ The urge for formal classroom education in newly independent nations drew many young people away from their farms. Here, in the Sudan in the early 1960s, the balance is redressed with practical education on the recognition of healthy crops.

▼ A traditional school in Germany at the outbreak of World War I. German schools had stern discipline but high achievement.

► "Like butterflies, mounted on pins, each one fastened to his place," was how Maria Montessori (1870–1952) described children in traditional academic schools. Montessori, here visiting one of her schools in old age, aimed to draw out the natural creativity of children by designing materials from which they could learn by self-discovery. Informality was the keynote of the Montessori classroom.

► Caught in one of the most competitive education systems in the world, this harrassed-looking boy, like the majority of his age-group in 1980s Japan, is off to attend nightschool (*juku*).

◄ Everyday hygiene education in China is encouraged through a poster campaign. After the Revolution of 1949 there were massive attempts to educate China's peasant population into new skills and correct behavior. Public education campaigns, especially in health matters, have been undertaken in most countries.

Datafile

The increasing integration of the world economy at the beginning of the 20th century is reflected in the growing volume of trade and the near doubling in size of the world merchant fleet between 1890 and 1914. The expansion of commerce and of colonialism, driven by the rivalry of the Great Powers, and the first steps in industrialization outside Europe and America helped to bring about social change in the "Third World" of Africa, Asia and Latin America. The formation of a working class began. The pattern of change depended also on the social structures and value systems of the colonial territories and on the way in which these were understood or misunderstood by the colonists.

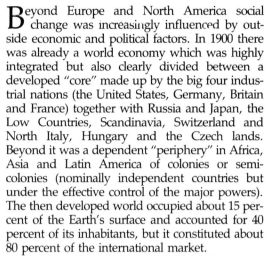

▲▼ Part of the drive behind colonial expansion was demand for commodities such as oil and rubber and, with the growth of the electrical industry, copper. Mexico's status as an informal colony of the United States is shown in the response in 1907–08 of its copper production – developed by foreign capital – to a down turn in the US economy (below). The demand for precious metals created the largest black labor force of all in South Africa (above), drawing in men from surrounding territories.

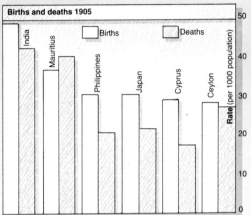

▲ Birth rates in "Third World" countries were in some cases no higher than in the West. Death rates were much higher so that population growth rates were often modest.
The diversity in the demographic patterns of the colonial territories is striking, and there is evidence that they have varied also over time.

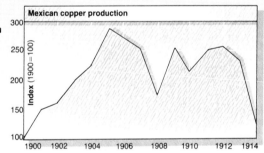

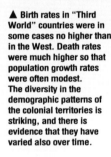

◀ British colonial attempts to classify and measure the Indian population in terms of castes (named groups of people defined by intermarriage and in part by distinct hereditary occupations, ordered in a district hierarchy) are reflected in the 1891 census. Such exercises made Indians themselves more conscious of caste.

▲ Variations in the social structure in different parts of India are shown in the wide differences that existed in the share in the whole population of the Brahmans, the priests who are at the top of the caste hierarchy. British administrative and legal arrangements ignored these differences, sometimes causing social change.

Beyond Europe and North America social change was increasingly influenced by outside economic and political factors. In 1900 there was already a world economy which was highly integrated but also clearly divided between a developed "core" made up by the big four industrial nations (the United States, Germany, Britain and France) together with Russia and Japan, the Low Countries, Scandinavia, Switzerland and North Italy, Hungary and the Czech lands. Beyond it was a dependent "periphery" in Africa, Asia and Latin America of colonies or semi-colonies (nominally independent countries but under the effective control of the major powers). The then developed world occupied about 15 percent of the Earth's surface and accounted for 40 percent of its inhabitants, but it constituted about 80 percent of the international market.

The competition between the Great Powers increased colonial governments' attention to economic questions as the costs of empire rose. Increased concern with the economy took the form of improvements in agriculture, veterinary services and irrigation. In India, almost 65,000km (40,000mi) of canals were built to irrigate 8 million ha (20 million acres) of the Indus Basin in the late 19th century.

IMPERIALISM AND SOCIAL CHANGE

The expansion of colonial work forces

To expand exports of agricultural and mining goods from colonies required infrastructure – roads, railroads, ports. This called for a substantial waged labor force, and colonial administrations devoted much ingenuity throughout the world to secure an adequate supply of workers – from the imposition of cash taxes (forcing peasants to undertake wage labor to secure cash with which to pay them), the use of terror or, as in the 19th century, instituting large-scale labor migrations – Indians to Africa, the Caribbean and Malaya; Chinese to Malaya, Australia, the Caribbean; Europeans to North and South America, southern Africa and Australia.

In Africa the period was one of active colonization and settlement, punctuated with wars of popular resistance, such as the Herero war in German South West Africa in 1905–06 and the Maji Maji rebellion of 1906 in Southern Tanganyika. They were put down with great force. Administrations sought steadily to increase revenues from direct taxation; for example, poll taxes were imposed on unmarried Kikuyu men in British East Africa (Kenya) to force them to work (desertion from work was simultaneously made a criminal offence). Expatriate administrations and

- The influence of European and US economic power
- Taxes, land seizures and mining in Africa
- Industrial expansion in Latin America and India
- Colonial governments and change in local societies
- The origins of native middle classes

▼▶ "France brings the blessings of civilization to Morocco" (right) according to a popular view of 1911. In practice the "civilizing mission" included the construction of railroads, here (below) in Madagascar, by laborers recruited and controlled by harsh and repressive means. The conditions of native employment in the colonies attracted criticism – sometimes censored – even in the colonial metropolises.

armies were expensive so the numbers in them were small, and governments relied heavily on indirect rule – selecting "traditional rulers or chiefs" to administer affairs – though of course, rapacious government demands for tax revenues and labor undermined any authority such rulers might have had. In settler societies – South Africa, the Rhodesias (now Zimbabwe and Zambia), British East Africa, Algeria – existing cultivators or herdsmen were driven off the land to make room for white farmers (as the Masai were driven off what came to be known as the Kenyan White Highlands). The discovery of important mineral deposits (gold and diamonds in South Africa, copper in Northern Rhodesia) exaggerated the demand for labor; the native reserves were raided and again cash taxes used to expel black farmers. The mines became a byword for the most ferocious working conditions, which were imposed upon an impoverished and terrified migrant labor force.

In Latin America the boom fueled by the overseas demand for raw materials was considerable, and supplied the means to absorb an enormous wave of immigration which created fashionable European cities across the continent. In Mexico, however, the pattern of growth produced a devastating social explosion. Under the long dictatorship of President Porfirio Díaz, foreign capital poured into the country to develop the northern silver and copper mines, the oil

▲ "A good specimen of a taxed hut", reads the contemporary caption. The picture was taken in Sierra Leone during a rising against the abolition of slave-dealing under British rule and the imposition of hut taxes. These were a widely favored system of colonial taxation.

▼ In the Congo, according to an account of 1911, "in the place of work the tax was assessed as so many kilograms of rubber. If the stated quantity was not delivered there were several methods of enforcing compliance, including the use of the *chicotte* – a rawhide whip".

industry (the 10,000 barrels of crude of 1901 rose to 13 million in 1911 by when Mexico was one of the leading oil exporters), agricultural exports (sugar and henequen from Yucatán), and major extensions to the transport system and to ports. US and British capital were said to own a fifth of the Republic's land by the turn of the century. The vast expansion in output seemed to be associated with increased landlessness and poverty; although three-quarters of the population lived off the land, 95 percent of them were landless and virtually enserfed to the 8–9,000 very large Mexican and foreign plantation owners. The scale of oppression – and the speed with which the land had been expropriated – explains the ferocity of the Mexican revolution; in the decade after 1911, possibly a quarter of a million people died.

In Latin America and in densely populated Asia (where the possibility of plantation agriculture was limited), industrialization was also becoming significant. By the turn of the century, some 18 percent of Argentina's national output was derived from industry, 14 percent of Mexico's. Employment in the Brazilian textile industry rose from 2,000 in 1895 to 26,000 in 1905 and 53,000 in 1907. The Indian textile industry was already of world significance by the turn of the century. Bombay alone then employed just over 80,000 workers (including 19,000 women and 2,000 children), and this rose to 105,000 by the outbreak of war. In 1911 the Indian Tata business group initiated the building of India's first iron and steel mill at Jamshedpur in the northeast, the same year in which Japan's first steel mill, Yawata, was begun. China, starting from a much lower base point, also began a modest industrialization, based upon a "putting-out" system to villages in the regions around the ports (for cloth, carpets, silk, tea, grass mats and flour). But in due course, a separate industrial sector emerged.

World Population c.1900

CANADA

NEWFOUNDL

USA

MEXICO

Bahamas

Cuba

DOMINICAN
REPUBLIC

BRITISH
HONDURAS

HAITI

Jamaica

PACIFIC

OCEAN

GUATEMALA

HONDURAS

EL SALVADOR

NICARAGUA

COSTA RICA

TRINIDAD

VENEZUELA

BRITISH GUIAN
DUTCH GUI
FRENCH

COLOMBIA

ECUADOR

PERU

ACRE

BRAZIL

BOLIVIA

PARAGUAY

CHILE

URUGUA

ARGENTINA

Population (millions)

100
50
10
5
1
0

Data not available

Scale 1 : 115 000 000
0   3000 km
0   2000 mi

Falk

In general the new workforces were most often recruited through agents. Employers hired agents to scour towns and villages to find members for work gangs. Sometimes they turned these over to the employer, but more often the agent became a ganger, supervisor of his group and often a subcontractor to the employer to deliver a certain volume of output in return for a fixed price; the ganger then paid his gang on whatever basis he chose.

Such a system tended to create loyalties to the gang rather than loyalties to either the collectivity of workers or to the firm, particularly where the gang was distinguished by a common language, caste, village of origin, religion, etc. This made it very much more difficult to organize trade unions. Furthermore, the system gave great power to the ganger who often took bribes to favor the recruitment of one worker rather than another, and also received a cut of what the workers saw as their earnings.

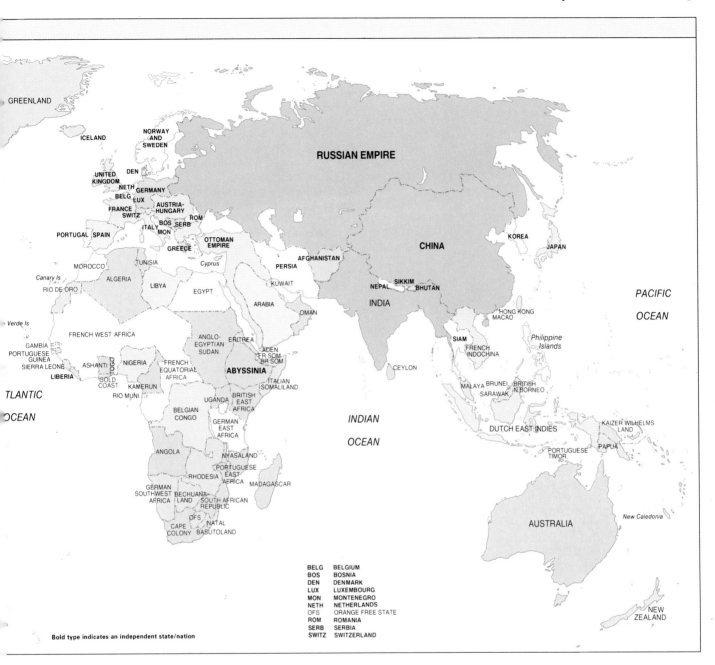

GREENLAND

ICELAND

NORWAY AND SWEDEN

RUSSIAN EMPIRE

DEN
UNITED KINGDOM
NETH GERMANY
BELG LUX
FRANCE
SWITZ AUSTRIA-HUNGARY
ROM
ITALY BOS SERB
MON
PORTUGAL SPAIN
GREECE OTTOMAN EMPIRE
MOROCCO TUNISIA
Canary Is
RIO DE ORO ALGERIA LIBYA
Cyprus
Verde Is
FRENCH WEST AFRICA
GAMBIA
PORTUGUESE GUINEA
SIERRA LEONE
LIBERIA
ASHANTI
GOLD COAST
NIGERIA
FRENCH EQUATORIAL AFRICA
KAMERUN
RIO MUNI
BELGIAN CONGO
ANGOLA
GERMAN SOUTHWEST AFRICA
BECHUANA-LAND
OFS
CAPE COLONY
BASUTOLAND
NATAL
SOUTH AFRICAN REPUBLIC
RHODESIA
PORTUGUESE EAST AFRICA
NYASALAND
UGANDA
BRITISH EAST AFRICA
GERMAN EAST AFRICA
MADAGASCAR
ABYSSINIA
ITALIAN SOMALILAND
ERITREA
ANGLO-EGYPTIAN SUDAN
EGYPT
ARABIA
ADEN
FR SOM
BR SOM
OMAN
KUWAIT
PERSIA
AFGHANISTAN
NEPAL
SIKKIM
BHUTAN
INDIA
CHINA
KOREA
JAPAN
HONG KONG
MACAO
SIAM
FRENCH INDOCHINA
CEYLON
MALAYA
SARAWAK
BRUNEI
BRITISH N BORNEO
DUTCH EAST INDIES
Philippine Islands
PORTUGUESE TIMOR
PAPUA
KAIZER WILHELMS LAND
AUSTRALIA
New Caledonia
NEW ZEALAND

PACIFIC OCEAN

INDIAN OCEAN

ATLANTIC OCEAN

Bold type indicates an independent state/nation

BELG   BELGIUM
BOS   BOSNIA
DEN   DENMARK
LUX   LUXEMBOURG
MON   MONTENEGRO
NETH   NETHERLANDS
OFS   ORANGE FREE STATE
ROM   ROMANIA
SERB   SERBIA
SWITZ   SWITZERLAND

Despite what seemed to be dramatic changes in the output of agriculture, mines and manufacturing in the "Third World", the overwhelming majority of people remained peasant cultivators or herdsmen. But colonial intervention did not leave them as "subsistence" producers outside the market economy. The need for cash to pay taxes and increasing needs for money to buy simple consumer goods brought in by European traders, drew these producers into the market and commonly into indebtedness and dependence upon traders and moneylenders.

The timing of government tax demands, sometimes at a time of the year when peasants had nothing left to sell, contributed to this process. A major share of colonial cash crops was produced by such apparently "independent" peasant producers, in circumstances which tended to break down arrangements which had previously provided them with some insurance against the effects of drought and other hazards.

Colonialism and the making of "tradition"

In his writings on India in the middle of the 19th century Karl Marx suggested that British colonial rule was bringing about the first major social transformation that the subcontinent had experienced. Modern historians have doubted this judgment on the impact of colonial rule in India and elsewhere and have found evidence of continuity, or of the adaptation, of supposedly traditional social institutions to modern purposes. A classic instance of this was thought to be the use of caste or tribal connections for political mobilization after electoral politics were introduced. But more recently historians have argued that much of what has been thought to be the "traditional" social structure in Asia and Africa is itself really the outcome of local responses to colonial rule, and sometimes the result of the way in which colonial administrators imposed their understandings of "native" societies upon the people they ruled.

▲ World population c. 1900 Thanks to lower death rates in the 19th century there were now relatively more Europeans than ever before (excluding the Russian Empire, about 16 percent of a total world population of about 1,640 million people), though Asians still made up more than half of the global population. As a result of the extraordinary population mobility of the 19th century there were now more Americans than Africans. Europeans and North Americans moved quickly to low birth and death rates and thus low demographic growth rates, whereas those in the "Third World" increased and have remained high for a longer time.

In India the British attempted to count the population by caste titles in the decennial census and thereby probably made caste more important for Indians themselves than it had been before. Certainly the legal system established by the British imposed ideas about the regulation of social relations from north India on the south, helping to change southern society in the process. And the economic circumstances of colonial rule also made caste affiliations more important. As labor scarcity gave way to labor surplus and indigenous owners of capital profited as never before by exploiting workers to the bone, those who were thus oppressed found some security for themselves by calling on the assistance of those to whom they could claim to be related by caste ties. Thus for them caste title became more important. Wealthier people sometimes found it expedient even to change rules about caste membership through marriage, as they sought to build up networks of alliances across much larger areas than before. Social collectivities or "communities" were constructed by the circumstances of colonial rule in much the same way, in fact, as they were by those of emigration to North America or movement to towns in Europe. In Africa too, it has been said that "tribes came into being on the way to town", referring to the way in which networks of kinship and neighborhood were built up by migrant workers and the new townsmen.

In much the same way that in Europe the sense of national identity or of membership in a group of people identified by common religious affiliation became important in the new circumstances of industrialization and democracy, so in the colonial territories religious loyalties could acquire new significance. Relations between Hindus and Muslims in India were not usually marked by conflict until late in the 19th century when competition over opportunities for salaried employment gave birth to rivalry amongst middle-class Hindus and Muslims, and workers in the Calcutta jute mills began to be drawn into bloody conflicts on communal lines.

New middle classes and rising nationalism

In the older imperial possessions the growth in the size of administrations (particularly in land administration and irrigation, highways and railroads and in tax collection) as well as the emergence of modern professional classes (for example, in India, lawyers, journalists, business management, etc), created a small but influential Westernized middle class by the end of the 19th century. In the Ottoman Empire and elsewhere the officer corps of the armed forces often provided the source of a comparable modernizing elite. The Westernized middle classes were the children of traditional rulers and gentry, the staff of traditional courts or the priesthood, bound together by the common experience of Western education, of becoming in most respects European.

At the same time, the lower echelons of the civil and military bureaucracies (the local officers, the operating engineers on the railroads and in shipping and commerce), small businessmen supplying local markets, and some of the children of richer peasants who benefited from the extension of vernacular education also merged as a significant force: a non-Westernized middle class. Their rebellion was against not only imperial rule, but against those with Western education who excluded those with vernacular education. There was rising interest in the creation or recreation of traditional values, cultures and religions. Whereas the Westernized had an ambiguous relationship to imperial power, hostile but dependent, demanding access to power by being accorded equality with the Europeans, the non-Westernized were entirely excluded from participation and thus much more aggressively nativistic, religious (as a form of secular politics) and anti-imperialist. Furthermore, the Westernized tended to regard traditional culture – and the mass of the population – with contempt in their attempt to prove themselves as good as the Europeans.

India provides the clearest example of the parallel development of two social classes, in part embodied in the factions of the nationalist movement, the Indian National Congress (founded in

◄ A South Indian Christian family. Christian missionaries had urged their converts to give up Hindu habits and culture. At this time members of the Indian elites, Christian or not, usually wore Western dress and through their education were quite anglicized in manners and outlook. But by 1900 there was a strong Hindu revivalist movement, responding to the challenge of Western influence. Christianity did not advance much beyond the lower castes.

My first contact with British authority was not of a happy character. I discovered that as a man and an Indian I had no rights. More correctly, I discovered that I had no rights as a man because I was an Indian.

M. K. GANDHI

▼ A classroom in Dar es Salaam, German East Africa, in 1905 with a German teacher. Financial provision was sufficient to provide for the education of only a small African elite, of clerks, teachers and a few who became independent professionals. They eventually became the leaders of the African nationalist movements.

1885). At first Congress had been led by an aloof and sophisticated group of lawyers who, in general, scorned traditional India and Hinduism (except in its sanitized reform versions); however, the most effective movement to link with mass agitations were the Hindu nationalist supporters of Bal Gangadhar Tilak. In the Dutch East Indies (Indonesia), meanwhile, the Sarekat Islam movement focused a nativistic opposition.

In China education in the treaty ports and elsewhere spread quickly as the new century dawned. Western missionaries were particularly important here, and as a result many of the significant figures in interwar nationalist politics were Christians. Gentry and merchant families began sending their children abroad for higher education; by 1906 there were 12,000 Chinese students studying in Japan. When, in 1911, after a long period of decomposition, punctuated by rebellions, the Manchu imperial dynasty fell, a small middle-class nationalist movement under Sun Yixian (Sun Yat-sen) – himself long exiled in

Japan – was one of the political alternatives on offer. The gentry, the former instrument of imperial power, was unable to supply an alternative order, and its families tended to ally with the fragments of the imperial and provincial military forces; the country disintegrated after World War I into what became known as the period of warlords. But the main social issue – the hideous oppression of the mass of the peasantry – still scarcely concerned any of the aspirant political alternatives.

In Latin America the emergence of new professional classes in the more advanced republics profoundly influenced politics, producing the beginnings of movements favoring representative democracy as opposed to rule by dictators, landowning oligarchs and foreign capitalists. But to achieve representative government a much wider stratum of the population had to be mobilized: this was the beginnings of mass populist politics in the big cities (frequently dominated by new immigrants from Europe).

▲ The watchful anxiety of these Mexican women reflects the confusion in their country following the downfall of the modernizing dictatorship of Porfirio Díaz (1911). The Mexican Revolution, involving agrarian unrest in the south led by Emiliano Zapata and dissidence in the dynamic but anarchic north, where Pancho Villa emerged as a revolutionary general, stemmed from the economic developments initiated by Díaz.

THE
CONSUMER
SOCIETY

	1900	1901	1902	1903	1904	1905	1906
Film	• Color photography simplified by Dugardin (Fr) • *Cinderella*, directed by G Méliès, magician and theater-manager (Fr) • Vaudeville strike; some theaters kept open by film shows (USA)	• 24 Oct: Incorporation of Eastman Kodak Co. (USA)	• First film-show area in an arcade opened in Los Angeles by T Tally (USA) • 1 May: *A Trip to the Moon*, first science fiction film, released by G Méliès (Fr)	• *The Great Train Robbery* by Edwin Porter, running to 12 minutes (USA)		• Opening of first nickelodeon in Pittsburgh (USA)	• First animated cartoon released by Vitagraph • *The Story of the Kelly Gang*, the first full-length film • Legislation on the minimum distance between cinemas, to c proliferation (Rus)
Media		• 11 Dec: Wireless telegraphy messages sent across Atlantic by G Marconi	• Voice modulator of "practically continuous waves" patented by R Fessenden (Can)	• Mar: Regular news service started by radio between London and New York (UK/USA) • 4 Jul: Message from President Roosevelt circled world in 9½ minutes via Pacific Cable • *Daily Mirror* was the first paper to have photos throughout (UK)	• Mar: Color photos published in London *Daily Illustrated Mirror* (UK) • Offset lithography process became commercially available (USA) • Three-electrode valve (audion) patented by Lee De Forest (USA)		
Music	• Patent granted on first molded recording cylinder (USA) • First jazz band claimed by Buddy Bolden (USA) • International craze for the cakewalk	• Shellac 10in (25cm) diameter gramophone record with spiral-groove introduced • "Rags" popular (USA) • Adoption of Victor trademark (USA)	• Enrico Caruso's first recording (It)	• First amplifier patented, by Charles Parsons (UK) • *Babes in Toyland*, an operetta by Victor Herbert, opened (USA)	• First music radio broadcast (Aut)	• First double-sided disks released • First preselective jukebox (USA) • Franz Lehar's opera *The Merry Widow* opened (Aut)	• 17 Oct: Photographs sent by telegraph over 1000 miles (1600km) (Ger) • Typecasting machine allowed large display ty for headlines and bills (USA)
Fashion and Design	• Brownie camera introduced (USA) • 14 Apr: Opening of the Paris International Exhibition (Fr) • Button-down shirt introduced to USA by Brooks Bros (from UK) • Glassmaker and designer LC Tiffany created Tiffany Studios, New York (USA)	• Apr: The first mass-produced gasoline-driven car, an Oldsmobile, introduced (USA) • Société des Artistes Décorateurs founded (Fr)	• Cartier (Fr) opened its first London branch • Turin International Exhibition (It) • Sew-on press studs invented (Fr) • Pepsi-Cola Co. founded (USA)	• The first Harley-Davidson motorcycle built (USA) • Safety razor with disposable blades manufactured by King C Gillette (USA) • Wiener Werkstätte founded as a craft cooperative (Aut) • Jun: Foundation of Ford Motor Co. (USA)	• Electric machine that permanently waved hair introduced (UK) • 30 Apr: Opening of St Louis World's Fair (USA)	• Fauvist paintings exhibited at annual Salon d'Automne in Paris, introducing fashion for bright colors (Fr) • *Die Brücke* magazine founded to revive the graphic arts (Ger) • Alfred Stieglitz opened a gallery in New York to exhibit photography as a fine art (USA)	• Saddlery shop opene in Florence by Guccio Gucci (It)
Sport	• Jul: Second modern Olympic Games held in Paris (Fr) • 10 Aug: Davis Cup competition (tennis) held for first time; won by American team • First motorcar race with international competitors, Paris to Lyon (Fr)	• Boxing recognized as legal sport in Britain	• First French soccer team played in England • Jan: Inaugural Rose Bowl game between leading college teams (American football) • Rubber-cored golfball invented (USA)	• First Tour de France cycling race held • 13 Oct: First World Series in baseball, won by the Boston Red Sox (USA)	• 21 Jul: Rigolly (Fr) became first man to drive at over 100mph (160km/h) • Aug: Olympic Games held in St Louis (USA) • Foundation in Paris of Fédération Internationale de Football Association (FIFA)	• Jul: May Sutton (USA) became first non-Briton to win a Wimbledon tennis title	• First Victorian Footba League (Australian rules) final at Melbourne (Aus) • Jun: First Grand Prix motorcar race held, nea Le Mans (Fr)
Misc.		• 22 Jan: Death of Queen Victoria (UK)		• 17 Dec: The Wright brothers made first flight in a heavier-than-air machine (USA)			

122

	1908	1909	1910	1911	1912	1913	1914
Slow-motion film •ented by A Musger •Foundation of •llywood as •nmaking center •SA)	• 11 Feb: Patent rights over moving-picture camera granted to Edison and major companies (USA) • Florence Lawrence became known as "The Biograph Girl" (USA) • May: Movies placed within copyright laws (USA)	• 1 Jan: US Motion Picture Patents Co. set up, licensing nine producers, including two French (USA)	• First movie publicity stunt, with Gertrude Lawrence mobbed after reports of her death • Biograph made its first films in Hollywood (USA) • Opening of largest cinema yet built, the 5000-seat Gaumont Palace in Paris (Fr) • Aug: Kinetophone, with moving picture and simultaneous sound, demonstrated by TA Edison (USA)	• 1 May: Color talkie released, with sound on Biophon synchronized disk (Swe)	• Jun: Universal Studios founded by Carl Laemmle (USA) • Sep: Keystone Co. founded by Mack Sennett (USA) • Motor-driven movie cameras introduced (USA)	• Charlie Chaplin's first film for Keystone Co. released (USA) • First films from Paramount Co. were released (USA)	• *The World, the Flesh and the Devil* – the first full-length color film (UK)
•First regular studio •dio broadcasts, by • Forest Radio •lephone Co. (USA)		• First newsreels released (USA) • May: First radio press message, from New York to Chicago (USA)	• Metropolitan Opera, with Caruso, broadcast on radio (USA) • First radio receivers in kit form on sale to public (USA)		• May: First issue of *Pravda* (Rus)	• First crossword puzzle published, in *New York World* (USA)	
Ziegfeld Follies revue •ened in New York •SA)		• First transcription of blues – WC Handy's *Memphis Blues* (USA)	• Craze for the tango • March band leader John Philip Sousa (USA) toured world	• *Alexander's Ragtime Band*, by Irving Berlin	• Dixieland Jazz Band opened at Reisenweber's Cabaret, New Orleans (USA)		• Feb: Foundation of American Society for Composers, Authors and Publishers (ASCAP)
•Nov: Maiden voyage •HMS *Mauretania*, •gest and fastest •ean liner for 20 years •K) •First Cubist paintings •own in Paris, •uencing avant-garde •hion (Fr) •Deutscher Werkbund •rman Association of •aftsmen) founded in •nich to promote •ustrial design (Ger) •First Rolls Royce •er Ghost produced •K)	• Dance triumphs of Isadora Duncan in London and New York, in flowing costumes based on ancient Greek styles (UK) • Aug: Model T Ford, first successful mass-produced car (USA) • Hoover company founded to market vacuum cleaner invented in 1902 (UK) • Sep: General Motors founded (USA)	• Sergei Diaghilev's Ballets Russes opened in Paris, creating a fashion for oriental dress and decor (Fr) • Process for manufacturing bakelite developed by L Baekeland (USA) • CR Mackintosh's Glasgow School of Art completed (UK) • Silk-pleating process patented in Paris by Mariano Fortuny (Sp) • *Vogue* magazine bought by Condé Nast (USA)	• Hairdresser Antoine (Pol) created bobbed hairstyle in his Paris salon	• Atelier Martine (Fr) founded by Paul Poiret, as design studio modeled on Wiener Werkstätte (Fr)	• Fashion designer Coco Chanel opened her first salon, in Deauville (Fr) • Foundation of arts and fashion magazine *La Gazette du Bon Ton* (Fr)	• First electric refrigerator for home use (USA) • Oct: Moving-belt conveyor used in assembly of Ford cars (USA) • Slide fastener (later called a zipper) developed (USA) • *Harper's Bazaar* magazine bought by WR Hearst	• First major exhibiton of industrial art by Deutscher Werkbund, in Cologne (Ger) • Jun: Le Syndicat de Défense de la Grande Couture Française founded, to protect copyright (Fr) • Live models used in US fashion shows for the first time • Edna Woolman Chase became editor of *Vogue* (USA) • First brassière patented, by Caresse Crosby (USA)
•May: First Isle of Man • motorcycle race •K) •un: Start of first •g-distance motorcar •y, Paris to Beijing	• Jul: Olympic Games held in London (UK) • Dec: Jack Johnson (USA) became first black world heavyweight boxing champion • WG Grace retired from first-class cricket (UK) • International Swimming Federation (FINA) formed	• Imperial (later International) Cricket Conference founded (UK)		• May: Inaugural Indianapolis 500 motorcar race (USA) • First Monte Carlo motorcar rally (Mon)	• Jul: Stockholm Olympic Games, with the first women's swimming events (Swe) • International Lawn Tennis Federation founded in Paris (Fr)	• First Far Eastern Games held in Manila (Phil) • Charter for International Amateur Athletic Federation (IAAF) drawn up in Berlin (Ger)	
•More than 1 million •migrants entered •A		• R Peary reached North Pole (USA)			• 15 Apr: Sinking of the SS *Titanic* (USA)		• Aug: Outbreak of World War I

Datafile

In the final years of the 19th century the dominant design esthetic had been related to the arts and crafts movement, which valued crafts and skills and traditional design. The Art Nouveau movement of the 1890s developed this by the adoption of organic and irregular forms in opposition to the mechanical modern world. This movement also involved the reassertion of traditional European values over those of America.

Skyscrapers were beginning to appear in New York and Chicago, and came to be seen as symbolic of the new world of technology and industrial organization. They expressed the idea that the form should derive from the structure – in this case from their crude metal frame – and that surface decoration was a mere embellishment to justify an object's cultural pretensions. In the early years of the century, however, this idea was challenged by the search for modernism via an undiluted functionalist machine esthetic. This movement was to gain supremacy in the 1920s.

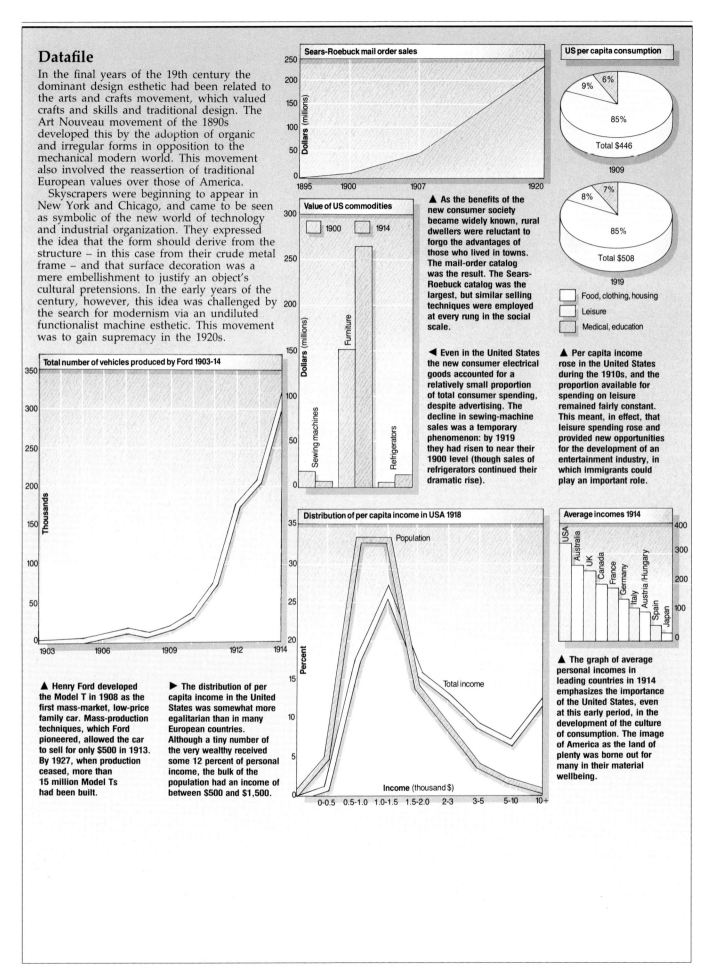

Sears-Roebuck mail order sales

US per capita consumption

Total $446
1909

Total $508
1919

☐ Food, clothing, housing
☐ Leisure
▨ Medical, education

Value of US commodities

☐ 1900 ▨ 1914

▲ As the benefits of the new consumer society became widely known, rural dwellers were reluctant to forgo the advantages of those who lived in towns. The mail-order catalog was the result. The Sears-Roebuck catalog was the largest, but similar selling techniques were employed at every rung in the social scale.

◄ Even in the United States the new consumer electrical goods accounted for a relatively small proportion of total consumer spending, despite advertising. The decline in sewing-machine sales was a temporary phenomenon: by 1919 they had risen to near their 1900 level (though sales of refrigerators continued their dramatic rise).

▲ Per capita income rose in the United States during the 1910s, and the proportion available for spending on leisure remained fairly constant. This meant, in effect, that leisure spending rose and provided new opportunities for the development of an entertainment industry, in which immigrants could play an important role.

Total number of vehicles produced by Ford 1903-14

Distribution of per capita income in USA 1918

Average incomes 1914

▲ Henry Ford developed the Model T in 1908 as the first mass-market, low-price family car. Mass-production techniques, which Ford pioneered, allowed the car to sell for only $500 in 1913. By 1927, when production ceased, more than 15 million Model Ts had been built.

► The distribution of per capita income in the United States was somewhat more egalitarian than in many European countries. Although a tiny number of the very wealthy received some 12 percent of personal income, the bulk of the population had an income of between $500 and $1,500.

▲ The graph of average personal incomes in leading countries in 1914 emphasizes the importance of the United States, even at this early period, in the development of the culture of consumption. The image of America as the land of plenty was borne out for many in their material wellbeing.

LEARNING TO BUY

By 1900 all major industrial countries had become aware of the importance of the consumption of goods by their citizens as well as production. As a result a "culture" of consumption emerged, which played an important role in the shaping of a country's social, economic and cultural identity. One feature of this new culture was a heightened awareness of social status and a strong desire at all levels of society to show off newly acquired wealth. New social aspirations were expressed most visibly in the "world of goods", and the concept of style became increasingly significant as a measure of social status.

This culture of consumption grew as a direct result of the process of industrialization within capitalist economies. It became increasingly necessary for manufacturers to produce and sell more and more goods to more and more people in order to guarantee their company's profits. The

- **The culture of consumption**
- **Adding style to goods**
- **Department stores and mail-order selling**
- **Standardization and variation**
- **Mass-produced fashion**
- **The new female shape**
- **Underwear and outerwear**
- **Poiret and avant-garde fashion**

▼ By 1900, advertising signs on stores, billboards and public transport urged people to identify themselves through what they consumed.

success of this formula also depended on the growth of the mass market. As the general level of affluence rose, there were increasing numbers of new consumers who sought new goods to reflect their enhanced social status. Most of them emulated their "social superiors" by imitating their purchases and as far as possible reproducing their lifestyles. The approach varied: in Britain the middle classes aspired to the lifestyle of the country gentry, whereas in the United States the new industrialists and businessmen sought to overturn the values of the traditional aristocracy. Everywhere, the new consumers displayed their new-found wealth and demonstrated the nature of their social ambitions through the many goods they bought.

One of the ways in which manufacturers tried to encourage consumption was by identifying a particular market and deliberately making their

goods look attractive to their potential customers. Even in the 18th century, when Britain was showing the first signs of becoming a consumer society, some entrepreneurs had achieved this by employing fine artists to design products for them. Goods that offered obviously "artistic" qualities conformed to the fashionable styles of the day and were particularly appealing to the newly affluent, status-conscious consumers for whom they were intended.

Adding style to goods

By the late 19th century manufacturers were addressing a sizable fashion-conscious mass market that included members of the working classes. The guarantee of taste or status was still connected with the visible presence of "art" in a product. This was a period of rampant estheticization in which almost any and every consumer product – in particular those that fell into the category of the traditional decorative or applied arts – could be seen to have an "artistic" content. This led to an extensive use of surface ornamentation that seemed to guarantee allegiance to the world of style for a market that was unfamiliar with fine art. The great vogue for "art furniture" and "art

pottery" in the 1880s and 1890s produced not only a spate of expensive, exclusive items designed for a middle-class market by such craftsmen as William de Morgan and E.W. Godwin, but also countless ranges of cheaper, mass-produced "art goods".

The dissemination of goods to a mass market depended on more than the efforts of manufacturers and designers to inject style into products. It also required a whole network of activities and institutions. These included changes in production methods so that more goods could be manufactured; the development of new kinds of retailing outlets; and the expansion of advertising and activities to promote sales. The introduction of a credit system of buying which was initiated by the Singer Sewing Machine Company in the United States in the 1860s, and adopted some decades later by the manufacturers of furniture and electrical appliances in Europe and the United States, also went a long way toward making more goods available to more people.

There were also changes in retailing. The department stores established in the second half of the 19th century – Bon Marché in Paris, Macy's in New York, and Derry and Toms, Whiteleys, and Harvey Nichols in London – were joined, at

▶ Trade cards provided one of the most direct forms of marketing at the turn of the century. They served to advertise a shop and to indicate, through the graphic style employed, the kind of market at which its goods were directed.

▶▶ This spread from a Sears Roebuck catalog, showing the wide variety of boots and shoes on offer by that company, would have been seen by a large sector of America's rural population at the turn of the century. Unable to make frequent shopping trips to the cities, these customers relied upon mail-order companies which brought an enormous range of goods to them.

▼ The cosmetics and drug department in an American store at the turn of the century. By this time the department store had become a vital means of retailing. Grandiose styling transformed these shops into the "temples" of the modern age.

about the turn of the century, by multi-branch retailing firms appealing to the lower end of the market, such as John Jacobs' furniture stores in England. American department stores appealed to as wide a market as possible through dramatic visual means. Interior spaces expanded and large shop windows were introduced to show off the new products to their best advantage. Electric lighting increased their visual appeal. The idea was pioneered in 1877 by John Wanamaker who persuaded Thomas Edison to install electricity in his store. The techniques of window dressing were also refined.

In the United States, where there were large distances between urban centers, the mail-order catalog became a vital means whereby the rural population could acquire goods that they would not otherwise have been able to buy. Montgomery Ward pioneered the concept, producing a single-sheet catalog in 1872. Three years later the catalog had nearly four thousand items listed in it. Sears followed suit, producing his first catalog in 1891 and moving on to become, with Roebuck, the largest mail-order company in the 20th century. They offered goods as diverse as agricultural machinery, applied art products, clothing and other utility goods. By 1900 electrical appliances had joined these earlier items.

The most direct way of making goods desirable was by modifying their appearance. Britain had gone a long way toward making the products of the traditional "art" industries available to the mass market through improved production techniques and distribution methods, but it was in the United States that the first consumer machines – automobiles, sewing machines, typewriters and domestic appliances – were made generally available. From the 1860s these began to take over from furniture as primary status symbols. Mass consumption of these consumer durables developed very quickly after their first

appearance on the market, as a result of the consumer boom that took place in the United States in the last decades of the 19th century. The market was quickly saturated with these new goods, however, and as supply began to exceed demand new ways were needed to market and sell these products. Credit buying was joined by aggressive sales programs in which salesmen toured the country offering demonstrations in their customers' homes.

Like the Singer sewing machines of the 1860s, which had gold scrollwork on their metal surfaces to give them greater domestic appeal, the first Hoover suction cleaner, a crude workshop-produced model, was adorned with decorative motifs in the fashionable Art Nouveau style. Product elaboration was thus transferred from ceramics and furniture to electrified machinery for the home. Electric fans, toasters, hot-plates and coffee-makers soon appeared on the market displaying the same decorative motifs as more traditional goods. Coffee pots resembled silver samovars and kettles looked like silver teapots from an earlier era.

The relationship between mass production and mass consumption was crucial in these years. High capital investment in a product meant that it had to sell in vast numbers to justify its initial costs and as a result marketing, advertising and design became increasingly important. However, the one product that dominated mass production and consumption in the first decades of the 20th century – the automobile – did not rely on "art" input to appeal to the mass market. Henry Ford's formula for mass production was based on product standardization; hence his famous statement that his cars were available in any color – providing it was black. The appeal of the Model T Ford lay less in its appearance than in its low price. Ford also used advertising and other marketing techniques to increase sales.

The spread of fashion

The "flapper" of the 1920s has long been considered the symbol for women's emancipation in the 20th century. In fact the freedom of manners and morals that she represented had begun to erode the old, stiff codes and conventions well before World War I. By the late 19th century middle-class and respectable working-class women were to be seen unchaperoned in city streets. One reason was that many more young women were now employed in offices, shops and department stores, while these department stores themselves – temples of 19th-century commerce – were places in which leisured women might wander alone or with their friends. Their refreshment rooms and cloakrooms, and sometimes even reading rooms and libraries, were social havens that even unaccompanied women could frequent without damaging their reputations.

One result of the growth of cities was the advance of fashion as a popular pursuit. Anonymity in the crowd was one new result of urbanization, and fashionable clothes provided an opportunity for people to express themselves in their daily business. The enormously increased demand for smart apparel at a reasonable cost found a solution in the mass production of fashionable garments. The mass production of clothes had begun with the making of uniforms in the early 19th century, but this had been extended well before 1900 as the independence and consumerism of city life fostered the growing appetite for fashionability. The factory process was first extended, in the 1830s and 1840s, to urban daywear for men – young clerks and shop assistants in London and other large cities whose pretensions to style were made possible by ready-made outfits.

It was between 1890 and 1910, however, that the mass production of fashionable clothing really took off. Blouses or shirtwaists and petticoats began to be made in bulk. Department stores sold ready-made women's suits, dresses and coats, which could be altered slightly for each customer, echoing the moves towards standardization and product variation pioneered in other areas of mass-market manufacture, such as furniture.

The great cities of the industrial world gradually took on a different air. Although the gulf between rich and poor remained, and although a whole underclass of the very poor still barely had clothes enough to keep them warm, women and men from the lower and upper middle classes now dominated city pavements, and among the vast urban masses clothes became as much an index of personality and of purpose as of simple social status. Dress in the city street was a performance, a subtle indicator of calling or leisure activities, hinting at sexual proclivities as

▼ By the early 1900s the S-bend figure had superseded the previous tight-laced look. The new corset still nipped in the waist and thrust the bosom upwards, but stretched lower down over the stomach, tilting the whole body backwards. In the Edwardian period too, the corset did not so much produce a cleavage as a "monobosom". To our eyes today the finished effect is of a human lampstand rather than a woman's body.

► The middle-class woman of the 1900s was less constrained than her mother would have been in the 1870s. She was still stiffly corseted and usually her blouse did up high at the throat. Her appearance would be completed with a towering edifice of hat and hair. Hair was often padded out artificially while hats were vast and often covered with flowers and fruit, or more gruesomely with dead birds.

much as at rank, and symbolizing countless allegiances. For men as well as women, to dress in fashion was to make a statement about yourself and your aspirations.

At the beginning of the 20th century women's clothing was changing more rapidly than men's. The growth in popularity of women's sports – particularly tennis and bicycling – meant that women were no longer quite so rigidly confined within the tight, voluminous garments that they had been wearing since the 1820s. Initially women laced themselves tightly even when running about the sportsfield; the bicycle at last made bloomers, or breeches, acceptable for women – if still rather "fast", or daring. A fashion for exercise, dance and calisthenics indicated the evolution of a new attitude toward the body. Women's exploits at hockey and cricket, on the bicycle and at the wheel of that most glamorous of fashion accessories, the motor car, inaugurated a new ideal of beauty that was soon to become dominant: the youthful, lissom, boyish woman. By the second decade of the 20th century her hair might well be bobbed (cut short), while long, loose clothes had replaced the hourglass figure.

STYLE BOOK

FALL 1911
The Ladies' Home Journal Patterns

◄ A new esthetic for street wear was the "coat and skirt", developed by Redferns and other British tailors from hunting and riding dress, but so functional for urban life that as a concept it has never really gone out of fashion.

▼ Some of the most daring women cyclists took to a cycling outfit which consisted of breeches, sometimes worn with a man's shirt, jacket and tie. It was widely accepted in France, as shown in this painting of the Bois de Boulogne, Paris, by Béraud.

▲ The American "Gibson Girl", drawn by Charles Dana Gibson, modified the severe tailored look of the New Woman and she became acceptably feminine, while retaining an air of dash and independence to typify the new woman of the 1900s.

Luxury and severity

Sportswear, the artistry of the great dress designers, and the ideas of dress reformers combined to create a new esthetic of dress to match the evolving new style of beauty. "Reform dress" had long been preached, and sometimes worn, in radical and artistic circles. Dress reformers objected to corsets, and to fashions such as the crinoline and the bustle which distorted the figure, for they believed that dress should follow the natural shape of the human form. The most famous example of reform dress was Amelia Bloomer's trousered costume of 1850 – named "bloomers" after its originator. Similarly reformers disliked men's trousers and preferred breeches, since they revealed the calf; the Irish playwright George Bernard Shaw was a dress reformer and habitually wore "plus fours".

Sportswear influenced women's daytime costumes. The firm of Redferns in London, which had originally specialized in riding habits, developed a modification of riding wear that became the "coat and skirt", or woman's suit. This rapidly became virtually a uniform for women's street wear, both in Europe and in the United States. It created a new kind of sobriety, almost a masculinity, in women's outdoor wear. In the United States the magazine artist Charles Dana Gibson created the epitome of this style in his famous "Gibson Girl", a tall, graceful young woman whose severe white blouse and dark, svelte skirt only enhanced her femininity. A fashion developed for frothy petticoats which peeped from beneath the hems of these sober skirts. It was during this period, when women's ordinary daywear became less feminine, that glamorous lingerie began to be popular.

Before 1800 underwear as we know it hardly existed. A shift was worn to protect the body from the rough material of the clothes, and the clothes from dirt of the body. The advance of hygiene and emphasis on modesty contributed to the popularity of underwear in the 19th century, but until about 1900 it was strictly utilitarian. With the turn of the century women were being more overtly sexual, as the rigid distinctions between the "respectable" and the "fallen" woman began to dissolve, and in the first decade of the 20th century fashionable women revelled in *crêpe de chine* underwear in "sweet pea" colors, covered in lace and ribbons. Unlike outerwear, these confections were still mostly hand-made.

The paradox of reserved outerwear and luxuriously sensual lingerie symbolized the way in which public life and private life had both become more elaborate and more distinct from each other during the industrial period. Social life was now more ritualized for most classes, and this found expression in equally elaborate rituals of dress. The new, lithe beauty of the sportsfield and dance floor, however, was born in the attempt to escape just this elaboration.

The story of Western dress in the 20th century, when for the first time fashionable clothes became widely available, has been one of oscillation between high artifice and studied simplicity, between fashions that glory in their useless glamor and those that are severely functional.

Poiret and Avant-garde Fashion

Paul Poiret was the leading Paris designer from 1908 to World War I. Possibly influenced by the ideas of the German dress reform movement, he designed loose, straight coats cut like kimonos and straight, often high-waisted dresses which hung from the shoulders. He claimed to have made women throw away their corsets, but Vionnet and other designers have also taken credit for the ending of the tight-laced silhouette. (In fact, women continued to wear boned corsets until well after World War II.)

Poiret was influenced by the fashion for oriental colors and styles, and also by the Ballets Russes, Diaghilev's dance company, which took Paris by storm with their exotic productions. These included vibrant backcloth and costume designs by Leon Bakst and Jose Maria Sert, and unfamiliar "modern" music and choreography. Poiret himself minimized the significance of Bakst's influence on his work, but few believed this claim. He achieved his greatest fame with his "hobble skirts" of 1911, which brought public outcry and even Papal denunciation. He used striking, even violent color combinations and his reds, violets, orange, rose and turquoise moved radically away from the pastel prettiness of more conventional *Belle Epoque* tints and equally from the half tones and "off" colors of the Liberty style. Poiret's designs were beautifully illustrated by Paul Iribe and Georges Lepape. He was a great publicist for his designs, and established a training school for young women in which they could learn the art of dressmaking.

▲ An evening coat by Paquin, influenced by Poiret.

Datafile

The great American cities, with their diverse populations, were the first centers of popular culture as now understood. Newspapers, movies, recorded music and advertising found their earliest markets in the metropolis, and New York was the cauldron in which popular culture's familiar forms were first produced. But few pioneers anticipated the speed with which these new industries of leisure would grow.

Types of film 1914

UK

US

- Crime/war/spies
- Drama/literary
- Historical
- Fantasy/horror
- Romance
- Documentary/current affairs
- Comedy
- Action/adventure
- Westerns
- Others

Victor record sales 1901-14

7,686,709

▲ Eldridge Johnson's Consolidated Talking Machine Company of Camden, New Jersey, began marketing gramophone records with the distinctive "His Master's Voice" label in 1900. In 1906 his company, now called Victor, introduced the Victrola player for domestic use.

▶ The spectacle of movement was cinema's earliest attraction, and "scenics" and "topicals" made up much of the program. Narrative fiction films in a variety of genres dominated American output after 1906, nevertheless most of the genres that would become staple fare in Holywood had been established by 1914.

Average number of feature films produced

| 1906-08 | 1909-10 | 1911-12 | 1913-14 |

224

78

Australia, Germany, Hungary, Italy, UK, USA, Russia

▲ Films grew steadily in length during the early years of the century. In 1903 the 10-minute long *Great Train Robbery* was one of the longest films then made, but by 1914 feature films lasting an hour or more were common.

▶ The first 15 years of the century saw the last great wave of immigration into the United States, to provide the workforce for its industry. The new immigrants were heavily concentrated in urban areas.

Immigration into USA

1,285,349

The first media moguls of the 20th century were the publishers of large-circulation American and British newspapers. As in so many other aspects of popular culture, British or American examples set precedents that were followed by the rest of Europe, and then by the world. The newspaper as we recognize it today was an invention of the great American cities: a mixture of news, entertainment and advertising, not formally attached to any political party, and financed as much or more by the advertising it carried as by the income from its low sales price. In 1900 half the world's daily papers were sold in the major cities of the United States.

The press and city life

Concentrating large numbers of people into small and tightly defined geographical areas, American cities provided the mass readership that made the distribution of a daily press practical. Many of the new city dwellers had immigrated from small country towns or from other countries or continents, and their sense of dislocation provided a context for the rise of newspaper reading. Through the wire services and news agencies, newspapers provided word from the migrants' homes. At the turn of the century there were more than a thousand foreign-language daily newspapers published in the United States. Immigrants were many times more likely to read a paper in New York than they had been in their native Minsk or Naples, whether that paper was written in their own language or in the English they were learning as part of their process of Americanization.

Even more importantly, newspapers offered their readers explanations of city life. In their exposés of government corruption, their gossip about the metropolitan elite, and in their scandal-mongering pursuit of "human interest" stories – as William Randolph Hearst put it, stories about "crime and underwear" – they gave substance and form to the anxieties of metropolitan existence. The newspapers proclaimed themselves the people's guardians, in small matters as well as large. One Hearst editorial declared, "The force of the newspaper is the greatest force in civilization. Under republican government, newspapers form and express public opinion. They suggest and control legislation. They declare wars. They punish criminals, especially the powerful. They reward with approving publicity the good deeds of citizens everywhere. The newspapers control the nation because they REPRESENT THE PEOPLE."

In many respects the popular press did represent the people, as part of a conscious policy of appealing to their readership. Hearst and his great rival, Joseph Pulitzer of the *New York*

ENTERTAINMENT IN THE CITY

World, campaigned against corrupt city government and the trusts that controlled railroads and other major industries, and declared their support of laborers, small businessmen and "ordinary people". More spectacularly, the American daily press and their British and European imitators were major proponents of the wave of imperialist sentiment at the turn of the century. Hearst and Pulitzer campaigned furiously for the United States to go to war with Spain over Cuba in 1898, and claimed responsibility for both the war and the victory. In Britain Alfred Harmsworth (later Lord Northcliffe), who launched the *Daily Mail* in 1896 in imitation of the New York papers, doubled that paper's circulation during the Boer War, which it charted with maps and columns of impassioned prose. During World War I Northcliffe, owner of *The Times*, was placed in charge of British propaganda.

Although the press barons were very often

▼ Cities bred newspapers, and made possible the mass distribution of a daily press. From 1906 the residents of London suburbs could have their papers delivered.

politically active as individuals, the popular dailies were not primarily agencies of political opinion. The tycoons were speculators and promoters much more than they were newsmen. Hearst, a millionaire rich enough to indulge even his most extreme fantasies (and the figure on whom Orson Welles' film *Citizen Kane* was based) frequently felt that the news that actually happened had two disadvantages: it was dull, and it was equally available to his rivals. His answer was to invent news, either through straightforward fakery or through self-publicizing reports of "newsworthy" events his papers themselves promoted. *Collier's Magazine*, describing Hearst's tastes in 1906, was exaggerating only slightly when it suggested, "An ideal morning edition to him would have been one in which the Prince of Wales had gone into vaudeville, Queen Victoria had married her cook, the Pope had issued an encyclical favoring free love,...France had declared war on Germany, the

▲ Crowded by their poverty into tenement ghettos in New York, immigrants were exhorted by the press to abandon their Old World customs. Simon Lubin and Christina Krysto satirized the idea of the Melting Pot: "Jump into the cauldron and behold! You emerge new creatures, up to date with new customs, habits, traditions, ideals. Immediately you will become like us; the taint will disappear. Your sacks will be exchanged for the latest Fifth Avenue styles. Your old-fogey notions will give way to the most modern and new-fangled ideas. You will be reborn. In short you will become full-fledged Americans. The magic process is certain. Your money back if we fail."

President of the United States had secured a divorce in order to marry the Dowager Empress of China... and the Sultan of Turkey had been converted to Christianity."

The daily press catered for a new market of urban readers, who were not exclusively interested in news. The press adapted an older formula, used by the 18th-century English radical press and 19th-century Sunday papers, of scandal, crime and popular education. The press barons developed the formula to include new features: comics, advice columns, interviews, sport and fashion pages, and photographs. They also devised ever more elaborate promotional schemes (such as free insurance with a subscription), stunts and guessing competitions. Many of these new developments indicated the importance of women readers. One of the earliest uses to which newspaper photographs were put in the United States was as a way of running beauty contests, which, like fashion, gossip and human interest stories, were thought to appeal more to women

than to men. Evening papers such as Hearst's *New York Evening Journal* were aimed quite specifically at women readers, and at the major retail advertisers seeking their custom. Harmsworth launched the *Daily Mirror* in 1903 as a paper for women.

The rise of advertising

The real novelty of the daily press was not so much its content as the scale of its enterprise and its financing. In the last years of the 19th century, as the range of packaged food and drugs and manufactured goods intended for private consumption dramatically increased, advertising became the mechanism by which the distribution of goods within the economy was stimulated, and regulated. In the 1890s advertising agencies no longer simply sold space in newspapers or magazines. They began to advise their clients on the design and appearance of their advertisements, and as they did so they created a crucial instrument, by which a mass public could be educated to desire the pleasures of consumption. Harmsworth and his American counterparts recognized that the new technology of Linotype typesetting machines and the fast rotary printing presses made possible the rapid mass production of millions of copies of a newspaper or magazine. Circulation became crucial because the larger a paper's circulation the more it could charge advertisers for space. Display advertising replaced the uniform columns of classified advertisements. This new source of revenue and the demands of mass circulation meant that the costs of each copy to the reader were cut to a minimum: in Britain the *Daily Mail* sold for a halfpenny, and took nearly half its income from advertising sales.

The press followed the example of other industries in incorporating into larger chains or groups of publications. New owners such as Hearst, Northcliffe and Arthur Pearson (who founded the *Daily Express* in competition with the *Mail* in 1900) came to recognize the advantages of economies of scale. By 1923 Hearst owned 22 daily and 15 Sunday papers, nine magazines, including *Cosmopolitan* and *Harper's Bazaar*, news and syndication services and a Sunday supplement, the *American Weekly*. His publicists claimed that one American family in four read a Hearst publication. He was the biggest user of paper in the world.

In France, the Parisian press operated in a similar way to the American and British dailies, and *Le Petit Journal* even exceeded them in circulation. The French news agency Havas shared the telegraphic distribution of European news with Reuters of London. However, the extreme centralization of the mass-circulation press in Paris led it to depend too heavily on Parisian high culture and government support, and undermined its commercial popularity. In the rest of Europe the press retained its 19th-century organization until well after World War I, with a much larger number of papers, many of them affiliated to a political party, and most having a small local circulation.

◄ The *Ladies Home Journal* had been founded in 1883 as one of the new breed of magazines aimed at a female readership. It was a lively and informative read, and celebrated its mass appeal ("the magazine with a million") rather than its exclusiveness.

◄ Newspaper-reading became an addictive habit of city-dwellers. This French cartoon comments wryly on the alienation brought to personal life by the anonymity of city life. Too engrossed in reports of disaster and scandal, the passers-by ignore the accident before their eyes.

◄ The staff of *Success*, one of several American magazines which emphasized the middle-class virtues of ardent nationalism, the gospel of work, and sincere admiration for the romance of business and the successful businessmen who figured prominently in both its factual articles and its fiction. Other general interest magazines such as *McClure's*, *Everybody's* and *Collier's*, however, also published some of the "muckraking" journalism which exposed the exploitation of the immigrants, the scale of civic corruption and "the Shame of the Cities", during the Progressive era.

The early film industry

None of cinema's inventors envisaged the vast entertainment industry that would develop from it, for no such industry, and no public for such an industry, had existed before. The motion picture became *the* central commodity of an amusement industry rather than primarily an instrument of science, an educational tool, or a form of family entertainment, more because of the social organization of the modern industrial city than as a result of any properties inherent in the technology itself. Louis Lumière's *cinematographe*, first exhibited in December 1895 in Paris, was regarded as "the crown and the flower of 19th-century magic"; early in the 20th century Hollywood provided the prototype for a new way of life, teaching the United States and the world the fashionable pleasures of conspicuous consumption.

In the earliest years of cinema no one knew quite what they had invented, or to what purposes it could be put. The technology of motion pictures, like that of magazine printing, was the culmination of 19th-century mechanical research. The goal of recording animal and human motion preoccupied inventors such as Marey and Edweard Muybridge during the third quarter of the century. Marey's "photographic gun", designed in 1882, was a prototype of the film-camera mechanism. With the development of celluloid roll film the technological requirements for cinema were complete; they merely awaited assembly. But Marey and Muybridge had little interest in developing their inventions further. Some, including Muybridge himself, thought that one of the principal uses for film would be as mechanical memories, preserving the moving images of individuals for their family and friends after death. Thomas Edison intended to market the Kinetoscope, which he invented with his assistant William K. Dickson in 1893 as home entertainment for wealthy families. It did not project, so the Kinetoscope could be viewed by only one person at a time, and Edison made his profits from sales of the machines rather than of films. Hoping to sell the Kinetoscope in department stores to middle-class customers, Edison was anticipating television rather than movies.

Cinema was a new commodity, unlike anything previously devised, and its early history was preoccupied with defining what that commodity was. Debates over whether the cinema imitated the theater or was itself a new form provided the esthetic aspect of that preoccupation, but there was more concern about how the new commodity should be sold, and to whom. The

▲ E.J. Marey's moving picture camera.

▼ A nickelodeon in 1906: "Last year it was probably a pawnshop or cigar store. Now the counter has been ripped out, there's a ticket-seller's booth where the show-window was, and an automatic musical barker thunders its noise down on the passer-by." Joseph Medill Patterson.

Early European Film

For much of the century's first decade, innovation in film production came more from Europe than the United States, where making movies was still seen as an offshoot of the more profitable business of making equipment. In France Georges Méliès exploited the cinema's capacity for illusion in a series of widely-copied science fiction and fantasy films such as *Journey to the Moon* (1902). At the Gaumont studios Max Linder pioneered the character clown achievements of silent cinema. European innovation kept the American market open; until 1908, nearly half the films shown in New York were European imports, and the largest single producer of films shown in America was the French firm Pathé. Using actors from the *Comédie Française*, the *Film d'Art* company introduced a subtler, less extravagant acting style to the screen. The overt appeal to a higher art tradition was also important in the feature films – expensively produced multiple-reel costume dramas and Biblical epics, such as *Cabiria* – which were first produced in Italy.

World War I drastically curtailed European production, and American distributors used this opportunity to secure a monopoly in their home market and expand their share of world

▲ *Journey to the Moon* (Méliès)

business, by selling at prices with which other companies could not compete. From then on through the twenties Hollywood provided not only the overwhelming majority of the world's movies, but also the stylistic model against which all other national cinemas – even those of India and Japan – would define themselves. The French, Italian, German and British industries never regained their pre-war size.

▼ Thomas Alva Edison, "the Wizard of Menlo Park", where his first research laboratory was situated. Einstein called him "the greatest inventor of all time". As much an entrepreneur as a scientist, he was only interested in experiments that had an immediate industrial application. The tickertape machine, the electric light, and the phonograph were among his inventions, as well as the Kinetoscope he devised with William Dickson.

novelty of moving photographic images was at first enough to guarantee its success, and the Lumières and others exploited this by sending their cameramen/projectionists (the *cinematographe* functioned as both camera and projector) around the world to photograph exotica for exhibition in Europe and United States. The earliest films lasted little more than a minute, and typically featured scenic views, topical events, boxing matches, and circus or vaudeville acts. Music hall and vaudeville theaters became the cinema's first permanent home. A dozen films would be presented together as a single turn among the performing animals, singers and comics, and soon managers noticed their popularity, particularly with the more "select" class of patrons.

The sale of films to vaudeville theaters indicated that manufacturers continued to be unsure of what it was they had to sell. The biggest producers were companies such as Edison, Biograph and Vitagraph, who made films – cheaply and with little technical equipment – merely as a necessary adjunct to their primary business of selling projection equipment. Vaudeville provided a convenient outlet as it spared producers the expense of investing in exhibition facilities of their own, but it provided little incentive for the development of the medium beyond its appeal as visual spectacle.

At first prints of films were sold outright, and vaudeville circuits or individual showmen putting on "tent-shows" would exhibit a film until the end of its physical or commercial life. In 1903 came the first film exchanges, middlemen who bought prints from their producers and rented them out to exhibitors. They created a low-cost distribution system that proved vital to the industry's rapid expansion from 1905 onward. Once films were available for rent rather than

purchase, it became possible to show films not as just one attraction among many on a variety bill, but to open theaters devoted to their exhibition, and to sell a movie show more cheaply than other forms of amusement – for no more than the price of a glass of beer. The first "nickelodeons" (the name came from their five-cent admission charge – in Britain they were called "penny gaffs") opened in 1905, and proved immediately and immensely profitable. Five years later there were 10,000 such theaters in the United States alone, attracting 30 million customers a week.

The increased demand for products from the nickelodeons encouraged American producers to revise their strategies. Since 1897 the leading

◀ By 1912 nickelodeons were rapidly being superseded in the United States by larger, purpose-built theaters, some of them seating over a thousand spectators. With their more comfortable and refined decor, they were designed to attract middle-class audiences, and situated in the more affluent parts of cities. Middle-class women on shopping trips were particularly sought-after customers, their presence a guarantee of the theater's respectability.

◀ The huge set for the Babylonian sequences of *Intolerance*, released in 1916, was probably the most lavish yet constructed. The film's complex structure intercut four stories of intolerance in different epochs, but audiences found its multiple plots difficult to follow, and it did not repeat the success of Griffith's spectacular but controversial *Birth of a Nation* (1915).

▼ Griffith (directing with megaphone) saw himself as a reformer, spreading the message of high culture through the movies, but the Victorian view of family and society which his films presented was rapidly being overtaken.

companies had been engaged in endless legal battles over patents, but in 1908 they combined to form the Motion Picture Patents Company to secure a shared monopoly control over the industry. This decision stabilized the American market and restricted the flow of imports.

The increase in demand from nickelodeons caused changes in the pattern of film production, too. From 1907 there was a marked shift towards the production of fictional narratives, rather than the "scenics" and "topicals" that had featured in earlier programming. This was inspired less by audience preference than by the fact that fictional films could take advantage of the economies of scale provided by mass production in a way that other kinds of filmmaking could not. Unlike topical films, a constant supply of story films could be produced from a purpose-built studio at a predictable cost, and released on a regular schedule. With the development of studios employing stock acting companies, the division of labor in production became more elaborate: the single cameraman responsible for everything was replaced by the director system, in which a director would prepare a scenario, supervise the cast and edit the film, while a cameraman handled the lighting, and shot and processed the film. Studios took their actors from provincial and touring companies.

The increased emphasis on narrative encouraged producers to make longer one-reel films, lasting about 15 minutes. This in turn stimulated the development of more complex techniques. By 1911 films derived their narrative mechanisms, and many of their plots, from the popular theater, from novels, and from magazine short stories. The nickelodeon business took over more and more vaudeville theater buildings and occupied more attractive sites in business or shopping districts to provide comfortable and genteel surroundings for their patrons. The Patents Company's acquiescence to a system of film censorship was also evidence of their strong desire to court respectability.

The Patents Company's monopoly was never complete, and their relatively conservative attitude towards production left room for independent exhibitors such as Adolph Zukor and William Fox to offer the public more innovative films from Europe. Their success provoked independent American producers to imitate them, by reproducing Broadway plays and adapting literary classics. By 1915, when D.W. Griffith made *The Birth of a Nation* from Thomas Dixon's novel *The Clansman*, the photoplay, a four- or five-reel feature film telling a complete story and carrying a moral lesson, had become the norm for most producers. By then, too, the stylistic techniques for constructing a narrative had been established. A continuous line of action was provided, with events closely linked together to ensure spectator involvement, and the way time and space were used was firmly controlled to ensure that the audience could follow the action.

Hollywood and its stars

Hollywood itself had also come into being. From 1908, production companies sent film units to California to make use both of its reliable climate and of the range of scenery, far wider than that available in New York, Chicago or Florida. Cheap real estate prices and labor costs, together with a cooperative civic administration, made Los Angeles an obvious choice, and production was concentrated there during the 1910s. Hollywood's "commercialized amusement" offered the world something more than mere entertainment; the American film industry was already learning how to teach America, and then the world, how to consume. As early as 1917 "Hollywood" was no longer just a suburb of Los Angeles; it had become an almost mythical place in which work and play were indistinguishable. Young, beautiful, successful movie stars with high incomes provided role models for their audiences and demonstrated the pleasures of the culture of consumption and the enjoyment of leisure. Stars projected a new morality, which demonstrated that leisure, and even sensuality, were no longer sinful.

Nevertheless, the "lower" elements in early American film production have endured more firmly than the feature films – perhaps because they now seem in keeping with the idea of the American cinema as a working-class and immigrant entertainment. The slapstick comedy short

films of Mack Sennett and Charlie Chaplin were criticized for their vulgarity. In their joyous celebration of chaos, knockabout comedies ridiculed some of the most treasured values of contemporary society. Property and the law were treated with an anarchic contempt that in another context might have seemed subversive. Yet, the Sennett characters were never imbued with individual personality. In their hectic collisions with machines, their automobiles might explode or career off cliffs, but the heroes always emerged unscathed. Chaplin's work also revealed a strong streak of sentimentality which made his humor much less threatening even while celebrating the exuberance of a less restrained social order.

◄ As films became longer and narrative more complex, so techniques and conventions of story-telling were developed – notably intercutting, close-ups, fade-outs and flashbacks. Posters advertised the complexity of their narrative line to draw in the audience.

▼ Mack Sennett took his Keystone comedy troupe to Hollywood in 1912, and by the following year their anarchic mix of clowning and car chases had won a wide audience.

► In 1905 Hollywood was little more than a farming village, almost a week's traveling time away from New York. The first movie studios were established in the next three or four years, and the Biograph Company made its first film in the area in 1910. By 1915, when the Universal Studios were opened, Hollywood's climate and convenient access to Los Angeles had encouraged the establishment of all the major American filmmaking companies there.

Ragtime and dance

To one veteran songwriter and publisher the 1910s marked a crucial turning point: "The public of the nineties had asked for tunes to sing," Edward S. Marks remarked nostalgically, "but the public from 1910 demanded tunes to dance to." The tunes in question, provided by the songwriting production lines of New York's Tin Pan Alley, were "rags", snappy, syncopated numbers; the dances were close-contact "animal" dances like the Turkey Trot and the Grizzly Bear. The sources for both of these lay in the black subculture of the late 19th century.

Ragtime had emerged in the United States in the post-Civil War era, rapidly maturing in the hands of pianist-composers such as Scott Joplin (whose "Maple Leaf Rag" was composed in 1899) into a meticulously crafted piano music in which European marching tempos and harmony engaged in a subtle dialog with Afro-American approaches to rhythm. Meanwhile, the cakewalk – a stylized display dance that combined black mockery of white dance steps with the black culture's own approach to movement – had begun to appear in polite white society, where it met with the energetic two-steps of the March King, John Philip Sousa. The establishment of public venues – cabarets, dance halls, restaurants – meant that dancing ceased to be a predominantly private affair. By the 1910s, discovery of the physically emancipating effect of black folk dance had led to a flood of popular new steps.

For the first time styles of music and dance for white America positively encouraged individual expression and suggested that the immediate moment was to be fully savored, even though dancers still had to share in a prescribed pattern. The premier dance couple of the era, Britons Irene and Vernon Castle, led the way.

The Castles managed to combine a trend-setting image as liberalizers of behavior with an air of middle-class moral respectability. This helped to resolve the controversy that developed as custodians of moral and esthetic standards argued over the merits of the new music and dance. Where one critic delighted in the "delicacy of ragtime's inner rhythms", another deplored its "jerk and rattle"; what to some eyes embodied the new "spirit of America" was to others decadent drivel. Underlying the arguments of opponents lay the (by no means always unspoken) fear of racial contamination, not only from the black source of the music and dance, but also from the white ethnic (especially Jewish) groups who dominated Tin Pan Alley's modernized song machine. The marginal status of these groups in American society allowed them readily to identify with the black approach, and also encouraged the use of popular culture as a means of social and economic advancement.

The moral opponents' argument was correct in one respect: more than mere entertainment was at stake. The part of American society that espoused the new styles of music and dance began to absorb, via white ethnic groups, attitudes and practices from the black community. It also raised fundamental questions about the family, about gender and race, and – above all – about the

Sheet Music

The mass production of popular songs in sheet-music form began in the United States in around 1885. Sales reached their zenith in the 1910s, when, with the price as low as 10 cents, stores like Woolworth's helped push annual totals up around 200 million copies. Rags and novelty songs abounded, responding to the demand for songs to be danceable. But the ballad outsold them all, peaking in 1918 with Egan and Whiting's World War I hit, *Till We Meet Again*, said to have sold 3.5 million copies in a matter of months.

A less precisely focused kind of sentimentality distinguished these ballads from their predecessors. But other factors were even more important. Here were songs which, more widely disseminated than any before, were also more capable of being privately owned by each listener. By a strange, often repeated paradox, the better a song was known, the more people seemed able to use it as a way of managing private emotion. This was achieved partly through the lyrics, as songwriters gradually developed the skill of making their words seem relevant to the widest possible audience, but principally through the music – very largely the work of immigrant or second-generation Jewish songwriters. In this music there began to emerge that hard-to-define interplay between subtly shifting rhythms and plaintive harmony which became characteristically American.

Sheet music for cabaret, operetta and music-hall songs was widely available throughout Europe, although the popular-music publishing industry was not so highly developed in Europe as across the Atlantic. In many countries sheet music brought a popularized version of music. Already it was rare for popular-music trends to flow westwards across the Atlantic.

▶ Sheet music covers of the 1900s.

► Dances such as the Grizzly Bear, derived from black styles, spread rapidly to Europe. Here, in pre-war Paris, actress Gaby Deslys and her husband demonstrate the potent combination of vigorous movement and bodily contact. While some dancers tempered sexual explicitness, others were less ambiguously sensual.

◄ The wonders of recorded sound are experienced for the first time – for a nickel in the slot – in turn-of-the-century Kansas. Listening to this early juke box, one girl later remembered, was a "magic treat". The sound might have been a Sousa march or an operatic aria – whichever, the potential of recording to offer entertainment was recognized early on by the inventor of the revolving disc, Emile Berliner, whose company soon began marketing the gramophone specifically for the home.

body; for it was to the body's still unexplored capacity for expression that the music and dance most obviously related. The music still had a predictable, march-like meter, the legacy and symbol of a relentless, regularizing value system; what gave it a new, unique character was syncopation, the "offbeat", with the accent placed against the expectations of the pulse. Jazz would soon take this much farther than ragtime, but a crucial point had been made: the control of the regular meter could be challenged – not by outright opposition, but by a change of emphasis.

Black performance style and musicality had interacted with European conventions before, but this was the first time its impact had been so clear. Yet even while appropriating this music, mainstream society neutralized its more expressive qualities. Unsure emotionally, self-conscious in display, at once fascinated and repelled by the implications of the music, the dancing public – taking their cue from leaders like the Castles – attempted to resolve the dilemmas by quickening the rhythms. What had been a subtle music became a display of good-humored impudence and respectable candor, which offered the sexes greater opportunity for intimacy, but froze the hand and eye in order to speed the foot.

The dance craze of the 1910s can be seen as an early example in 20th-century popular culture of the conflict between a liberating force and a conservative tendency. Opposition to developments was to play a part in the story of popular music but the mainstream's capacity for assimilation was to prove even more important.

VAUDEVILLE AND MUSIC HALL

Before ragtime and the new dances captured the public imagination the musical stage was pre-eminent in the provision of commercial entertainment in both Europe and America. A range of closely related styles had been developed (minstrelsy, vaudeville, music hall, burlesque, revue), presented in a sequence of separate performers. Only revue made an attempt at dramatic cohesion, thereby growing close to comic opera, another popular form. In all except the latter, the transatlantic traffic in people, styles and ideas was two-way. The European variety show, particularly as practiced in British music halls, provided the main model for American vaudeville, while the growth in blackface minstrelsy in Britain had quickly followed its rise to popularity in America.

The origins of British music hall lay in the disparate types of stand-up entertainment common in working-class pubs and supper-rooms. By the 1850s it had coalesced into an identifiable yet heterogeneous form. At first associated with making profits for the drink industry, the halls gradually developed a form of entertainment which was itself marketable, and by 1880 this formula, commercially underwritten and professionally executed, was dominant. Around this time, too, the audience widened to include the middle classes.

Music hall and vaudeville intertwined culture and commerce, setting up the tensions so frequently encountered in 20th-century popular culture. But an equally important legacy was the way in which that tension was undermined through a collaboration between humor and musical eclecticism.

▼One form of American entertainment never established itself across the Atlantic. The Wild West show, first staged at an open-air arena in New York in 1883 by erstwhile Indian fighter "Buffalo Bill" Cody, marketed its own version of the history of the West to vast audiences for over 20 years. It remained popular, so long as it remained outdoors.

▶The standard format for music-hall entertainment – a succession of unconnected acts – permitted performers to appear at several venues each night. As programs grew longer, dramatic sketches became more ambitious and the number of novelty acts increased. But the comic song retained its popularity, and the comic singer reigned supreme.

▲ The popularity of minstrelsy – white musicians singing black music with blackened faces – in the United States has been ascribed to a complex of factors involving the social function of racial stereotypes. The same conclusions are harder to draw elsewhere. Curiosity about America and – ironically – abolitionist sympathies were chiefly responsible for its popularity. Minstrel shows were usually staged as family entertainment.

▼ Whoever owned the music halls, nobody could make a London audience feel the culture was theirs better than Marie Lloyd (1870–1922). Appearing in her regal finery, her songs full of street innuendos, she established a "collusive intimacy" with her audience – "one of us", hobnobbing with respectable folk, hinting at subversion. Whether the actual result was subversive or whether it tended to persuade people to accept established society is still a matter of debate.

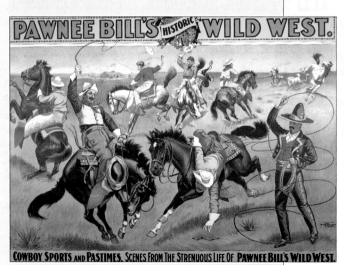

COWBOY SPORTS AND PASTIMES. SCENES FROM THE STRENUOUS LIFE OF PAWNEE BILL'S WILD WEST.

▲ Riotous behaviour was not unknown in music-hall audiences, but when Marie Lloyd sang *Boy in the Gallery* rapt attention was more likely. Walter Sickert's painting of an engrossed gallery audience also reveals that music halls were fairly opulent.

◀ By the turn of the century in Europe the revue had spread from its Parisian base to other centers, most notably in Berlin. In the years before the outbreak of war an international circuit of performers developed, one as open to the British song-and-dance troupe called the "Gala-Girls" as to more established stars.

THE FIRST STARS

Before 1910 the movies had discovered that stars sold cinema tickets; the earliest stars were former stage actors like comic John Bunny or Bronco Billy Anderson, billed in 1912 as "The World's Greatest Photoplay Star". But the greatest stars of Hollywood's formative years were Douglas Fairbanks and Mary Pickford. From 1914 they, with Charlie Chaplin, achieved a celebrity quite unlike anything ever seen before them. More than the scale of their popularity, what made stardom a new phenomenon was that it detached fame from achievement in the strenuous life of work or battle.

Readers of the fan magazines that began to appear in 1912 became as familiar with their idols' off–screen lives as with their movie appearances. Chaplin's "little tramp" first appeared in 1914, and was an immediate success with audiences. But Charles Chaplin the actor behaved quite differently from Charlie the clown. Pickford and Fairbanks projected the same image on screen and off, and between them they offered their audiences new role models.

Fairbanks' comedies ridiculed Victorian restrictions on fun. In newspaper columns and books such as *Laugh and Live* and *Make Life Worth-while*, he advocated sport as a means of regenerating the urban masses. In *His Picture in the Papers*, made in 1916, Fairbanks played the rebellious son of a dour cereal manufacturer. He learned to box, became attractive to women, and rescued a big businessman from criminals. Asked the secret of his strength, he advertised his father's cereal. Sales improved now it was associated with robust fun-lovers.

Mary Pickford embodied the "new woman": healthy, robust, self–reliant, she combined sexual allure with chastity. "Little Mary", "America's Sweetheart", was more popular even than Chaplin. In 1916, she became the first star to be the producer of her own films. In them, she brought out the spontaneity and playfulness which Victorian culture had repressed in women. Emancipated and even a suffragist, in her performances she questioned the female role in the family and at work. When she married Fairbanks in 1920, the Hollywood mansion they built, Pickfair, became famous as a paradise in which high-level consumption was advertised as the basis for a secure and stable family life.

▲▶ **Douglas Fairbanks and Mary Pickford**, the first King and Queen of Hollywood, taught America that success could best be expressed in the world of leisure. His good-humored athleticism celebrated the male body. She became the "most popular girl in the world" by combining independence and innocence in a "radiant image of girlish beauty" that showed she was "old fashioned but not a prude". After marrying they toured Europe; in Moscow a crowd of 300,000 greeted them.

▶▶ **In 1918 Fairbanks**, Pickford, Chaplin and Western star William S. Hart traveled the country, raising millions of dollars for Liberty Loans to help the war effort (center image and far right). The next year, together with director D.W. Griffith, they founded United Artists to market and exploit their pictures. One Hollywood wit observed, "So the lunatics have taken charge of the asylum," but in the fast-growing Hollywood of 1920 (main image) it made sound commercial sense to protect their interests.

Datafile

The years around 1900 saw both a rise in interest in organized sport throughout Europe and the United States, and a tendency for international organization and serious competition. The ethos of much sport was strictly amateur: at the 1912 Olympics, the American athlete Jim Thorpe, winner of the decathlon and pentathlon, was stripped of his medals after admitting to having once accepted $25 for playing baseball in a minor league.

There was widespread concern to improve the physical fitness of the working classes, which led to an interest in gymnastics. The political dimension of this concern meant that, between 1914 and 1918, almost half the volunteers for Britain's armed forces had been recruited at soccer grounds.

The pressure for urban recreational facilities led to increased municipal provision of facilities such as recreation grounds, gymnasia and public swimming pools in many countries.

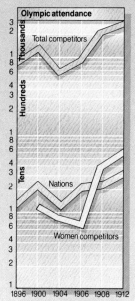

Olympic attendance

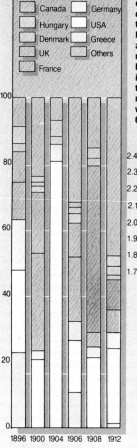

Gold medals 1896-1912

Canada | Germany
Hungary | USA
Denmark | Greece
UK | Others
France

◀ The United States established its domination of the modern Olympics at the second meeting, in Paris, but their superiority at St Louis was fairly meaningless as few European countries took an interest in the Games. For the London Games, a large new stadium was built, with a crowd capacity of 66,000.

▲ In the first three modern Olympic Games, at Athens, Paris and St Louis, there was no real national team organization; the Games were treated as a part of the World's Fairs going on at the same time, and some bizarre events (such as barrel-jumping) were included. The 1908 Games were the first organized by sporting bodies.

▶ Through the century improved standards of training and conditions for competition have meant that sporting standards have increased inexorably as exemplified by the Olympic-winning performers. The gap betwen men's and women's records has also narrowed as opportunities for women have grown.

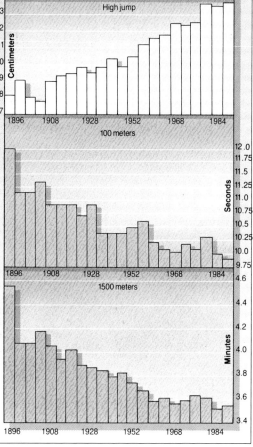

Before 1900 many sports had developed from local adaptations of traditional folk games into organized activities with uniform rules, special playing kit, cups and trophies, team colors and caps. The most influential setting for the modernization of sports was provided by the British public schools.

British school sports

In the 19th century, football and cricket – the two major British sports – were unrestrained affairs, played in different ways in different schools, not much more than savage battles in which older boys could assert their dominance over younger ones. Their transformation into modern sports resulted largely from the reforming influence of the new industrial middle classes who sent their sons to the public schools to be educated with the gentry; they turned games into a form of discipline. Organized school sports became compulsory instruments of socialization and moral education for the elite young men destined to become leaders of the Empire. Rules limited aggression and ensured "fair play". The games-playing cult, designed to produce disciplined, self-reliant and socially responsible "muscular Christians", had, as its central theme, *Mens sana in corpore sano* (A healthy mind in a healthy body). Games were also seen as channels of sexual sublimation, sufficiently ascetic and exhausting to eliminate "indecent" expressions of sexuality.

Matches between schools became social events watched by huge crowds. The athletic public schoolboy was revered as a hero at school and exalted in the press. During the first decade of the 20th century the fiercely amateur cult of athleticism became an obsession in the public schools. But the idea of moral excellence and character training associated with sports did little to inhibit the aggressive display of physical power.

Sports in public schools were never truly virtuous and "civilized" activities. The desire to win was always part of the amateur sporting tradition of the British. The sports cults of the public schools celebrated competitiveness and expressions of brute male power. Violent competitive sport provided a dominant image of sport in Britain and throughout the world.

Organized sport proliferated in universities and independent sports clubs formed by ex-public schoolboys. By 1900 national associations, responsible for codifying rules and administering competitions, existed for football, rugby, cricket, yachting, skating, boxing, rowing, lawn tennis, croquet, hockey, gymnastics, lacrosse (originally a North American game) and badminton. Britain, the world's major sporting nation, exported its sports (and usually their rules) as an element of its

SPORT: THE BRITISH INHERITANCE

cultural imperialism. But while football went to Europe and Latin America in its Association form, in Australia and North America it developed indigenous forms, based on Gaelic football.

International sporting events

The inauguration of international associations, for football in 1904 and lawn tennis in 1913, accelerated international competition. The modern Olympic movement and its organizing body, the International Olympic Committee (IOC), was founded in 1895 by Pierre de Coubertin. It was the exemplar for international amateur sport, in which the contestants participate without being paid. In common with other international bodies, it was controlled by middle- and upper-class men with economic power and elitist ideas. Almost all the athletes who competed in the first Olympics, and the bulk of those who took part in Olympic competition before World War I, were wealthy

Sport and British public schools

International organization

The Olympic movement

Women and sport

Sport and the working classes

The organization of boxing

► A gold medal from the first modern Olympics, held in Athens in 1896.

▼ Jingoistic Londoners urge on marathon runners in the 1908 Olympics.

Beauty of face and form is one of the chief essentials (for women), but unlimited indulgence in violent, outdoor sports, cricket, bicycling, beagling, otter-hunting, paper-chasing, and – most odious of all games for women – hockey, cannot but have an unwomanly effect on a young girl's mind, no less on her appearance. Let young girls ride, skate, dance and play lawn tennis and other games in moderation, but let them leave field sports to those for whom they are intended – men.

BADMINTON MAGAZINE

▼ Winter sports gained in popularity during the second half of the 19th century, and figure skating was one event open to women at the 1908 Olympics. The first Winter Olympics were held in 1924.

◀ Although gymnastics was accepted as a form of therapeutic exercise for women, competition was deemed unladylike and even unhealthy. The male-dominated organizing body of the modern Olympic movement, the IOC, barred women's gymnastics and track-and-field events until the 1928 Olympics.

▼ During the early 20th century, golf was among the few sports considered acceptable for women of fashion and leisure. Amateur golfing championships for women were first held in Britain in 1893, and in the United States in 1895.

amateur, as opposed to professional, sportsmen, which left an indelible mark on the development of international sport and militated against athletes from less privileged backgrounds. The Olympic movement was inspired by the ideal that the Games would promote harmony between nations, but as early as 1908 there were nationalistic conflicts, commercial interference and disputes over amateur status.

During the 19th century plebian sports such as folk football had virtually been eliminated by legal prohibitions. During the 20th century, new patterns of recreation for the working classes developed. Preoccupied with the moral character of workers' activities inside and outside the factory, churches, schools, local government, industry and the military established clubs to provide them with respectable, organized sports.

Golfers

Many professional football clubs had religious or industrial origins. Socio-religious organizations such as the Young Men's Christian Association (YMCA) and the Boy Scouts introduced drill, gymnastic exercises and sports that demanded strict control of the body, to promote the "habits of obedience, smartness and order" that were required for work in the factory and action on the field of battle.

There was also growing interest in sport in political circles. The Boer War had shown how few British recruits were physically fit. Success on the playing fields was related to success on the battlefields of the Empire. But the imperialist ideology of "training mind and body for the Empire's need" was applied differently to young men from different social classes: while public schoolboys were being urged to "play up and play the game" to develop their initiative and leadership qualities for military conquest abroad, working-class youths were being encouraged to develop fitness and alertness for following orders. Sport could induce habits of deference as well as dominance.

Many sports clubs had an exclusively middle- and upper-class membership; polo and yachting clubs, for example, restricted membership and charged fees only the rich could afford. Golf was also a predominantly upper- and middle-class game though there were some municipal golf courses. Tennis proliferated in the garden suburbs, and water sports, riding and other field sports were popular with the middle classes. There were sports available for people from all backgrounds, such as cycling, rambling and athletics as well as football, cricket and rugby, but they took place in separate clubs for people with different class backgrounds. There was little mixed-class sport of any sort.

Women and sport

There was a popular idea that women were unsuited to take part in vigorous sports. Only moderate exercise, without overindulgence or risk of strain, was considered suitable for females and their potential to have healthy children. They might enjoy sports such as tennis and gymnastics, which were considered appropriate for women, or remedial and therapeutic forms of exercise, but women faced serious opposition and harsh ridicule if they wanted to participate in traditional male sports, which were supposed to have disabling and de-sexing characteristics.

Nevertheless, the first two decades of the 20th century saw the gradual expansion of a variety of female sports. Croquet, tennis, golf, badminton and skating were all fashionable middle-class sports. Cycling allowed women a new physical independence, and symbolized their revolt against the restrictions of tight-lacing. Women's participation in hockey, netball, lacrosse, rounders, gymnastics, cricket, athletics and swimming was possible only because they were played in "ladylike" fashion. These sports were played separately from the sports of men, in clubs, girls' schools, universities and colleges, and so did not constitute a direct challenge to men. In urban areas many women's sports clubs were attached to polytechnics and attracted young working women from nearby shops and offices. The "Poly" girls became the pin-ups of the sporting world, providing the impetus for a more general acceptance of female sport and a gradual increase in working-class participation. As sport became increasingly popular, the public image of the new sportswoman was reproduced elsewhere.

The modern Olympics remained a bastion of male sporting privilege and an unambiguous celebration of male supremacy and physical prowess. Prolonged struggle and protest were required before women were officially permitted to take part. In 1908 only 36 women competed, in lawn tennis, archery, figure skating and yachting; there were 2,023 male athletes.

The rise of spectator sports

British football, as it developed in the state school system and clubs, transformed ideas about what modern sport means. By 1910 there were 300,000 football players in 12,000 clubs registered with the Football Association (FA). After 1900, market forces increasingly replaced paternalism, and professional football was promoted by business patrons who saw opportunities to exploit the new mass demand for entertainment. Football led the way toward the general commercialization of sport. Larger, professional clubs were successful commercial ventures, attracting huge crowds and deriving their revenue from gate money and sales of food and drinks. The FA Cup Final attracted enormous numbers of spectators: 120,000 in 1913. Watching professional football became central to the culture of the working classes, and spectators deeply concerned for victory and vociferously partisan, gave it a unique character. The popularity of football developed into a mania. Professional football teams from Britain toured abroad. Players and coaches became emissaries of the game, transmitting skills around the world.

Other spectator sports had also become highly popular and profitable. In 1913 there were 1-kilometer (half-mile) queues on Men's finals day at the Wimbledon Tennis Championships, and touts were selling £1 tickets for £10. The popularity of spectator sport had a knock-on effect, acting as an incentive for people to participate themselves, and for entrepreneurs to profit from sales of sports equipment, clothing and medication. Working-class people avidly followed sports of all kinds: by 1900 there were 25 sporting newspapers in London alone and daily papers were sprouting sports pages. A foreign visitor declared, "All is sport in England.... It is sucked in with the mother's milk."

By World War I sport had become a major industry, and the essential characteristics of professional sport were established. There were separate amateur and professional leagues and competitions, sporting heroes and unruly fan behavior. Sport was increasingly used as a publicity medium by politicians and other public figures. Those who owned sport wielded power: most professional players were working-class, owned and controlled, bought and sold, and subjected to strict disciplinary procedures imposed by wealthy businessmen. There were struggles

The Spread of Boxing

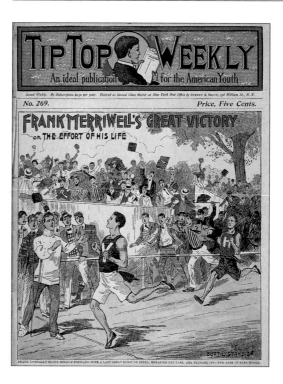

◄ The American magazine *Tip Top Weekly* celebrated the middle-class ethos of the amateur sporting endeavor in this cover illustration. The ideal, that participation and fair play was more important than victory, derived from the British public-school tradition, but even there, winning remained a significant objective.

between players and employers over the minimum wage and the transfer system, and though players' unions were formed, the players nonetheless remained in a weak position.

Popular spectator sport was promoted as an escape from the hardships and poverty of working-class life, and became an extremely effective vehicle of social control. The ruling classes valued it as a socially more acceptable pursuit than political or criminal activities, but working men found football exciting. Its hard physical contact reflected the tough life they were accustomed to. It became an integral part of their lives, and an important setting for male bonding.

► The British Soccer club Manchester United in its FA Cup-winning year of 1909. As in most football clubs of this period, the players were professionals, coming from a working-class background, but the club was in the hands of a local brewing magnate. It was unusual for such a club to be controlled by one man: by 1914 most British clubs were limited-liability companies, with a wide range of shareholders.

Boxing was encouraged at amateur level by moralists who argued for the benefits it would bestow on working-class boys: "Like dancing, boxing should be rescued from its evil associations and its educational force put to do moral work. At best, it is indeed a manly art, a separate school for quickness of hand and eye, decision, 'force of will' and self-control. The moment this is lost, stinging punishment follows. Hence it is the surest way of all cures for excessive irascibility and has been found to have a most beneficial effect upon the peevish or unmanly disposition."

The amateur sport was organized and given new rules in Britain in 1880, and in the United States four years later. Professional boxing before 1914 in the United States was dominated by Irish and European immigrants, although Joe Gans and Jack Johnson were black fighters who became world champions in the early 1900s despite encountering strong racial prejudice.

◄ An impromptu boxing match in 1905.

◄ Charlie Murphy, the American bicycle champion, was the first man to cycle one mile (1.6 km) in 60 seconds, and won a brief celebrity for his achievement. The interest in such sporting records as achievements in their own right, distinct from the fact of winning or losing, was developed through the sporting press and became particularly important in the 1920s.

BIOGRAPHIES

Adler, Alfred 1870–1937

Austrian psychiatrist who founded Individual Psychology and was strongly influenced by his social concern. Studied medicine in Vienna and became a prominent member of Freud's psycho-analytical group before differences led to a split in 1911. Emphasizing social factors in personality development rather than sexual factors, unlike Freud, Adler established his school of Individual Psychology. He asserted that people are motivated more by goals and expectations, even though they may be unobtainable (fictional finalism), than by their past, thus creating their own personality. The principal human goal is perfection; as this is patently unachievable, inferiority feelings arise. Adler believed the unique way in which an individual strives for perfection, the "style of life", forms in early childhood. He insisted that the individual should be considered within the social context and that perfection can be approached only by people collectively in cooperation.

Agnelli, Giovanni 1866–1945

Italian industrialist. Educated at military academy and an officer in the 1880s, he founded FIAT (Fabbricca Italiana Automobile Torino) in Turin in 1899. Under Agnelli the company diversified production to include airplanes, buses, tractors, diesel engines and ball-bearings with the acquisition of the RIV company (1907). Fiat soon developed an international reputation, becoming Italy's biggest motor company and during World War I adapted to military needs, running its large Turin plants at full capacity. Agnelli became president of Fiat in 1920. He employed over 30,000 people and favored a paternalistic form of leadership with an emphasis on workers' welfare. However, when militant workers occupied the factory in 1921, he retired and left them to it, soon to return to his post at their urgent request. He supported Mussolini, who made him a senator in 1923. Fiat was again the chief military supplier in World War II, and in April 1945, the Italian Committee of National Liberation removed Agnelli and his top executives from control, although his family later maintained a role in the running of the company.

Arbuckle, Roscoe "Fatty" 1887–1933

US film actor, director and screenwriter. Vaudeville preceded comedy one-reelers for Selig Polyscope, from 1907. In 1913 came the move to Sennett's Keystone Cops and starring roles with Chaplin, Conklin and Mabel Normand. By 1916 he was writing and directing himself; in 1917 he went independent. A large, baby-faced, remarkably agile man, he was one of Hollywood's most popular stars when his career ended in a brutal sex scandal (1921). He later directed pseudonymously but his attempts to perform were doomed.

Arden, Elizabeth 1878–1966

Canadian-born US businesswoman. Born Florence Nightingale Graham, she studied nursing before opening her first beauty salon on New York's Fifth Avenue in 1909. She eventually became one of the world's leading producers of beauty aids, selling over 300 different items and owning two luxury beauty resorts at her death. She was a pioneer in the advertising of cosmetics.

Asquith, Herbert H. 1852–1928

British prime minister. In 1886, Asquith was elected to the House of Commons as a Liberal. A barrister by profession, in 1887 he defended the Irish nationalist Parnell. He served as home secretary from 1892 to 1895, but was in opposition from 1895 to 1905. During this period, he advocated free trade, and sided with the imperialist wing of the party during the South African (Boer) War (1899–1902). He became Chancellor of the Exchequer in 1905, and prime minister in 1908. In 1911, he abolished the House of Lords' right of veto, after they had rejected a radical budget. In 1912, he introduced an Irish Home Rule Bill. Both unionists and nationalists then joined paramilitary organizations in Ireland, and army officers at the Curragh near Dublin declared that they would not coerce Ulster into becoming a self-governing dominion. The bill was suspended when World War I broke out. In 1915, he became head of a coalition government, and shortly after, a succession of crises occurred. The Dardanelles campaign failed, and there was still no breakthrough on the western front. 1916 saw both the Easter Rising in Dublin and the battle of the Somme, in which the British lost 500,000 men, and Asquith resigned. He entered the House of Lords in 1925, later received the Order of the Garter, and resigned the party leadership in 1926. In his retirement he wrote several books.

Baekeland, Leo Hendrik 1863–1944

Belgian-US chemist, whose name is commemorated in "Bakelite", the first major industrial plastic. He settled in the USA in 1889, initially as chemist to a photographic manufacturer. While there, he developed a fast-printing (Velox) photographic printing paper which he made and sold through his Nepara Chemical Company: this he sold to George Eastman for 1 million dollars in 1898. He then turned to electrochemistry and, in seeking a substitute for shellac, a widely used insulator, studied the reaction product of phenol and formaldehyde, normally a useless conglomerate. He discovered that if the reaction is conducted at raised pressure an easily molded resin is obtained, eminently suitable for electrical equipment. This he manufactured worldwide through his Bakelite Corporation, subsequently merged into Union Carbide and Carbon Corporation (1939).

Balla, Giacomo 1871–1958

Italian painter. A lithographer from 1883, he attended Turin Academy, and in 1900, in Paris, encountered Neo-Impressionism, and came under the influence of the poet Marinetti, progenitor of Futurism. In 1910 Balla signed the manifesto of Futurist painting. *La Lampe Électrique* (1909) embraces Futurist principles, but Balla's work, although innovative, remained lyrical, like *Dynamism of a Dog on a Leash* (1912). He also moved further than his fellows into Abstraction. In 1916 he was the acknowledged leader of the new Futurist movement, but his work lost its force, and he reverted to a traditional, decorative style.

Baring, John 1863–1929

British merchant banker. He entered Baring Brothers merchant bank, his family firm, in 1883 and was made a full partner in 1890. Baring played a major role in the successful reconstruction and recovery of the house after the Baring Crisis of 1890, when the bank's collapse was averted only by the intervention of the Bank of England, and in its incorporation as Baring Brothers and Co., Ltd. Succeeding to the title Lord Revelstoke in 1897, he became senior director of the bank in 1901. He cultivated strong overseas connections, the house specializing in the issue of loan stock in London for governments, municipalities and railway companies in the Americas and Russia. After World War I, issues and commercial credit were moved away from there and toward Europe. Revelstoke was director of the Bank of England and advisor to governments, the Treasury and the Foreign Office. British representative at the Committee of Experts to renew the Dawes Plan in 1929, he advocated the establishment of the Bank for International Settlements.

Bartók, Béla 1881–1945

Hungarian composer. Bartók's mother taught him piano from the age of five; he began to compose at nine, and studied at the Budapest Academy (1898–1903). His earliest compositions were Straussian in flavor – *Also Sprach Zarathustra*, heard in 1902, was a revelation to him. He also became a nationalist, and began to notate Hungarian folk songs. In 1905 his lifelong collaboration with Zoltan Kodály began; they recorded thousands of folk-songs from Europe and elsewhere. This music led Bartók to employ pentatonic and modal systems in his own music. His music was unpopular until 1917, when his ballet *The Wooden Prince*, followed by *Bluebeard's Castle* (1918), brought him fame. *The Miraculous Mandarin* (1926) initially offended audiences with its sexually explicit and farcical subject-matter. In 1927–28 Bartók toured the USA, playing his own and Kodály's music. His palindromic "Brückenform" is exemplified in the superb choral *Cantata profana* (1930). In 1940, devastated by his mother's death, as his tragic

Sixth Quartet shows, he moved to the USA, but although awarded a doctorate, and a post researching folk-music, he missed public acceptance, and his home; in 1942 a blood disease was diagnosed, and he died before completing his third piano concerto.

Becquerel, Antoine Henri 1852–1908

French physicist remembered chiefly for his discovery of radioactivity. He entered the École Polytechnique in 1872, received his doctorate in 1888 for a thesis on the absorption of light and in 1895 was appointed professor. From 1882 to 1892 Becquerel investigated the phenomena of phosphorescence and fluorescence and took an immediate interest in the X-rays discovered by W.K. Röntgen in 1895. He supposed that strongly fluorescent substances, like certain uranium salts, might emit X-rays and found that they did in fact produce penetrating rays that blackened a photographic plate, but these were not X-rays. They were in fact not strictly waves but streams of electrically charged particles. In 1898 Marie Curie named this phenomenon radioactivity. In 1903 Becquerel shared the Nobel Prize for Physics with Marie and Pierre Curie.

Behrens, Peter 1868–1940

German architect and designer. Behrens, then a painter, joined the Darmstadt artists' colony in 1900. Influenced by William Morris, he believed in the esthetic integration of an environment, and that national pride and dignity could be fostered by architecture. Co-founder of the *Deutscher Werkbund* (1907), in 1909 he built Germany's first steel-and-glass building, the AEG (Berlin) turbine factory. From 1920, as director of the Vienna Academy School of Architecture, he produced International Modern white cuboid buildings; he held a post at the Berlin Academy under the Nazis. Behrens lacked vision, but was an important teacher of more talented architects.

Berg, Alban 1885–1935

Austrian composer. Berg turned from literature to music in his teens, and in 1904 met Schoenberg, who taught him and remained, with Mahler, a lifelong influence. His first mature works (1907–10) were a piano sonata, four songs and a string quartet. In 1913 uproar broke out at the première of two of his *Altenberglieder*, with lyrics taken from postcards sent by the poet Peter Altenberg. Mahler's widow helped to publish *Wozzeck* (1922), the first atonal opera; it was hailed as a masterwork. His *Lyric Suite* (1925–6) contains musically-coded "messages" to his mistress. Berg traveled widely, and in 1930 was elected to the Prussian Academy of Arts, but he refused a teaching post under the Nazis. His last and perhaps finest work, the lyrical *Violin Concerto* (1935) was premièred posthumously.

Bernhardt, Sarah (H. Bernard) 1844–1923

French actress. Educated at a convent school and for the stage at the Paris Conservatoire, Bernhardt, daughter of a Dutch courtesan, made her Comédie Française debut in 1862. Sacked after a row with a senior actress, she worked as a singer, had an illegitimate son by Prince Henri de Ligne, and organized a military hospital during the Franco-Prussian war, before returning to the Comédie Française in 1872; with two lead roles (Phèdre and Voltaire's *Zaïre*), achieving instant celebrity not only for the caliber of her acting but also for her physical and vocal beauty. In 1879 she formed her own company and toured, playing Phèdre in London and New York to international acclaim: 1881 saw her first performance of the classic "Lady with the Camellias". For most of the remainder of her life, Bernhardt lived in London, or touring the world. In 1893 she opened the *Théâtre Sarah Bernhardt* in Paris. Also a painter and sculptor, she played almost all the great classic roles, including *Hamlet*; "the Divine Sarah" was as great in comedy as tragedy. She continued to act even after a leg amputation, because of gangrene, in 1915. *L'Art du Théâtre*, her treatise on acting, was published in 1923.

Bernstein, Eduard 1850-1932

German Social Democrat "father of revisionism", who inspired the German SPD to its revisionist position of 1920, and the fleeting establishment of a democratic state.Bernstein, a bank clerk who joined the SPD in 1872, believed in German unity and democracy; Bismarck's repressive anti-socialist legislation pushed him to a radical stance.Expelled from Germany and Switzerland, he continued (from 1888) to publish the underground SPD paper from London, where he got to know Engels and the Fabians. Back in Germany from 1901, he expounded his theory of Socialism as a natural manifestation of inborn human liberalism, and his disagreement with Marx vis a vis the inevitability of the collapse of capitalism and the utter undesirability of the bourgeoisie; he espoused gradualism, and his party followed him, rejecting Kautsky's advocacy of radical Marxism. A member of parliament from 1902 to 1928, Bernstein quit the SPD in protest at their support of World War l, returning postwar to become minister of finance.

Bethmann-Hollweg, Theobald 1856–1921

German imperial chancellor. In 1905, Bethmann-Hollweg was appointed Prussian minister of the interior. In 1907 he was state secretary in the imperial interior office, and in 1909, he became chancellor. He failed to end naval rivalry with Britain, and Germany's actions in the third Moroccan crisis of 1911 led to a British guarantee of military assistance to France. Bethmann-Hollweg did, however, in conjunction with Britain, manage to prevent the escalation of the Balkan wars into a confrontation between Austria-Hungary and Russia. He expanded the army, and did not oppose the Austro-Hungarian action against Serbia in 1914, which preceded World War I. Bethmann-Hollweg opposed the introduction of unrestricted submarine warfare and in 1916 tried to obtain US mediation. In 1917, he announced plans for electoral reform and was forced to resign.

Binet, Alfred 1857-1911

French pioneer of experimental psychology and developer of IQ tests. In 1878 Binet turned from the study of law to psychology, initially concentrating on hypnotism. In 1892 he began work in a research laboratory at the Sorbonne, becoming its director in 1894. He specialized in child study, working first with his own daughters as subjects; his collaborator was the educational psychologist Théodore Simon. In 1895 Binet co-founded the journal *L'Anneé psychologique*. In 1905 the first Binet-Simon intelligence tests were conducted, and the second series in 1908. In 1911 their introduction of the concept of "mental age" permitted the measurement of "IQ". Their findings were published in "A Method of Measuring the Development of Young Children" (1913). Binet was the first to attempt a precise measurement of intelligence, and the first to include in such tests questions demanding cognition.

Birkeland, Kristian 1867–1917

Norwegian inventor (with Samuel Eyde) of the first commercially successful process for the fixation of atmospheric nitrogen. He was appointed professor of physics at Christiania University in 1898. Research on the aurora borealis led him to experiments with electric discharges through gases. In 1784 Henry Cavendish had showed that the nitrogen and the oxygen of the air combine in an electric spark and in 1901 Birkeland and Eyde, an engineer, joined forces to develop this as a viable industrial process. In 1905 they founded the now well-known Norsk Hydro-Elektrisk Kvaelstofaktieselskab. They continued manufacture until the early 1920s when the process was displaced by one invented by Fritz Haber.

Boccioni, Umberto 1882–1916

Italian painter and sculptor. Boccioni, whose first ambition was journalism, began painting in 1900, in Rome, under the tutelage of Giacomo Balla. In 1907 he moved to Milan and worked as a commercial artist. He joined the *Famiglia Artistica* group, meeting Marinetti, and was the main writer of two Futurist art manifestos (1910, 1912). In 1911, with other Futurists, he visited Paris and met avant-garde artists; he also painted *The City Rises*, using brushwork to express animation. Energy imbued Boccioni's work – he saw even still objects as moving. *Unique Form of Continuity in Space* (1913) exemplifies this perception.

▲ Bernhard H. Bülow

▲ Andrew Carnegie

▲ Vernon and Irene Castle

Bohr, Niels 1885–1962

Danish physicist who applied Planck's quantum theory to atomic structure. He studied physics in Copenhagen and in 1912 went to England to work with Ernest Rutherford, who had proposed a model of the atom in which negative electrons circled a positive nucleus. This failed to explain why the electrons did not simply spiral down into the nucleus, losing energy. Bohr proposed that the electrons' orbital momentum is quantized, and that radiation is emitted only when an electron jumps from one orbit to another. In 1916 he returned to Copenhagen and became director of a new Institute for Theoretical Physics, soon a leading international center. He was awarded a Nobel prize in 1922. In 1943 he left German- occupied Denmark and went to Britain, and then to the USA, to advise on the Manhattan atomic bomb project. In the 1950s he was concerned with establishing CERN.

Bonnard, Pierre 1867–1947

French painter. After failing law examinations, Bonnard studied art in Paris. In 1890 he took a studio with Vuillard and Denis, exhibited in 1891, and produced many illustrations, some for *La Revue Blanche*, and prints; in 1894 he met Vollard, who published his lithographs and, in 1896 had his first one-man show. He was a member of *Les Nabis*, known as *Le Nabi Japonard* from his fondness for Japanese art. By 1905 he was painting exclusively, producing the sunlit interiors for which he is renowned, usually featuring the female figure, like *The Breakfast* (1907). Bonnard made dazzling use of color and light, but painted from memory. His style was christened "Intimism" for his use of domestic scenes. From 1910 he worked increasingly in the Midi, and his colors became more vivid, as in *Getting Out of the Bath* (1930).

Bragg, William Henry 1862–1942 and William Lawrence 1890–1971

British physicists, father and son, who pioneered the application of X-ray diffraction to the determination of crystal structure. After graduating at Cambridge, W.H. Bragg was appointed professor of mathematics and physics at Adelaide University (1886). While he was there he began to investigate the newly discovered X-rays and alpha particles. In 1912, after Bragg had taken a chair in physics at Leeds, Max von Laue announced his discovery that X-rays can be diffracted by crystals. Bragg immediately saw that this could be used to work out the exact positions of atoms and ions in a crystal lattice. He and his son, W.L. Bragg (then a research student at Cambridge), used X-ray diffraction to reveal the structure of many single crystals. In 1915 they shared the Nobel Prize for Physics. In 1923 W.H. Bragg became director of the Royal Institution, London, an appointment to which his son succeeded (1953–66).

Brancusi, Constantin 1876–1957

Romanian sculptor. Already a fine woodcarver, in 1898 he entered the Bucharest School of Fine Arts. In 1904, influenced by Rodin, he went to Paris, and worked at the Ecole des Beaux-Arts. Breaking with custom in doing his own carving, and painstaking in his pursuit of the essence of things, with *The Prayer* (1907), Brancusi began to produce more abstract forms, including the superb *The Kiss* (1908). In 1913 his work appeared in the American Armory Show. From 1918 he produced several *Endless Columns*, culminating in 1937 in one 30m (100ft) high, in a Romanian park. These, like his bird sculptures, well expressed his spiritual aspiration. Works like *Caryatid* (1915), and *Socrates* (1923), showed his love of primitive art. Brancusi was a towering figure, who influenced such great artists as Epstein, and Gaudier-Brzeska.

Braque, Georges 1882–1963

French painter and co-founder of Cubism. After attending Le Havre Art School, in 1900 Braque moved to Paris, where from 1902 to 1904 he studied at the Académie Humbert. In 1906 his work appeared in a Fauvist exhibition. The Cézanne Retrospective (1907) impressed him deeply. In 1907 he began a close collaboration with Picasso, to last until 1914, which fathered Cubism. In 1908 H. Kahnweiler put on a Braque one-man show. In 1910, Braque began to use collage. The *Canéphores*, a series of paintings of women with fruit and flowers, were produced in the 1920s. By 1930, Braque was an internationally acknowledged master of still life, with frequent retrospectives held worldwide. He began a series of drawings in white on black ceramic, influenced by Greek art. From 1948 to 1955 he painted the eight *Ateliers*, probably his finest work. In 1961 he became the first living artist to be exhibited in the Louvre.

Bülow, Bernhard H. 1849–1929

German politician. In 1897 Bülow, a diplomat, became foreign secretary under Kaiser Wilhelm. He secured territories in the Pacific, and extended German influence in the Middle East. In 1900, he was promoted to chancellor, overseeing the formation of the Triple Entente between France, Britain and Russia. Germany alienated Britain, adopting a proBoer stance in the South African War, and enlarging its navy to rival that of Britain. In an attempt to break the Anglo-French Entente of 1904, Germany supported Moroccan independence in 1905. Russia allied with Britain and France in 1907, and Russo-German relationships were irrevocably damaged when Bülow forced Russia to accept the Austro-Hungarian annexation of Bosnia-Herzegovina. He was dismissed in 1909, after failing to vet the transcript of the Kaiser's interview with the British newpaper the *Daily Telegraph*, in which he had made remarks about anti-English opinion in Germany.

Calmette, Léon Charles Albert 1863–1933 and Guérin, Camille 1872–1961

French bacteriologists who developed the BCG (Bacille Calmette-Guérin) vaccine for protection against tuberculosis. Calmette qualified in medicine in Paris before serving in the French Navy (1883–90) to study the incidence of malaria and sleeping sickness in Gabon. In 1889 he investigated bubonic plague in Oporto before moving to Saigon to establish a Pasteur Institute there (1891), developing vaccines against plague and snakebite. In 1895 he returned to France to found another Pasteur Institute in Lille. In 1917 he was appointed administrative head of the Pasteur Institute in Paris, where he spent the rest of his working life. His most important work was done over the years 1906–24 when, with Guérin, he developed an effective vaccine against tuberculosis. BCG was dramatically effective, reducing the incidence of the disease by 80 percent and giving protection for up to ten years.

Carnegie, Andrew 1835–1919

Scottish-born US steel industralist. His family emigrated to Pittsburgh in 1848. Carnegie worked in menial positions for the Pennsylvania Railroad Co. (1853–65), became superintendent of the Pittsburgh railroad division and introduced sleeping cars. He successfully invested his savings into oil lands in 1864 and left the railroad in 1865, turning his attention to iron, steel, oil and other business interests. In 1868 Carnegie built the Union Iron Mills at Pittsburgh and in 1873, began to specialize in steel, owning the largest mill in the US. His business operations grew and prospered as he bought sources of supply of raw materials, and transportation lines, and introduced new methods and technology. In 1901 he retired and sold his interests, which became the United States Steel Corporation, to the baker, J.P. Morgan, for $400 million. He devoted his retirement to philanthropy, believing in the distribution to others of the surplus wealth of the rich few. He provided for public libraries throughout the USA and Britain, endowed trusts and institutions and pension funds, Hero Funds and large gifts to Scottish and American Universities.

Castle, Vernon (1887–1918) and Irene (1893–1969)

US husband-and-wife dancing team. They were married in 1911 and achieved world fame, creating the one-step and the turkey trot and bringing the glide, hesitation waltz, cast;e [p;la. cast;e wa;l. tango, maxixe and bunny hug to a wider audience through their exhibition dancing and a book, *Modern Dancing* (1914). Vernon was killed in an airplane accident while training cadet pilots during World War I.

Marc Chagall

Cixi

Joseph Conrad

Cézanne, Paul 1839–1906

French painter. Cézanne studied art in Paris, and his early work was crude, with often violent subjects, and he was repeatedly rejected by the Salon, exhibiting instead at the *Salon des Refusés* (1863). He met Renoir and Monet (1867–68), and from 1872 worked with Pissarro. He had works in the Impressionist Exhibitions of 1874 and 1876. From then, he worked mainly in Provence, with its brilliant light and dark foliage, producing many paintings of Mont Ste Victoire. Public acclaim came in the 1880s and in 1890 he exhibited in Brussels with *Les Vingt*. Vollard set up his first one-man show in 1895. Although he had virtually no public career, Cézanne pursued his art assiduously. He rejected Realism and Impressionism, and broke forms into facets, using color and modeling with care, seeking an underlying abstract structure. The posthumous Retrospective of 1907 was a great influence on the whole of 20th-century art.

Chagall, Marc 1889–1985

Russian-Jewish-born French painter. Introduced to modern French art by his teacher Léon Bakst, Chagall, already producing paintings of Jewish life, encountered Cubism in Paris in 1910, and turned its methods to his own use, in works like *I and the Village* (1911). In 1915 , detained in his hometown of Vitebsk by the war, he married Bella Rosenfeld, subject of many of his paintings. Made Commissar of Fine Arts after the Revolution, he left in 1919 after conflict with Malevich, and designed for the Moscow State Jewish Theater. Back in Paris from 1923, Ambroise Vollard commissioned many illustrations, notably a series of etchings for Gogol's *Dead Souls*. 1930 saw the publication of his autobiography *Ma Vie*. In 1944 Bella died, and Chagall's sorrow was reflected in paintings like *Around Her* (1945); that year he also created designs for Stravinsky's *Firebird*. In the 1950s he took up sculpture and ceramics. He created the stained glass windows for the New York United Nations building (1964). Chagall's work was unique, using symbols from his Jewish heritage and his own poetic images to create works of ecstatic fantasy.

Chekhov, Anton 1860-1904

Russian dramatist and short-story writer. Chekhov's family moved in 1879 to Moscow, where in 1884 he qualified as a doctor and supported them all. He started writing comic tales to supplement his income; they became extremely popular, and serious writing overtook him, starting with "The Steppe" in 1888. As well as stories, he wrote a play, "Ivanov"; his reputation grew, but he was considered lacking in moral purpose. In 1890 he withdrew to the remote island of Sakhalin, where he studied social conditions, writing a thesis on his return. He helped to fight the cholera epidemic of 1892-93; and in 1889 he

wrote "The Wood Demon", later converted to "Uncle Vanya". In 1892 he bought a country house, becoming the local doctor and philanthropist. "The Seagull" was first, unsuccessfully, performed in 1896, finding success in Moscow in 1898. Afflicted from 1897 with TB, in 1899 he built a villa in Yalta and wintered there or in the South of France. Now famous, he also sold his copyrights to the publisher A.F. Marx for a derisory sum, and a 10-volume edition of his work appeared forthwith. Chekhov continued to produce great plays, like "Three Sisters" (1900-01) and "The Cherry Orchard" (1903–04); he dealt habitually with the tension between the life of the soul and worldly contingency. He intended his drama as comedy, and disliked its often heavy treatment. International acclaim came after his death.

Cixi 1834(5)–1908

Chinese Empress-Dowager and regent, who dominated the last years of the Manchu dynasty. Cixi, the beautiful daughter of a minor official, became concubine to the emperor Xianfeng and bore the son, Tongzhi, who succeeded him in 1861, aged five. Cixi, as co-regent, with the late emperor's chief wife, Cuan, and at the instigation of his brother, Prince Gong, made some moves toward modernization, and struck at government corruption. After the emperor's early (and questionable) death in 1875, Cixi adopted his heir, her three-year-old nephew, and remained regent. In 1881 Cuan died, and in 1884 Cixi crushed Gong's attempts at further westernization and imprisoned him, remaining sole regent. In 1890 she moved to the splendid summer palace she had had rebuilt using money intended for the renovation and expansion of the Chinese navy. Corruption proliferated as Cixi sold high-ranking posts. In 1898 the emperor attempted to re-establish the process of modernization, but Cixi led a coup to overthrow him, and put him under house arrest. Her increasingly entrenched reactionary and isolationist position probably caused the Boxer Rebellion; after her defeat, in 1902, she finally and belatedly began to introduce Gong's reformist plans. As Cixi lay on her deathbed, the emperor died, probably poisoned at her command.

Conrad (Korzeniowski), Joseph 1857–1924

Polish English writer. Son of a revolutionary Polish poet, and orphaned in 1869, Conrad always admired England, and read English books as a child, although it was his third language. In 1874 he became a sailor, qualifying in 1886 as master seaman. He studied English, and in 1884 became a British subject. His first novel, *Almayer's Folly* (1895) shows a mature command of English; in 1896 he settled in Kent. The brilliant novels *Lord Jim* (1900) and *Nostromo* (1904) show the power and beauty of his style, and the depth and complexity

of plot and character which mark his work out. In 1910 he suffered a mental breakdown; his second political novel, *Under Western Eyes*, appeared the following year. Conrad wrote of men put to the utmost test; the settings are often menacing – the sea, the jungle, even the world of political espionage – but the real threat comes from the "heart of darkness" within.

Coolidge, William D. 1873–1975

US industrial scientist, remembered for the development of ductile tungsten and the hot-cathode X-ray tube. He studied electrical engineering at MIT, physics at Leipzig and chemistry once again at MIT; he taught at both establishments. In 1905 he joined the General Electric Research Laboratory at Schenectady, New York, eventually becoming its director (1932–61). He quickly had a major success. An urgent need of the day was to draw the very refractory metal tungsten into wires fine enough to use as filaments in electric lamps. This he succeeded in doing in 1908. In 1914 the invention reduced the cost of electric light in the United States alone by around two billion dollars. His second major invention, in 1913, was an X-ray tube in which current and voltage can be varied independently; his design formed the basis of modern X-ray tubes.

Croce, Benedetto 1866-1952

Italian philosopher and historian. Croce, who came from a traditionally conservative background, was orphaned in 1883 as the result of an earthquake. He left university without graduating, and later, a self-taught solitary, founded and edited the journal *La Critica* (1903-44). His major work, the four-part *Philosophy of the Spirit* (1902-17), presented a fourfold division of human activity: mental, comprised of the intuitive (1902), covering esthetics, and the conceptual (1909), covering logic; and practical (1909), comprised of the particular, covering economics, and the universal, covering ethics. These were all properties of the immanent spirit. Part IV (1917) dealt with the theory of history as the only possible key to understanding the nature of human consciousness and the only way to observe the operation of spirit; Croce stated that consciousness was non-determined; he expanded on this in *History as Thought and Action* (1938). He initially supported fascism, seeing in it a possible counter to the violence of postwar leftism; but after 1925 he led the opposition to it worldwide. Seen as Italy's moral and ethical mentor, he inspired his country's democracy after World War II. He then returned to solitary study; he established a research center "The Italian Institute for Historical Studies" in his own library. Massively influential, he defined works of art as vehicles communicating a transcendent "art"; he valued above all liberty, and the "true and creative human spirit".

▲ Marie Curie

▲ Harvey Williams Cushing

▲ Clause Debussy

Curie, Marie 1867–1934 and Pierre 1859–1906

French pioneers in the phenomenon of radioactivity. Marie Sklodowska, daughter of a Warsaw physics teacher, worked as a governess before entering the Sorbonne in 1891 to study physics and mathematics. There she met, and soon married (1897), Pierre Curie, director of laboratory work of the newly founded École Municipale de Physique et Chimie. Both were intensely interested in the newly discovered phemonena of X-rays and radioactivity. They decided to collaborate in a search for substances with properties similar to those of uranium. The discovery in 1898 of polonium and radium brought fame to both. In 1904 Pierre was appointed professor of physics in the Sorbonne but, tragically, was killed in a street accident in 1906. Marie succeeded to his chair, and was awarded a Nobel Prize for Chemistry in 1911.

Cushing, Harvey Williams 1869–1939

US physician, founder of modern neurosurgery. After qualifying in 1895 he practiced general surgery before going to work with the Swiss surgeon E.T. Kocher. This aroused his interest in neurosurgery and he spent some time with C.S. Sherrington in Oxford before returning to the USA. There he spent 30 years developing new techniques of brain surgery, in which there had hitherto been a depressing lack of success. They involved meticulous attention to preoperative diagnosis and readiness to carry out operations lasting many hours. He made a study of the pituitary gland, inaccessibly situated at the base of the brain, and showed a particular form of wasting disease (Cushing's Syndrome) to be associated with a tumor of the pituitary.

Debussy, Claude 1862–1918

French composer. Debussy began to study piano in 1871 with a pupil of Chopin. In 1872 he entered the Paris Conservatoire, and in 1884 won the Prix de Rome – but absconded from Rome and returned to Paris; his first major work, *La Demoiselle élue*, was completed in 1888, when he fell for a time under Wagner's influence; Debussy's more lasting influences were gamelan music, Mussorgsky, and Satie. *Prélude à l'après-midi d'un faune* (1894) earned him the epithet "Impressionist", though he repudiated this. Debussy's subtlety of touch did not lend itself to opera – *Pelleas et Mélisande* (1902) was his only successful opera. As well as the poetry of Mallarmé, Maeterlinck and others, Debussy was inspired by painting, as in *La Mer* (1905). The *Préludes* (1910–13) contain some of his best-known pieces, like *The Sunken Cathedral*. Debussy retained the discipline of the classical tradition, but introduced unusual harmonic procedures, employed chromaticism and the whole-tone scale, and employed orchestral color as a structural element in itself.

De Chirico, Giorgio 1888–1978

Italian painter. Born in Greece, de Chirico studied engineering, then art, in Athens and Munich, where his family settled in 1906. *The Enigma of the Oracle* (1910), painted in Milan, is an early imitation of Böcklin. In 1911 he was inspired by the colonnaded architecture and empty piazzas of Turin to depict a strange and menacing world in works like *Mystery and Melancholy of a Street* (1914) and *The Disquieting Muses* (1917), where he used flattened perspective, looming statues, sharp shadows, distant or peripheral figures, surreal images and deadened lighting, to convey a trancelike mood of muffled horror and pain. De Chirico influenced the Surrealists in his fluent articulation of "unconscious" imagery; he had in 1917 a short but important partnership with Carlos Carrà, founding the "Metaphysical School". After 1919, when he left Paris, he abandoned metaphysical imagery, except for a brief period, 1924–30, when he returned to Paris and to Surrealist acclaim.

De Coubertin, Pierre 1863–1937

French educationalist. He was responsible for the revival of the Olympic Games. One of the first Frenchmen to see the need for physical education, he studied educational methods in Europe and the USA. He visited the excavations of the Olympic site in Greece, and in 1892 began proposing a modern revival, believing international competition among amateurs would lessen world tension. He was president of the Olympic Committee from 1896 to 1925.

Delaunay, Robert 1885–1941

French painter. After apprenticeship to a stage designer, and studying painting in Paris, Delaunay became a full-time artist in 1904. His work was influenced by Fauvism and Cubism, and in 1907–08 he studied Neo-Impressionism and color theory; color was Delaunay's main concern. Delaunay painted many pictures of Paris, like *Eiffel Tower in Trees* (1909), and investigated the rhythmical effects of color. Apollinaire named his style Orphism. In 1911 he contributed to, and influenced, *Der Blaue Reiter*. He soon left natural forms for Abstraction and cosmic symbolism, eventually producing a "color disk", emotionally-related colored shapes, mosaic-like, on a wheel – *Disks: Sun and Moon* (1913). From 1921, when he painted a second *Eiffel Tower* series, his work lost its spontaneity. Delaunay influenced many other painters, especially Klee.

Delcassé, Théophile 1852–1923

French politician. Delcassé, a journalist, entered the Chamber of Deputies in 1885(?9). In 1893 he became under secretary for commerce, industry and colonies, and then minister for colonies (1894–95). Foreign minister from 1898 to 1905, he negotiated the Anglo-French Entente of 1904, and approached Russia, paving the way for the 1907 Triple Entente. As marine minister (1911–13), he made crucial arrangements for Anglo-French cooperation in case of war. He continued to exercise his diplomatic skills as ambassador to Russia and then foreign minister once again, from 1914 to 1915.

De Vries, Hugo 1848–1935

Dutch plant geneticist. He studied medicine in Holland and Germany and then taught botany in Amsterdam. With J. von Sachs, he investigated the physiology of water uptake in plants. In the 1870s he prepared for the Prussian Ministry of Agriculture a series of monographs on cultivated plants and this aroused his interest in heredity; he began breeding plants in 1892. He quickly found evidence for the 3:1 ratio discovered by Mendel in the 1850s. When he first came across Mendel's neglected work in 1900 he exerted himself to make it widely known. He took a particular interest in mutations (sports), plants showing atypical characteristics, and believed that these might cause evolution to proceed more rapidly than Darwinian principles suggested. In the event, however, this proved to be an overestimate.

Diaghilev, Sergei 1872–1929

Russian impresario. His vision of a ballet which integrated the best of music, painting, drama and dance revitalized an almost moribund art. In 1906 he left Russia for Paris, and in 1909 opened his first Ballets Russes season with Pavlova, Nijinsky and Fokine. His choreographers, Fokine and Massine, found a style of action ballet which relied heavily on mime. Leon Bakst, a friend from his student days, produced brilliant stage design for him. *The Firebird* (1910), *Petrushka* (1911) and *The Rite of Spring* (1913) were Diaghiler's major, and monumental, achievements.

Diesel, Rudolf 1858–1913

German engineer, remembered for the internal combustion engine that bears his name. He grew up in Paris and England, was later sent to an uncle in Augsburg and attended the Munich Technische Hochschule, where he studied thermodynamics. In 1880, while working in Paris, he experimented, unsuccessfully, with an expansion engine based on ammonia. About 1890 he conceived the idea of an engine in which ignition would be effected by the heat generated by highly compressing a fuel/air mixture. Having patented this (1892) he published a detailed account of its theory and design. On the strength of this, two German companies supported its development, Maschinenfabrik of Augsburg and Krupp of Essen. It was exhibited in Munich in 1898 and aroused worldwide interest. Diesel was soon a millionaire but did not live to see his invention fully exploited.

Isadora Duncan

Thomas Alva Edison

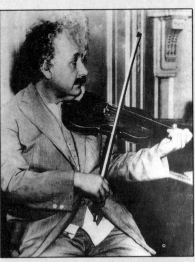

Albert Einstein

Duchamp, Marcel 1887–1968

French artist and art theorist. In 1911 Duchamp joined the Parisian *Section d'Or* group. His supra-Cubist and erotic *Nude Descending a Staircase* (1912) caused a furore at the New York Armory Show in 1913. He then turned to "ready-mades", signing a bottle-rack and a urinal in an attempt to eradicate estheticism, to pinpoint the artist as chooser, and admit chance to the field of art. He was important in Dadaism; his copy of the Mona Lisa, bearded and superscribed "L.H.O.O.Q." (*elle a chaud au cul*) became a symbol of the movement. From 1915 he lived in New York, where he produced his major work, the glass, metal and painted *The Bride Stripped Bare by her Bachelors, Even* (1915–23), unfinished. After this, he devoted himself to chess, producing optical devices, and propounding his artistic philosophy.

Duncan, Isadora 1878–1927

US dancer. Duncan rejected the rigidity of ballet in childhood; in 1894, after moving to England, she was popular as a dancer at parties. In 1905 she toured Europe. She aimed to bring expressive life to dance; her movements came from the solar plexus, and she worked with, not (as in classical ballet) against gravity; her dances were improvised. She modeled her flowing, draped costumes on those of ancient Greece. Tragedy struck in 1913 with the death of her two children, drowned when the car they were in ran into the Seine. In 1921, by invitation, she founded a school of dance in Moscow; in 1922, she left the USA. She married a Soviet poet, Yesenin; the marriage foundered, and in 1925 he killed himself. She lived a lonely and dissipated life in Nice until her own tragic death. Duncan's vision of the dancer as a creator has infused modern choreography.

Durkheim, Emile 1858–1917

French sociologist. Viewed as one of the founding fathers of modern sociology, Durkheim taught at the University of Bordeaux and later at the Sorbonne in Paris. Believing that sociologists should study social facts rather than individuals, he argued that society has its own reality which cannot be reduced to the actions and motives of its members. In this social environment, with its constraints and pressures, the individual is molded and shaped. Durkheim's classic works included *The Roles of Sociological Method* (1899), in which he demonstrated that social facts, such as the rule of law, are not dependent upon individuals or upon any specific act of enforcement. In *Suicide* (1897) the apparently individual act of taking one's life was explained in terms of different social settings, while in *The Elementary Forms of Religious Life* (1912) Durkheim suggested that the idea of society was celebrated in primitive religions and that objects only became sacred when they were seen to symbolize the community.

Edison, Thomas Alva 1847–1931

US inventor. He had little formal education, being regarded as retarded, and had a series of casual jobs as a youth. While working as a telegraph operator during the American Civil War, he read Michael Faraday's *Experimental Researches in Electricity* and gained a technical insight into the principles of electrical communication. In 1869 he invented the ticker-tape machine used to distribute stock exchange prices nationwide. This he sold for 30,000 US dollars, which he used to fund a research laboratory where from 1887 he devoted himself to invention. In all he lodged over 1,000 patents. His major inventions included the carbon-granule microphone, the phonograph, and (independently of Joseph Swan in Britain) the incandescent filament lamp. He also discovered the Edison effect (the one-directional passage of electricity between filaments in a vacuum lamp), which was later to become the basis of the thermionic tube (valve).

Ehrlich, Paul 1854–1915

German pioneer of hematology (the study of blood and blood forming organs) and founder of chemotherapy. He studied medicine at several German universities, finally graduating at Leipzig (1878). While a student, with the help of amline dyes, he discovered all the different types of white blood cells (1877–81). In 1881 he began to use methylene blue as a stain and the specificity of this for certain bacteria suggested to him that such substances might be used to destroy infective organisms without harming their host. In Liverpool, UK an arsenical drug had been used to treat trypanosomiasis without success. By systematically ringing the chemical changes in this he eventually discovered a compound effective against the organism that causes syphilis. This was marketed as Salvarsan.

Einstein, Albert 1879–1955

German-Swiss-US mathematical physicist who conceived the Theory of Relativity. In 1896 he entered the Polytechnic Academy, Zurich, after some delay because of his weakness in mathematics. On completing his studies he acquired Swiss citizenship and got a junior post in the Berne Patent Office. After the publication of the first of his remarkable papers on relativity, he held senior academic appointments in Zurich and Prague and in 1913 became director of the Kaiser Wilhelm Institute of Physics, Berlin. He traveled widely, and when Hitler came to power in 1933 he was in California, and never returned to Germany, taking up a position at the Institute of Advanced Study, Princeton. In 1905 he published three seminal papers on the Special Theory of Relativity: his General Theory was published in 1915. The latter gained him a Nobel prize in 1921. In 1952 he was offered, and declined, the presidency of Israel.

Escoffier, Georges Auguste 1846-1935

French chef of international renown. Escoffier, a blacksmith's son, began to cook aged 13 in his uncle's restaurant, and was apprenticed in 1865 to a famous Paris chef. An army chef in the Franco-Prussian war, he worked from 1883 as head chef at the Grand, Monte Carlo, for César Ritz. Using teamwork to enhance efficiency, Escoffier refined and simplified contemporary French cuisine. He also ran the Ritz kitchen in London. Regarded as the supreme chef of all time, he cooked for the great, for kings and emperors, and created dishes such as peach Melba, and Melba toast. From 1899 to 1919, still in partnership with Ritz, he was in charge of the Carlton Hotel kitchen. He was awarded the Légion d'Honneur in 1920. In his retirement, he helped run L'Hermitage restaurant. Escoffier wrote several cook books.

Ferranti, Sebastian Ziani de 1864–1930

British electrical engineer and inventor. Began his career at Siemens Brothers in 1881 and the following year patented the Ferranti alternator which gained him recognition among electrical engineers. In 1883 he established a business in London which manufactured electrical apparatus. In 1886 he became engineer for the Grosvenor Gallery Electric Supply Corporation. As chief electrician to the London Electric Supply Corporation, Ferranti planned and initiated the building of Deptford power station, which was to supply electricity to London north of the Thames; this was never completed, owing to the restrictive terms of the Electric Lighting Act of 1888. It was Ferranti who first proposed the use of alternating current, later universally employed. After 1892 he concentrated on his private business as a manufacturing engineer and founded Ferranti Ltd in 1896. Between 1882 and 1927 he took out 176 patents, and was a pioneer of high-voltage systems. He was the originator of long-distance transmission of high-power electrical current. He was made a Fellow of the Royal Society in 1927.

Fischer, Emil 1852–1919

German organic chemist. He was successively professor in Erlangen (1882), Würzburg (1885) and Berlin (1892–1919). The last was the major chair of chemistry in Germany and with the appointment went the promise of a new laboratory, completed in 1899. There he built up a flourishing school of chemistry with a particular interest in natural products. His earliest work was on nitrogenous substances known as purines – which include guanine and adenine, identified years later as constituents of DNA – and sugars. Later, he turned his attention to proteins, breaking them down into amino acids, and achieving some success in recombining them to form polypeptides. He received the Royal Society's Davy Medal in 1890, and was awarded a Nobel prize in 1902.

Sigmund Freud (right)

André Gide

Samuel Gompers

Ford, Henry 1863–1947

US automobile industrialist who constructed his first automobile in 1896, and set up the Ford Motor Company (1903) which in 1908 produced the Model T Ford, the first inexpensive standardized car, in production until 1927, and whose sales – 15 million – totaled half the world's auto output. Increased demand soon led to the introduction of mass-production methods, which enabled rapid expansion of the automobile industry worldwide. Ford also introduced a new $5 minimum wage for an eight-hour day and profit-sharing plans for employees. He produced motor vehicles for the government during World War I and survived the postwar crisis of 1920–21 but failed to cater to the changing car market, which now demanded style and speed as well as economy; the company lost its dominance of the car market under increasing competition especially from General Motors. In the 1930s Ford took a strong stand against organized labor. His political aspirations led him to run for the Senate as a Republican. He was a pacifist during both world wars and dispatched the "Peace Ship" to Scandinavia in 1915 to seek mediation. Most of his estate was placed in the Ford Foundation (a philanthropic institution) before his death. He resigned in 1919, in favor of his son.

Freud, Sigmund 1856–1939

Austrian pioneer of psychoanalysis. After graduating in medicine in Vienna in 1881 he specialized there for a time in neurology before going to work in Paris with the eminent French neurologist J.M. Charcot. Returning to Vienna, he set up in practice as a consultant on nervous disorders. Disillusioned with existing forms of treatment, notably hypnotism and electrotherapy, he developed a technique of "free association" to penetrate the patient's subconscious, thus founding what is now known as psychoanalysis. For a time (1906) he was associated with Alfred Adler and Carl Jung in the International Association for Psychoanalysis. Freud identified repressions of the subconscious with infantile sexuality. He believed in the significance of dreams and formulated the concept of the "id" – the subconscious drive – and the "ego", the executive force. His theories had a considerable effect on contemporary art and literature.

Funk, Casimir 1884–1967

Polish biochemist. After studying in Berne and London he became biochemist in the Pasteur Institute, Paris (1904–06). After appointments with the Cancer Hospital, London, and in New York, he returned to Warsaw as director of the State Institute for Hygiene (1923–27). Returning finally to New York as a research consultant, he founded the Funk Foundation for Medical Research in 1953. He published many papers in the field of nutritional science and discovered that yeast is effective for

curing beri-beri. As it appeared that all food factors associated with deficiency diseases belonged to the chemical group known as amines, he suggested the name vitamine. When this assumption was proved wrong the modern form, vitamin, was introduced in 1920.

Gaudí, Antonio 1852–1926

Spanish architect. The son of a coppersmith, he studied architecture, after training as a blacksmith, and in 1877 began work on a fountain in Barcelona. He was commissioned by Count Guëll to create many buildings, including the Casa Guëll (1885–89) and Guëll Park. From 1884 he took over the construction of the church of the Sagrada Familia in Barcelona, working exclusively on it from 1914. It remained unfinished. Gaudí's extraordinary work is distinguished by a Gothic profusion of forms, with sculptured and pictorial detail, and an imitation of living organic forms.

Geiger, Hans Wilhelm 1882–1945

German pioneer of atomic physics and inventor of the Geiger counter. After graduating in physics in Germany he did postdoctoral research on the discharge of electricity through gases, before going to Britain to work with Ernest Rutherford in Manchester. They devised a method for counting alpha-particles and showed that these have two units of charge. In 1909, with E. Marsden, he demonstrated that, exceptionally, the particles showed a very large deflection when directed at gold leaf. This led to Rutherford's initial concept of the nuclear atom. In 1912 Geiger returned to Germany and in 1925 became professor of physics at Kiel. There, with W. Müller, he perfected his famous counter. This consists of a tube fllled with a mixture of argon and halogen gas down which passes a high- voltage wire. If a charged particle passes through the tube it causes a discharge from the wire, which is quenched by an electronic circuit, activating a counter.

Gide, André 1869–1951

French writer. *Les Nourritures terrestres* (1897), published four years after his realization of his homosexuality, advocates an impulsive hedonism. 1902 saw the publication of *L'Immoraliste*. In 1909 he helped set up the *Nouvelle Revue Française*. World War I left Gide more introspective. In 1926 his most ambitious novel – the book which, indeed, he described as his only novel – *Les Faux-Monnayeurs*, appeared – it dealt with sexual ambivalence in teenage boys; the autobiographical *Si le grain ne meurt* also came out this year. Gide wrote plays, like *Oedipe* (1931), libretti, essays, and his finest work, the *Journal* (1939 onward). He battled with religious ideas (becoming finally an agnostic), traveled Africa, wrote on colonialism, was briefly Communist, until put off by a visit to Russia in 1936. He won the 1947 Nobel Prize.

Golgi, Camillo 1844–1926

Italian histologist, pioneer of research on the microstructure of the nervous system. After graduating in medicine at Pavia he was for seven years physician in the hospital there. In 1875 he was appointed professor of histology, and later professor of general pathology in Pavia. He was much interested in the dye-stain techniques being developed by bacteriologists and in 1873 discovered that nervous tissue could be differentiated by staining with silver. He classified nerve cells and showed that their fibers did not join directly but were separated by short gaps (synapses). In the 1880s he discovered significant differences between the intermittent and the pernicious types of malaria parasite. In 1898 he described an important feature (Golgi body) present in the cytoplasm of many cells. In 1906 he shared a Nobel prize with S. Ramón y Cajal: he was the first Italian to achieve this honor.

Gompers, Samuel 1850–1924

US labor leader. Gompers, a US immigrant from Britain with his family in 1863, joined a union in 1864. As president of a local group he led an unsuccessful strike in 1877. In 1881 he established the US and Canada Federation of Organized Trades and Labor Union. He founded the American Federation of Labor (AFL) in 1886, leading it, barring one year, until his death. A pragmatist, Gompers supported collective bargaining, and strikes for basic necessities. He considered socialist ideology and intellectualism to be diversions from fundamental issues, and deemed it necessary to work with capitalism to gain specific ends. He supported the formation of "guilds" for skilled workers. Under Gompers, wages increased by 250%, working hours decreased, and the AFL, with a membership approaching 3m., became the USA's biggest labor organization. His influence far outlived him.

Gris, Juan (Victoriano Gonzalès) 1887–1927

Spanish painter. After studying at the Madrid School of Industrial and Applied Arts, he worked as a caricaturist, moving in 1906 to Paris where he met Picasso and other avant-garde artists. In 1911 he began to paint seriously, using an analytical Cubist style in works like *Oil Lamp* (1912). His work was characterized by an austere clarity of line, and blocks of luminous color; he soon began to use collage, moving into Synthetic Cubism, of which by 1913–14 he was the foremost proponent; in 1912, under contract to Kahnweiler, he exhibited with the *Section d'Or*. During World War I he was supported financially by his friend Matisse. He also designed for Diaghilev and illustrated books. During the 1920s, as he became increasingly ill, his style, hitherto stern and mathematically structured, softened, with more curves and muted colors. Gris was a brilliant and articulate theorist, writing

Fritz Haber

F. Theodor Herzl

Harry Houdini

works like *L'Esprit Nouveau* (1921), with a deep understanding of Synthetic Cubism; rather than analyzing representational form, he applied the principles of Cubism to create a harmonious structure.

Haber, Fritz 1868–1934

German Jewish physical chemist. Educated in Berlin, he taught physical chemistry at Karlsrühe and pioneered research in electrochemistry. In the early 1900s there was grave concern about the rapid depletion of natural sources of nitrogenous fertilizers. With Carl Bosch Haber developed the method for the synthesis of ammonia from nitrogen and hydrogen. In 1911 Haber became director of the Kaiser Wilhelm Institute for Physical Chemistry in Berlin. During World War I, the Haber-Bosch ammonia process enabled Germany to manufacture explosives although the Allies prevented access to natural nitrate deposits; the Institute became a major military establishment and Haber played an important part in its development of poison gas. In 1918 he received the Nobel Prize for Chemistry. After the war the Institute became the world center for research in physical chemistry; but the rise of Nazism ended Haber's career, and he ended his life in England

Handy, W.C. 1873–1958

US jazz composer, bandleader and cornet player. Possibly composed, was certainly the first to set down on paper, numerous classic blues themes; his credits include *Memphis Blues, St Louis Blues, Beale Street Blues* and *Old Miss Rag*. He set up a publishing company in Memphis, moving it to New York's Broadway in 1918. He continued publishing throughout the twenties and thirties.

Harmsworth, Alfred Charles 1865–1922

Irish newspaper magnate and politician. With his brother Harold, he built a publishing empire, initially issuing periodicals, and buying the *Evening News* in 1894. In 1896 he started the *Daily Mail;* selling for 1 penny, its bold headlines and racy style had a great impact on British journalism. He founded the *Daily Mirror*, the first exclusively women's interest newspaper, in 1903. In 1908 he became chief proprietor of *The Times.*

Hearst, William Randolph 1863–1951

US newspaper publisher. His methods polarized the American press. He turned his father's *San Francisco Examiner* to profit (1887–9) and then bought the ailing *New York Morning Journal* (later *Journal-American*) in 1895. He reshaped the paper, using copious illustration, color-magazine sections, bold headlines and a sensation-seeking approach. By 1925 he owned newspapers and magazines all over the USA. In the thirties his empire was depleted by the Depression and his own extravagances, but it thrived from 1945 on.

Herzl, F. Theodor 1860–1904

Austrian founder of Zionism. A law graduate, Herzl was so shocked by the level of anti-Semitism in France exposed by the Dreyfus affair, that, in 1896, he issued a pamphlet (*Der Judenstäat*) advocating the creation of a Jewish state. He displayed diplomatic genius in bringing together Jews from dramatically different backgrounds, in Eastern and Western Europe, for the first Zionist Congress, in 1897. First president of the World Zionist Organization, Herzl was convinced that only global cooperation would solve the problem of anti-Semitism. However, when the British government offered Jews a homeland in Uganda, he was unable to reconcile the differences within the movement, as many Zionists were immovably attached to the idea of Palestine as their only possible home.

Hobbs, Jack 1882–1963

English cricketer. The world's greatest batsman in his time, he first played first-class cricket in 1905, scoring a century in his second game. He was a professional cricketer for 30 years, scoring a record 61,237 runs (including 197 centuries) and playing for England in 61 Test Matches. His greatest innings was against Australia in 1926, when his century helped England keep the Ashes. He was the first professional cricketer to receive the honor of a knighthood in 1953.

Houdini, Harry 1874–1926

Hungarian-born conjurer. His father, a rabbi, took the family to the USA and the child became a trapeze artist. By the early 1900s his amazing ability to extricate himself from shackles, ropes, handcuffs, straitjackets and locked containers, sometimes while weighted and submerged in water or suspended head down 23m (75ft) above the ground, had brought world fame. Also a successful conventional illusionist, he denounced mind readers and mediums as charlatàns, arguing his case in two books published in the twenties.

Ibsen, Henrik 1828–1906

Norwegian dramatist. As an apprentice chemist, Ibsen fathered an illegitimate son, whom he supported until 1860. His first play, *Catilina*, aroused little public interest, but initiated in his oeuvre the theme of the gulf between the possible and the actual human condition, which is the root of comedy and tragedy. *The Burial Mound* was his first play to be staged, in Christiania in 1850. From 1851 to 1857 he gained valuable theater experience in a post he disliked, as resident dramatist at the Norwegian Theater in Bergen. He was then artistic director of the Norwegian Theater at Christiania until it went bankrupt in 1862. During this time he married and had a son. After two unhappy and impoverished years as literary advisor to the Christiania Theater he moved in 1964 to Italy, and

divided his time until 1891 between Rome, Dresden and Munich. During this period he wrote most of his great plays. *Brand* (1865) saw instant success in Scandinavia; another indictment of bourgeois life, *Peer Gynt*, followed in 1867. *Pillars of Society* (187), his first social satire, brought Ibsen fame in Germany. *A Doll's House* (1879), a shattering attack on the virtual imprisonment of women in society, caused a furore. *An Enemy of the People* (1882), *The Wild Duck* (1884), *Rosmersholm* (1886) and *Ghosts* (1887), using venereal disease as a symbol of inherited moral disorder, followed. *Hedda Gabler* (1890) was inspired partly by his encounter in 1889 with two young girls who "lightened his life". *The Master Builder* (1892) was the last play before a move to a more visionary style as in *When We Dead Awaken* (1900). Soon after this, he suffered two strokes. The progenitor of modern drama, Ibsen influenced such great writers as Shaw and Chekhov; he was unflinching in his confrontation of social issues, a great poet and a masterly interpreter of the human psyche.

James, Henry 1843–1916

US British writer. James, son of a philosopher, and brother of the philosopher/psychologist William, settled in 1876 in London. His work can be divided into three periods: 1876–79, dealing with personal tragedies arising from the US-European culture clash; works include *The Europeans* (1878); explorations of feminist issues in *The Bostonians* (1886–99), and inter-generation conflict in *The Awkward Age* (1899); *The Golden Bowl* (1904) has a much more elaborate style and complicated webs of relationships which govern and dwarf the action. James consistent suspension of moral judgement aroused controversy; he was famed, and respected also, as an extraordinary and masterful prose stylist, with long, finely-balanced sentence structure.

Jaurès, Jean 1859–1914

French politician and socialist leader. Jaurès, a university lecturer and a fine speaker, entered the Chamber of Representatives in 1885, returning to teaching after an election defeat in 1889, and receiving his PhD in 1891. His support of a miners' strike helped him toward re-election in 1893, as an Independent Socialist, opposed to revolution. He lost the seat in 1898 after supporting Dreyfus, who was unpopular with radicals. He then (1901–07) wrote Socialist History of the French Revolution, and co-founded (1904) the journal *L'Humanité*. Returned to the chamber in 1902, Jaurès continued his advocacy of a democratic socialism, rejected at the 2nd International. Opposed to colonialism, he sought peace, and reconciliation with Germany. He mistrusted Russia, and therefore the Triple Entente. Unpopular with all political extremists, he was assassinated by rightwingers after his vehement denunciation of World War I.

▼ Franz Kafka

▼ Max von Laue

▼ Rosa Luxemburg

Johnson, Jack 1878–1946

US boxer. The first black world heavyweight champion (26 December 1908 to 5 April 1915), his professional career lasted from 1897 to 1928. He fought 114 bouts, winning 80 (45 by knockouts). His victory over a white increased his fight opportunities as white America sought a challenger. Conviction under the Mann Act forced him to flee abroad and he defended the title outside the USA several times, losing in 1915 in the belief the charge would be dropped. In 1920 he surrendered to serve sentence, working in vaudeville after his release.

Joplin, Scott 1868–1917

US ragtime pianist and composer. A saloon-bar player in St Louis, he was later based in Sedalia, in whose red-light district his music was a hit, and, after enrolling at a black academy (1896), he began to write down the rags he heard. In 1899 his *Maple Leaf Rag* was published, selling 75,000 copies in the first year. Other successes include *Easy Winners*, *Elite Syncopations* and *The Entertainer*.

Kafka, Franz 1883–1924

Czech-Jewish-born German-language novelist. A law graduate, Kafka worked in accident prevention and in his domineering father's shop – he had to write at night, producing short magazine pieces. In his most famous work, *Metamorphosis* (1912), he treats the theme of the impossibility of communication, represented by Gregor Samsa's own difficulties after his "metamorphosis" into a giant insect. In 1917, after TB was diagnosed, Kafka told his friend, Max Brod, to burn his unpublished work. Brod disobeyed, and the great unfinished novels, *The Trial* (1914–15) and *The Castle* (1922), were preserved, both of which develop further the theme of *Metamorphosis* – the "protagonist" (K) is at once driven and opposed in his actions by omnipresent and inscrutable forces, with whom he cannot adequately communicate, a projection, perhaps, of Kafka's relationship with his father. Kafka's intellectual honesty and anguished moral concern shed light on the human landscape in works of unparalleled lucidity and profoundly direct insight.

Kamerlingh Onnes, Heike 1853–1926

Dutch physicist. After graduating in physics at Gröningen, he went to Heidelberg in 1871 to work with R.W.E Bunsen and G.R. Kirchhoff. In 1882 he became professor of physics at Leiden and remained there. Influenced by J.D. van der Waals, he embarked on a lifelong study of the properties of gases and liquids over a wide range of pressures and temperatures. Eventually he concentrated on very low temperatures near absolute zero, and founded the famous Cryogenic Laboratory in 1894. In 1908 he succeeded in liquefying helium and he discovered the phenomenon of superconductivity (1911) whereby the resistance of electrical conductors vanishes at near-zero temperature. This is a phenomenon of major significance in solid state physics. He received a Nobel prize in 1913.

Kandinsky, Wassily 1866–1944

Russian painter. In 1896, abandoning a career in law, he went to art school in Munich. In 1901 he founded the Phalanx group. He traveled widely, often exhibiting in Paris, and experimented technically, often painting on dark paper; he used line both as content and to contain colored areas. In 1912, with Franz Marc, he formed *Der Blaue Reiter*. He became interested in Theosophy and wrote *On the Spiritual in Art*, advocating the use of color as emotional language. Disillusioned with the potential for change in post-revolutionary Russia, in 1921 he returned to Germany and taught philosophy of form at the Bauhaus. In 1924 Kandinsky, Jawlensky, Feininger and Klee were the "Blue Four", exhibiting together. 1926 saw the publication of his *Point and Line to Plane*. In 1933 the Nazis closed the Bauhaus, and Kandinsky went to Paris; impressed by Miró and Arp, he developed softer, biomorphic forms in his work – *Et Encore* (1940). The driving force of Kandinsky's always lively work was the search for life implicit in pure form.

Kautsky, Karl 1854-1938

Czech German Social Democrat leader. Kautsky, a graduate of the University of Vienna, became a Marxist in Zurich, where he met Eduard Bernstein. He also became a good friend of Engels, whom he met in London. In 1883 he founded the influential Marxist paper Neue Zeit, and co-created (with Bernstein) the Social Democrats' Erfurt Program (1891), espousing an "evolutionary" Marxism, which was criticized by Bernstein and Lenin. A critic of leftwing radicalism and rightwing revisionism, Kautsky, at one time the West German authority on Marxism, was isolated because of his moderate views and his opposition to World War l. In 1918 he edited the German foreign office archives dealing with the outbreak of war. From 1924 on he wrote books, chiefly applying Marxist analysis to historical subjects. He participated in the foundation of the Social Democrats' Heidelberg program (1925). Kautsky endorsed Marx's view of history as a natural process, and consciousness and ethics as biological functions, as laid out in his *Materialist Interpretation of History* (1927).

Kirchner, Ernst 1880–1938

German painter. Kirchner studied architecture, and then, at art school in Munich, absorbed *Jugendstil*. He produced stronger work, influenced by the Post-Impressionists, after 1905, when he cofounded the *Die Brücke* group: *Self-portrait with Model* (1910) is typical. He moved in 1911 with other *Brücke* members to Berlin, leading a bohemian life. His angular, tense urban paintings of this period, like *The Street* (1913) are superb. In 1913 he criticized other members in the "Brücke Chronik" – and the group broke up. Kirchner became increasingly hostile, and in 1916, while serving in the army, he had a nervous breakdown. During his convalescence in Switzerland his work was calmer, but 1922 saw a return of his nervous dynamism. In 1926 he painted a nostalgic group portrait of *Die Brücke*, including himself. Harassed, like many others, by the Nazis from 1933, he finally killed himself.

Laemmle, Carl 1867–1939

German-born film studio boss. Investment in nickelodeons caused him to set up a distribution network in 1907 and by 1909 he was challenging the monopolists. He founded a production company, the Independent Motion Picture Company (IMP), to evade their pressure and by skillfully manipulating publicity – especially for Florence Lawrence – invented the star system to establish his studio's image. In 1912 he effected a series of mergers to create Universal, one of the earliest major studios, in California.

Landsteiner, Karl 1868–1943

Austrian-US immunologist. He graduated in medicine in Vienna in 1891 and then spent five years studying chemistry at various European centers. He returned to Vienna for some years, before working (1919–22) in Holland. He then accepted an invitation to work in the USA at the Rockefeller Institute of Medical Research. His interests were wide, but his main contribution was in immunology, especially that associated with the blood. By 1909 he had identified the four main blood groups recognized today. This made blood transfusion – previously extremely hazardous – feasible as a routine procedure. He continued his research on blood and in 1940, with A. Wienes and P. Levine, announced the discovery of the rhesus (rh) factor in the red blood cells of certain individuals. In certain circumstances, this is of critical importance. Landsteiner was awarded a Nobel prize in 1930.

Laue, Max Theodor Felix von 1879–1960

German physicist. At an early age he abandoned classics for physics and became assistant to Max Planck at the Institute of Theoretical Physics, Berlin (1905–19) where he worked on Albert Einstein's Special Theory of Relativity. Moving on to Munich, he also did research on wave- optics and reached the conclusion that short- wave electromagnetic radiation should be diffracted by crystals. In 1912, using copper sulfate, his assistants Friedrich and Knipping verified this. His discovery was subsequently used by W.H. and W.C. Bragg to investigate the structure of crystals. He was

awarded the Nobel Prize for Physics in 1914, as were the Braggs in 1915. After subsequent appointments in Zurich and Frankfurt he became professor of theoretical physics in Berlin, resigning in 1943 in protest at Nazi racial policy. After the war he worked to revive German science.

Linder, Max 1883–1925

French director and actor. His highly original style of screen comedy anticipated Sennett and Chaplin and by 1910 he was the most popular comedian in Europe and the USA, writing, supervising and (from 1911) directing his own films. He made over 400 for Pathé. Their humor depended upon the contrast between his elegant self-possession and the ridiculous situations in which he found himself.

Lloyd, Marie 1870–1922

British music-hall artiste. Immensely popular, she was cheerful, alluring, fashionable, frank, witty and crammed full of vitality. Her best-known songs include *Oh, Mr Porter!*, *My Old Man Said Follow the Van*, *A Little of What You Fancy Does You Good* and *I'm One of the Ruins That Cromwell Knocked Abaht a Bit*.

Luxemburg, Rosa 1871–1919

Polish-born German socialist leader and theorist. A doctor of law and political economy, Luxemburg co-founded the Polish Social Democratic Party in 1892. In 1906, in the pamphlet *The Mass Strike*, she advocated this radical action which she deemed essential to spearhead a proletarian revolution, and to radicalize the workers. She opposed Lenin's nationalist ideas, believing that the cause, and effective action, of workers must transcend national boundaries; and also his approach to party organization, which Luxemburg held must emerge democratically. She fell out with German SPD colleagues on the issues of workers' radical action. The scholarly *The Accumulation of Capital* (1913) delineates her belief in the moral, and ultimately, economic, unsoundness of capitalism. In 1914, with Carl Liebknecht, she founded the Spartacus League. Imprisoned during World War I for her antimilitarist stance, she wrote the "Junius" letters, supporting Lenin's call to revolution. Released in 1918, she continued her activism, and established, with Liebknecht, the German Communist Party. They were both killed by counter-revolutionary troops. Although muted under Stalin, and modified in view of her differences with the revered Lenin, Luxemburg's influence on radical socialism has been massive.

Mackintosh, Charles R. 1868–1928

British architect and designer. After studying architecture, and apprenticeship, Mackintosh met Herbert MacNair, Frances and Margaret MacDonald. Known as "the Four", they originated

Art Nouveau in Glasgow. Mackintosh regarded architecture and design as one, and the Glasgow School of Art (1897–1909) is an elegant monument. In 1900 his designs were exhibited in the Vienna Secession; Hill House, Glasgow (1902), is another fine example of his work; however, in England, where he lived from 1914 to 1923, such fame eluded him, and he could not establish a practice. He moved to France, where he painted fine landscapes, but was forced by illness to return to London in 1928.

Mahler, Gustav 1860–1911

Bohemian-Jewish-born Austrian composer and conductor. Mahler learned the piano aged six, and aged ten gave his first recital. In 1875 he entered the Vienna Conservatory, where he met Anton Bruckner, whose music he later championed. After leaving the Conservatory in 1878 he wrote the cantata *Das Klagende Lied* (1880), achieving an original sound-world. He began a period (1881–91) conducting at Cassel, Prague, Leipzig and Budapest, until he became a chief conductor in Hamburg. It was at his friend Hans von Bülow's funeral that Mahler was inspired to use Klopstock's ode *Resurrection* in the finale of his *Second Symphony* (1888–94). In 1897 he was appointed director of the Vienna Opera, a post he held until 1907, when he went to New York as the conductor of the Metropolitan Opera, until his death. His works consist of ten symphonies (the *Tenth* left unfinished) and a sequence of song-cycles, of which *Das Lied von der Erde* (1907–09), a setting of Chinese poems, is the finest. In the greatest of his symphonies – the *Sixth* (1903–05) and *Ninth* (1909–10) – passion and poetry are balanced by a concise and chiseled structure. His music, though championed by Schoenberg and Webern among others, suffered neglect after his death until the 1960s when it began the climb to its present level of popularity.

Marconi, Guglielmo 1874–1937

Italian commercial radio pioneer. He was educated privately and then at the Leghorn Technical Institute where, in 1894, his imagination was captured by an article discussing the possibility of using for wireless communication the waves discovered by H.R. Hertz in 1888. Within a year he had sent and received signals at distances up to 2 mi (3.2 km). He took out his first patent in London in 1896. His invention interested the British government, particularly the Admiralty, and soon experimental equipment was installed in naval vessels. A cousin of Marconi's eventually helped financially and otherwise to establish Marconi's Wireless Telegraphy Company, Limited. The American Marconi Company was formed in 1899. In 1900 another company was founded to run services between ships and land stations. In the same year Marconi filed a patent allowing various

stations to work on different wavelengths without interference. In 1901 he succeeded in sending signals across the Atlantic. He invented a magnetic detector (1902) and a directional aerial (1905): during World War I he developed short-wave equipment for use over long distances. In 1909 he shared the Nobel Prize for physics with K.F. Braun.

Matisse, Henri 1869–1954

French painter. In 1890 Matisse left a career in law to study painting in Paris. In 1896 the State bought one of his works from an exhibition at the *Société Nationale des Beaux-Arts* in Paris. In 1897 he became interested in Impressionism, and met Pissarro. He studied sculpture from 1899. In 1904 he had his first one-man show. In 1905, he painted *Luxe, Calme et Volupté*, increasing the simplicity of his forms; and on his annual summer visit to the South of France to paint, he began to work with Derain, and with him and other friends, exhibited at the Salon d'Automne, earning the name *Fauvistes*. *Joie de vivre* (1905–06) is Matisse's finest nude. During the next few years he traveled throughout Europe and North Africa, and had exhibitions in Europe and the USA. In 1919 Matisse designed for Diaghilev, but returned to sculpture and painting. An invalid in his last years, Matisse continued to work with the help of assistants, using colored paper cut-outs. *The Snail* (1953) is an example of this work. Matisse believed painting should restore balance and well-being; he has been criticized for excluding dark and disturbing subject-matter.

Mayakovsky, Vladimir 1893–1930

Russian poet. Briefly an art student, Mayakovsky was imprisoned in his teens for his Bolshevik activism. He wrote poetry from 1912; his first publications *I* (1913), and *V. Mayakovsky* (1914) are self-centered and set out to shock. After the revolution, now a prominent Futurist, he did Bolshevik propaganda work at home and abroad. From 1923 to 1928, he edited the Journal *Lef*; his move to functionalism made him increasingly unpopular with the literary mainstream, though he still wrote lyrically. His best play, *The Bedbug* (1929) satirized the stifling boredom of the everyday. He committed suicide.

Méliès, Georges 1861–1938

French director and producer. In 1888 he sold his share in the family business to buy Robert Houdini's theater and earned a name as an imaginative illusionist. He began projecting shorts on a Bioscope in 1896, but was soon making films with a camera of his own design, building Europe's first film studio in 1897. His fantasy films, with their original optical and mechanical effects, were the most influential, particularly *Voyage to the Moon* (1902) and *A la Conquête du Pole* (1911).

Mistinguett

Claude Monet

Nicholas II

Mistinguett 1875–1956

Flemish-born music-hall artiste. Although she almost never appeared outside Paris, she won an international reputation as a symbol of the city for over 50 years. In her youth she performed Parisian low-life character sketches; later she mostly sang and danced – she had marvellous legs, saucy looks and a good line in repartee. She appeared at the Moulin Rouge, which for a time she co-owned, and later the Folies-Bergère, with Maurice Chevalier.

Monet, Claude 1840–1926

French painter. In 1856 Monet, already a good caricaturist, met Boudin, and began landscape painting. In the next few years he met Pissarro and Jongkind, and from 1862–64 studied art in Paris, and became friends with Renoir. He had his first show in 1865. His constant aim was to find more effective ways of representing light and color. *Impression: Sunrise* (1874), which gave the Impressionists their title, was one of a series of small landscapes; most of Monet's work was more fully executed. In 1883 Monet moved to Germany, and, ever more sensitive to changes in light, had to finish his paintings in the studio. *Haystacks* (1890–91) are fifteen paintings in exploration of light changes. From 1900 he produced his celebrated paintings of water-lilies and trees, culminating in 1914 in a set of huge canvases for the Paris *Orangerie*.

Morgan, John Pierpont 1837–1913

US financier. Involved in gold speculation and foreign exchange during the Civil War, he went on to specialize in railroad development and organization. By the 1890s he controlled the largest group of railroads in the US. In 1871 he established the New York firm of Drexel Morgan and Company, later J. P. Morgan and Company, which became a major source of government finance and one of the world's most powerful banking houses. After purchasing Carnegie's steel interests, in 1901 he formed the United States Steel Corporation, the largest corporation in the world, and controlled shipping lines. Morgan mainly decided how the government money in his banks was to be used for relief in the crisis of 1907. By 1912 he held 72 directorships in 47 large corporations. He donated many works to the Metropolitan Museum of Art.

Morgan, Thomas Hunt 1866–1945

US geneticist and embryologist. A zoology graduate, he spent most of his professional career at Columbia University (1904–28) and the California Institute of Technology (1928–45). A man of wide interests, he favored the direct experimental method over the then prevalent descriptive approach to biology. His research falls into four main phases: embryology, 1895–1902; evolution and heredity, 1903–10; heredity in the

fruitfly *Drosophila*, 1910–25; and embryology, again, in relation to heredity and evolution, 1925–45. Originally skeptical about the validity of J.G. Mendel's laws of inheritance, his own experiments with *Drosophila* convinced him of their basic truth and led him eventually to advance the chromosome theory of heredity. He identified several sex-linked characteristics and in 1911 he and his colleagues published the first chromosome map. By 1922 they had mapped more than 2,000 genes on *Drosophila's* four chromosomes. He was awarded a Nobel prize in 1933.

Moseley, Henry Gwyn Jeffreys 1887–1915

British physicist. It had been shown in Mendeleyev's Periodic Table that if the 60 disparate chemical elements then known are arranged in order of their atomic weights, chemically related elements recur at regular intervals. This left certain anomalies: many elements have atoms of different weights, only one of which may fit the table. In 1914, working at Oxford (where he had graduated in 1910) Moseley showed that the critical index was not the weight of the atom but the charge on its nucleus.

Munch, Edvard 1863–1944

Norwegian painter. One of Munch's first paintings, after he attended art school, was *The Sick Child* (1885), depicting his sister, who had died of TB, as had his mother, in Munch's teens. In 1885, he saw Impressionist paintings in Paris and was influenced by Van Gogh and Gauguin. The bleak and claustrophobic dramas of Strindberg also affected his work, and themes of dark sexual turbulence – *The Vampire* (1894), and *Puberty* (1895), and the self-portrait *In Hell* (1895) reflect his neurotic, tortured mental state, as does his best-known work *The Scream* (1893). His later work, like *Horse Team* (1919), or *Starry Night* (1924) could be as bright as that of Van Gogh. Munch was the major forerunner of Expressionism and controversy over his 1892 exhibition led to the Berlin Secession. Munch was also a fine portraitist.

Nicholas II 1868–1918

Russian czar. Nicholas, who took the throne in 1894, was an autocratic and repressive ruler, and in 1905 created the Duma to deal with revolutionary insurgence. Contrary to his promise, however, it was limited to a consultative role. In 1907, Russia formed an entente with Britain, and early in World War I, which Nicholas had tried his utmost to prevent, he appointed himself commander-in-chief. During his absence the country was effectively and disastrously ruled by Rasputin, and the government's authority collapsed. Nicholas was forced to abdicate after the revolution of February 1917, and after the October Revolution of the same year he and his family were imprisoned and finally killed by Bolsheviks.

Nietzsche, Friedrich W.

German philosopher. Nietzsche was awarded his doctorate – in classical philology – without being required to sit an examination, and made a professor, aged 24, before graduating. Ill-health made him give up his chair in 1879, and he lived reclusively, increasingly so after an unhappy love affair, devoting himself to writing, until insanity overtook him in 1889. He asserted that all human activity is fired by the will to assert and increase personal power, – by impinging, whether pleasantly or unpleasantly, on the consciousness of others – and posited the existence of an Übermensch (superperson) whose self-mastery shows itself in the equal valuation of all experience, and all experience being welcome. Nietzsche considered history to be a record of the events set in motion by such individuals, and deplored the "slave morality" of Christianity, in which the responsibility for making informed choices was devolved on to an omniscient God – who, in reality in our scientific age "is dead". The acuteness and impartiality of his observation of human motivation and consciousness opened the door for psychology as a subject of study. His ideas were set forth in works like "The Birth of Tragedy" (1872), "Thus Spake Zarathustra" (1883 onward), and "Ecce Homo" (1908, published posthumously) in a sublime prose, considered the finest in German literature. Crucial to the proper understanding of his work is the tenet that all "knowledge" is relative, and must be understood in relation to its holder's point of view. Nietzsche influenced such great thinkers as Adler, Foucault, Freud, Jaspers, Jung, Klossowski, Mann, Shaw and the Existentialists. His notorious influence on Hitler was due to the intervention of Nietzsche's pro-fascist sister, who edited, manipulated and even forged writings published posthumously in his name, and brought them to Hitler's notice. Nietzsche himself despised nationalism and denounced anti-semitism. His last sane (or first insane) act was to embrace a horse in the street, reportedly to prevent it being whipped.

Nijinsky, Vaslav 1889–1950

Russian dancer and choreographer. Nijinsky danced from the age of three. He attended the Imperial Ballet School (1898–1907) and from 1907 to 1911 danced lead roles in the Imperial Ballet, and the Bolshoi. In 1909 he began to dance with the Ballets Russes, joining them in 1911. He left Russia for good in 1911. He shone in Fokine's choreography for him, like *Le Spectre de la Rose*, and *Petrushka* (1911) and showed innovative choreographic power with *L'Après-midi d'un faune*, *Jeux*, and *Le Sacre du printemps* (all, 1912–13). In 1913 he married, and the jealous Diaghilev dismissed him. His career ended in 1917, with the onset of schizophrenia. Nijinsky paved the way for later virtuosi like Nureyev and Baryshnikov.

▲ Emmeline Pankhurst

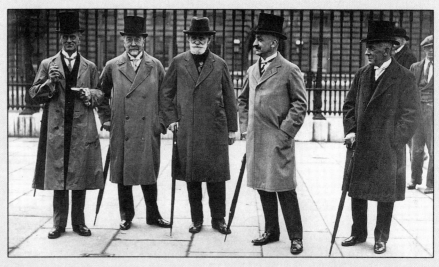

▲ Ivan Petrovich Pavlov (center)

Pankhurst, Emmeline 1858–1928

Militant leader of the British women's suffragette movement. In 1889 Emmeline formed the Women's Franchise League which went on to attain the right for married women to vote in elections to local offices (1894). In 1903 she formed the Women's Social and Political Union (WPSU), gaining much publicity through its campaigns of civil disobedience. Pankhurst was arrested and jailed several times. Her daughter Christabel spearheaded a WPSU campaign of extreme militancy from 1912. During imprisonment in 1913 Emmiline went on hunger strike, was released to regain her health and subsequently re-arrested twelve times in the next year. With the outbreak of World War I suffrage agitation ended and suffragist prisoners were released. During the war Pankhurst successfully campaigned for the entry of women in to industry and in 1918 women over the age of thirty received the vote. She died in 1928, shortly after the passing of the Representation of the People Act which gave equal suffrage for men and women.

Pareto, Vilfredo 1848–1923

Italian economist and sociologist. Pareto graduated in physics and mathematics at the University of Turin in 1868. He pursued a successful engineering career until turning in 1893 to social science, and was a professor at Lausanne university until withdrawing from society to write. He held that economics must be studied in a social context; and in *Cours de l'économie politique* (1897) introduced his law, stating that inequalities of income in a society vary according to the number of incomes above a certain level. He related inequalities also to income levels in other countries and at other levels. Pareto also propounded the "circulation of elites" – that society consists of elites who tend to become complacent and non-elites – the more gifted of whom push to achieve, unbalancing the previous elite, and replacing them. Elites must justify their own existence. In *Mind and Society*, Pareto described the three orders of motivation he had identified – sentiments or instinctual behavior, residues – based on sentiments, and derivations, systems for justifying the first two. Pareto's ideas were controversial; their major impact was in France and Italy, where in 1927, Mussolini made him a senator. Pareto appears to have regretted this before his death.

Parsons, Charles Algernon 1854–1931

Irish engineer. Son of an astronomer and mathematician, Parsons read mathematics at Trinity College, Dublin, and Cambridge University, and then became junior partner in an engineering firm. The inadequacy of reciprocating steam engines for driving high-speed dynamos led him to develop a steam turbine. He succeeded where earlier inventors had failed by recognizing that the steam pressure must be reduced in stages. His first engine (1884) developed 10hp at 18,000 revolutions per minute. He succeeded in founding a business of his own and turned his attention to marine propulsion. In 1897 his turbine-powered *Turbinia* created a sensation at the Spithead Review of the British Royal Navy's fleet. Within a decade turbines were widely used at sea.

Pavlov, Ivan Petrovich 1849–1936

Russian physiologist. After graduating in medicine at St Petersburg in 1883 he studied in Germany before becoming director of the St Petersburg Institute for Experimental Medicine (1891–1936). There he began a long series of experiments on the nature of the digestive process, identifying three distinct phases: nervous, pyloric and intestinal. His major work on this subject appeared in 1898, and he was awarded a Nobel prize in 1904. Ironically he is best known for the lesser, though still considerable, discovery of the conditioned reflex. He found that when dogs learnt to associate food with the ringing of a bell they began to salivate at the sound even in the absence of food.

Peugeot, Armand 1849–1915

French automobile manufacturer. Peugeot became famous and influential after the success of his machine-tool-manufacturing company. In 1891 he traveled to Germany in search of the ideal two-cylinder engine, finding it being manufactured by Daimler. He returned to France and converted a factory to the production of automobiles. By 1906 he had established factories throughout France. Initially his Sochaux plant concentrated on the production of trucks, demand increasing dramatically during World War II, as for all industrial vehicles, but receding when war ended. Before the war Peugeot cars won many races, including the 1913 Indianapolis 500. The company produced vehicles which had a reputation for sturdiness and innovation.

Picasso, Pablo 1881–1973

Spanish painter. Picasso began at the age of 14, in Barcelona, to produce avant-garde, experimental work. His romantic, melancholy "Blue Period" (1901–04) followed; then he moved to Paris, meeting many artists and writers, and numbering Gertrude Stein among his patrons. The lighter, poignant "Rose Period" (1904–06) followed. *Les Demoiselles d'Avignon* (1907) was a startling, iconoclastic piece, savage, influenced by primitive art, hinting at Cubism, and a major 20th-century work. From 1909 to 1914 Picasso collaborated intimately with Georges Braque, founding Cubism. In 1912, using collage, he moved into Synthetic Cubism. After working on ballets in Rome and London, he moved into his "neoclassical period", and by 1925 developed a reciprocal relationship with the Surrealists, which showed in his reorganized anatomies. During the 1930s he illustrated Ovid's *Metamorphoses* among other books. In 1936 he became director of the Prado; in 1937 his painting *Guernica*, of the destruction of a village in the Spanish Civil War, was exhibited at the Paris World Fair. This work is often considered his masterpiece. In 1946, in Antibes, he painted murals, and in 1947 began ceramic work. He became active in peace congresses, and became, for a time, a rather unconvincing communist. Picasso was the most influential figure in modern art, and an artist of volcanic creativity; he mastered many styles, but said he wanted style to be subsumed in emotional effect.

Planck, Max Carl Ernst Ludwig 1858–1947

German physicist. Abandoning an early intention to be a professional musician he studied physics at Munich and Berlin. He held professorships in theoretical physics at Kiel (1885–87) and Berlin (1887–1928). He published a series of papers (1880–92) on thermodynamics, summarizing his conclusions in his *Vorlesungen über Thermodynamik* (Lectures on Thermodynamics) in 1897. His research on radiant heat led him in 1905 to his revolutionary quantum theory, according to which radiation is emitted not continuously but in quanta (packets), the size of which are determined by the frequency of the radiation. He was awarded a Nobel prize in 1919. In 1930 he became president of the prestigious Kaiser Wilhelm Institute in Berlin, but resigned in 1937 in protest at the Nazi persecution of Jewish scientists. He was reappointed after World War II when the institute was reorganized as a Max Planck Institute.

Poiret, Paul 1879–1944

French couturier. Paris's most fashionable dress designer before World War I, his most influential design was the hobble skirt. After working for Worth, he opened his own small shop in 1903. He revived the Empire line and a flowing style based on the classical Greek tunic. But many of his clothes are theatrical; employing strong colours and decorated with pearls and feathers, they are much influenced by the Ballets Russes and Eastern art.

Porter, Edwin S 1869–1941

US film director. Porter immigrated to the USA from Scotland as a sailor. Initially a designer and builder of projectors and cameras, he became a director/ cameraman for Edison in 1899, making the first cutting-room assembly and the first US documentary, *The Life of an American Fireman* (1903); the first epic, *The Great Train Robbery* (also 1903), which influenced the Western genre profoundly and established his reputation, and a stop-motion animation film, *The Teddy Bears* (1907). In 1911 Porter founded Rex Films; but in 1912 he joined Adolph Zukov's Company. Porter's work revolutionized cinema; he retired in 1915.

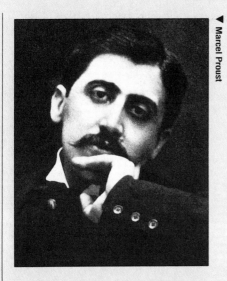

Marcel Proust

Santiago Ramón y Cajal

Maurice Ravel

Pound, Ezra 1885–1972

US poet. Pound, a philosophy graduate and M.A., was briefly professor of Romance Languages in Indiana before leaving for Venice in 1908, where his first volume of poetry, *A Lume Spento*, was published. He met Yeats, joined the Imagists, and became London correspondent for Chicago's *Poetry* magazine. He wrote the first Imagist manifesto, and in 1914 worked with Wyndham Lewis on the periodical *Blast*. He associated with Yeats, Joyce and T.S. Eliot, whose *The Waste Land* he was later to edit. Pound also published his own work, including fine translations of Chinese poetry and the much-praised *Hugh Selwyn Mauberley* (1920). In 1915 he began work on his poem-sequence, the *Cantos*. In Paris from 1921 to 1924, he wrote for *The Dial*, helped Hemingway and Eliot, and wrote an opera, *Le Testament*. He spent the next 20 years in Italy, writing the *Cantos*, arranging concerts – he "discovered" Vivaldi, and becoming increasingly pro-Fascist. Pound made wartime broadcasts against the Allies, and in 1945 he was arrested and imprisoned in Pisa where he studied Confucius and wrote the very fine *Pisan Cantos*. He spent the next 12 years in a hospital for the insane; he continued writing and translating. After pressure from Eliot, among others, he was released in 1958 and returned to Italy, in time for the publication of *Thrones* (1959), the final volume of the Cantos. After 1961 he fell virtually silent, producing only fragments. Pound's influence on 20th-century culture has been immense.

Proust, Marcel 1871–1922

French novelist. Asthmatic from 1880, and very close to his mother, Proust took degrees in law and philosophy, and absorbed most of the world's classic works in all art forms. From 1901 to 1922 he lived entirely in one soundproof room. After publishing a few stories and poems, he wrote his seven-part masterwork, *A la Recherche du temps perdu*; Volume I was rejected by two publishers, so in 1913 Proust paid for its publication. It was quite successful, and he further revised the whole work, and in 1919 received the Prix Goncourt, becoming world famous. *A la Recherche* is a nostalgic, self-analytic, comic autobiography, exploring sexuality, jealousy, the pain of love, disillusionment and psychological rebirth; his style is complex, with long, reverberating sentences.

Pulitzer, Joseph 1847–1911

Hungarian-born newspaper editor and publisher. One of the USA's most influential journalists, he began his career on a German language newspaper in 1868. By a dynamic series of purchases and mergers, he established *St Louis's Post-Dispatch* and New York's *The World*, founding the *Evening World* himself. He was sympathetic to labor interests and established the Pulitzer Prize for excellence in literature, music and journalism.

Ramón y Cajal, Santiago 1852–1934

Spanish neurohistologist. After graduating in medicine in Madrid in 1877, he held professorships in Valencia (1884–87) and Barcelona (1887–92) before returning to Madrid as professor of histology and pathological anatomy (1892–1922). Using Golgi's staining method of distinguishing nervous tissue Ramón y Cajal demonstrated that though impulses can be transmitted from one to another the nerve fibers always have a minute gap between them. While at Madrid he devoted nearly all his time to research on the mechanism of nervous transmission and the way in which severed nerves regenerate. In 1906 he shared with Golgi the Nobel Prize for Physiology or Medicine, the first Spaniard to achieve this honor.

Rasputin, Grigori 1871 (2?)-1916

Russian "mystic". Rasputin (=debauched), so named because of his behavior in boyhood, underwent a conversion at 18 and became pseudo-religious, holding that the psychic emptiness of sexual exhaustion was the best condition for approaching God. Married at 19, he left home and traveled to Greece and Israel, gaining a reputation for healing and prophecy. In 1905 he established a hold on the Czar and Czarina by helping their hemophiliac son Alexis. With them he pretended asceticism; otherwise, he was wildly dissolute, suggesting to the women he seduced that he was "good for them". The doting Czar exiled his accusers, until in 1911 Stolypin denounced him and he was at last expelled; only to be recalled at the Czarina's urgent plea. During the Czar's absence, and the Czarina's regency, in World War l, Rasputin, in the political ascendant, interfered perniciously with affairs of state. He was assassinated by a group of relatives of the Czar: poison did not work, so he was shot, continued to run until shot again, and was then tied up and thrown into the icy river Neva, and so died.

Ravel, Maurice 1875–1937

French composer. Ravel attended the Paris Conservatoire from 1899–1905, composing *Jeux d'Eau* in 1901, antedating the innovative work of Debussy, who is often cited as an influence. Ravel repudiated this (though admiring Debussy), claiming Fauré and Satie as influences. *Shéhérazade* (1903), an oriental song-cycle, shows Ravel's characteristic clarity and precision. He composed prolifically until 1914, and in 1920 declined the Légion d'Honneur (resentful that he had never been awarded the *Prix de Rome*). In 1925 he produced the powerful opera, *L'Enfant et les Sortilèges*. *Bolero* (1928) in many ways epitomizing, almost parodying, his incisive musical style, was his only popular success. He suffered a progressive nervous disease from 1932. His music was always crisp and elegant, with harmonic surety. He was an early proponent of objectivity in music.

Renault, Louis 1877–1944

French automobile manufacturer. After military service Renault persuaded his older brothers to invest in the establishment of an automobile firm, to be called Renault Frères. They sold their cars in 1899 and expanded rapidly. By 1901 Renault was the eighth largest automobile company, and the most important in France. Success was based on the manufacture of a small cheap, reliable car, though after 1905 the taxicab was the largest selling vehicle. Louis and Marcel Renault were successful international racing drivers but after Marcel's death while racing in 1903 this ended. The company was known for its technical and organizational innovations. Louis, more interested in the technical aspects of his business, took out approximately 700 patents for inventions and his transmission system was adopted by many smaller firms. Experience in developing French aviation was later put to use when Renault manufactured military equipment, including aviation engines, during World War I. The company continued growth after the war, but with the liberation of Paris Louis was jailed for collaboration for making military equipment under German occupation. He died in prison, and his company was nationalized.

Renoir, Pierre Auguste 1841-1919

French painter, and Impressionist leader. Renoir trained in decorating porcelain before working in Charles Gleyre's studio; in 1862 he met Monet; they often painted together. Influenced by Manet and C18 French painting, Renoir exhibited at the Salon. He began to focus more on color than on outline, introducing a "rainbow palette" of intense hues; he exhibited in the first three Impressionist exhibitions of the 1870s. He achieved success as a portraitist, and revised his technique, especially after a trip to Italy in 1881, when Raphael and the Renascence and Classical masters struck him deeply. His style became more structural; by 1890 he had regained his freshness. *The Umbrellas* (1884) shows both styles. Renoir's output was enormous and such great works as *Les Grandes Baigneuses* (1887) and *The Bathers* (1919) and his many gentle, colorful studies of landscapes and lovely women and children, endear him to a wide public. Arthritic at the end of his life, he continued to paint with the brush strapped to his hand.

Rhodes, Cecil 1853–1902

British mining pioneer and founder of Rhodesia (now Zimbabwe and Zambia). Son of a country vicar, in 1869 Rhodes went to South Africa and started diamond mining with his brother, moving to Kimberley, and living for a time between there and Britain; he graduated at Oxford in 1881. By 1888 he owned the Kimberley diamond mines. He was unscrupulous in the methods he employed in pursuit of his dream of a world federation dominated by the English-speaking peoples,

John Davison Rockefeller

Wilhelm Konrad Röntgen

Theodore Roosevelt

starting with the uniting of South Africa under British rule. In 1884 he took Bechuanaland (Botswanaland) and in 1889 set up the British South Africa Company, later developing the area later named Rhodesia. He deceived the Matabele ruler, Lobengula, into signing away the rights to much of his land, and in 1890 seized the rest of the Matabele lands by force; Lobengula later died trying to regain them. By 1891, as a prime minister of Cape Colony, he dominated Southern African politics and economics, except in the Dutch-settled Transvaal; he conspired to sabotage President Kruger's government. But in 1895, though his matabele administrator Leander Starr Jameson, Rhodes launched the "Jameson raid" in a hopeless attempt to dispose of these settlers. His men were utterly defeated, and his reputation shattered, and he resigned his office. This episode contributed to the tension which led to the Boer war. Rhodes left his £3m fortune to found the Rhodes scholarships, allowing gifted subjects of Commonwealth and other nations to study at Oxford University.

Rilke, Rainer Maria 1875–1926

Austrian poet. Rilke's unsympathetic father sent him to military academy, then business school, both of which he hated. In 1895, after publishing a book of poetry (1894), he went to university in Prague. On leaving after one year, he went to Germany, where he met Lou Andreas-Salomé and became her lover. She imbued in him a deep love of Russia, his "spiritual homeland", which inspired *The Book of Hours* (1905). In Paris, his second "spiritual home" (1902–14), he met Rodin, whose secretary he became. Rodin's down-to-earth approach to sculpting influenced Rilke's engagement with his own craft. The result was *New Poems* (1907–08). The novel *The Notebook of Malte Laurids Brigge* (1910) reveals a vastly sensitive being, too passive to use his gift creatively. A "barren" period of 13 years ensued, before the *Duino Elegies* which Rilke and the literary public considered his major work, and *Sonnets to Orpheus* (both 1922). Rilke's vision is of a hierarchy of life-forms, transcended by the human creative consciousness, which can "redeem" the visible, by rendering it invisible – see the *Ninth Duino Elegy*. He stands out as one of the towering figures in the genesis of modern western literature.

Rockefeller, John Davison 1839–1937

US industrialist, financier and philanthropist. He established his own food merchant's in 1859. When oil was discovered in Pennsylvania he became involved with oil refining. With his partners he quickly became the largest refiner in Cleveland and organized the Standard Oil Company in 1870 with a capital of $1 million. Rockefeller led the company in its development into the largest oil firm in the USA, symbol of the modern, efficient and ruthless American business

corporation, especially with its use of price-cutting offensives used to take over competitors. By 1879 Standard Oil controlled almost all of US refining capacity. To consolidate and be able to operate legally in other states, Rockefeller's concerns adopted a trust agreement putting all stock under the control of a board of trustees. Despite legislation aimed at breaking this organization the Rockefeller enterprises survived under different names but as a single unit. In 1897 Rockefeller formally retired from active leadership. His main concern became the distribution of much of his vast wealth in charitable and philanthropic ventures, helping to establish Chicago University and the Rockefeller Foundation.

Rodin, Auguste 1840–1917

French sculptor. Rejected by the Ecole des Beaux Arts, Rodin worked to pay for sculpture classes. Shocked by his sister's death in 1862, he became a monk, but the Father told him sculpture was his vocation. He worked as assistant to other sculptors, and in 1872 had a bust accepted in the Brussels Salon. In 1877, the showing of *The Age of Bronze*, a male nude originally a tribute to the war dead, caused uproar, because people could not believe an unknown had produced such brilliant work. Rodin was still a journeyman, until the showing of *John the Baptist* that year brought him acknowledgement as a master. Given money and studios, he was commissioned to design doors for the Paris Museum of Decorative Arts; he used imagery from Dante's *Inferno*, producing hundreds of figures, with *The Thinker* as centerpiece – he worked on this all his life. In 1884 he produced, on commission, *The Burghers of Calais*, and the profoundly erotic *The Kiss*, for the State, in 1887. In 1888 he was made *Chevalier de la Légion d'Honneur*, and in 1893 the president of sculpture at the *Société National des Beaux Arts*. He was disappointed in the rejection in 1898 of a monument to Balzac, which he considered his best work, but the State considered "unfinished". Rodin's greatness overshadowed later 20th-century sculptors; the fine modeling and emotional power of his work remained unsurpassed.

Röntgen, Wilhelm Konrad 1845–1923

German physicist. He entered the Polytechnic Institute in Zurich in 1855 and after a series of academic appointments was elected professor of physics at Würzburg and director of the newly founded Physical Institute there in 1888. His interests were wide and included the mysterious "molecular rays" emitted when eletric discharges are passed through gases at low pressures. In 1895, while experimenting with a Cookes' tube covered in an opaque shield of black cardboard, he noticed that a nearby sheet of paper painted with barium platinocyanide had begun to fluoresce. The cause proved to be a penetrating radiation which he

designated X-rays. He immediately announced his discovery in a report to the Würzburg Physical-Medical Society and the great potential diagnostic and therapeutic value of X-rays was quickly recognized. Röntgen was awarded the Nobel Prize for Physics for 1901.

Roosevelt, Theodore 1858–1919

26th US president. Roosevelt, a moderate Republican, became leader of the New York legislature in 1884. In 1897 he became assistant secretary for the navy and when war was declared on Spain, he helped to form a volunteer regiment, the Rough Riders, which he went on to lead in Cuba. He returned home a national hero, and in 1898 became governor of New York. In 1900 he became vice-president, and in 1901, after the assassination of McKinley, took over as president. He described his domestic policies as providing a "square deal" for all groups in the nation. He pursued a policy of "trust-busting" under the Sherman Anti-Trust Act, intervened on behalf of public interest in a coal strike in 1902, introduced the Hepburn Act to regulate railways in 1906, and in the same year introduced the Pure Food and Drug Act. Internationally, he based his policies on the principle "speak softly and carry a big stick". He supported a revolution against the Colombians in Panama, and consequently gained a lease on the canal zone, and began construction. He undertook to ensure that Latin American countries met their international obligations. As a mediator he was instrumental in 1905 in bringing the Russo-Japanese war to a close, for which he was awarded the Nobel Peace Prize in 1906, and intervened in the first Moroccan crisis between European Powers in 1906. He retired in 1908, but, regarding his successor Taft as too conservative, stood again, unsuccessfully, for the Republican nomination in 1912, and then founded the progressive Bull Moose party, but lost that year's election. He advocated neutrality in 1914, but then came to favor intervention.

Rouault, Georges 1871–1958

French painter. After an apprenticeship as a stained-glass worker, Rouault studied art in Paris, notably under Gustave Moreau, whose favorite student he became. He met Matisse and other Fauves, and although he painted in the same style, adhered in subject matter and sensibility to the Romantic and Baroque traditions. The dealer Vollard bought all his work in 1913, and in 1917 gave him a room to work in; Rouault produced several series of prints, including the *Miserere* (Psalm 51) set. From 1918 he painted strong oils, often on religious themes. He also (from 1908) produced a series of lawcourt paintings. The passionate, anguished moralism of his work fits his description of it as "A cry in the night, a stifled sob".

▲ Benjamin Seebohm Rowntree

▲ George Bernard Shaw

▲ Jean Sibelius

Rowntree, Benjamin Seebohm 1871–1954

UK industrialist, sociologist and philanthropist. He joined the family firm in 1889, was appointed director in 1897 and chairman from 1923 to 1941. He was a pioneer in the field of industrial welfare, and was director of the welfare department of the Ministry of Munitions (1915–18). Between 1897 and 1898 Rowntree investigated the state of the poor in York and in 1901 published *Poverty, a Study of Town Life* as a result. He published *The Human Needs of Labor* in 1918 and *The Human Factor in Business* in 1921. He undertook two further York surveys, and published reports in 1941 and 1951. Rowntree also worked with Lord Astor on studies of British agriculture. A man who felt deeply responsible for the poor, he significantly influenced the development of British social policy.

Rutherford, Ernest 1871–1937

The founder of modern atomic physics. Born in New Zealand, he was educated at Canterbury College (now University of Canterbury), where he did research on magnetism. In 1895 a scholarship took him to Britain to work under J.J. Thomson at Cambridge, where he did research on the conduction of electricity by gases. In 1898 he was appointed professor of physics at McGill University, Montreal, where he investigated the phenomenon of radioactivity discovered by A.H. Becquerel in 1896. He discovered that two kinds of radiation were involved, which he designated alpha and beta. In 1907 he was appointed professor at Manchester and subsequently at Cambridge (1919–37) as head of the famous Cavendish Laboratory. During these years he attracted a succession of brilliant research workers who laid the foundation of modern atomic physics. His supreme achievement was the concept of the nuclear atom – an atom with a relatively heavy nucleus surrounded by a cloud of much lighter electrons. Niels Bohr explained a final anomaly in this by applying quantum theory (1912). Rutherford was awarded a Nobel prize in 1908 – and was chagrined, as a dedicated physicist, to learn that it was the prize for chemistry.

Schiele, Egon 1890–1918

Austrian painter. While attending the Vienna Academy of Art, Schiele joined the *Wiener Werkstätte*. His early works, like *Orchard in Spring* (1907), were Impressionistic; the influence upon him of Gustav Klimt caused a rift with his teacher, and he left the Academy in 1909 and joined the *Neukunstgruppe*, exhibiting all over Europe. A fine draftsman, and influenced by the theories of Freud, Schiele produced vital, powerful works, frequently depicting tortured, brooding figures, and often erotic. In 1911 he was jailed for a month for "immoral drawings". During and after World War I, in which he served as a war artist, he painted major portraits like *Edith Seated* (1917–18).

Sennett, Mack 1880–1960

Canadian-born director, producer and actor. Initially a comic actor, Sennett learned about film-making from D.W. Griffith. A co-founder of the Keystone Studios in 1912, he soon made it a leader in the slapstick comedy genre. The early films were uninhibited one-reel farces which defied convention; sustained by the energy of their visual gags, they were improvised, then brilliantly edited by Sennett. The "Keystone Cops" were quintessential Sennett and among his stars were Mabel Normand, "Fatty" Arbuckle, Gloria Swanson, W.C. Fields and Chester Conklin.

Shapley, Harlow 1885–1972

US astronomer, the first to formulate a clear picture of the size and structure of our galaxy. Originally a crime reporter, he soon found astronomy more to his taste. Discovering a disproportionate density of stars in the direction of the constellation Sagittarius he reasoned that this must be the galactic center and that the Sun must be some 50,000 light years from it. He further calculated the overall diameter of the galaxy as about 300,000 light years, though later estimates tripled this.

Shaw, George Bernard 1856–1950

Irish playwright. Shaw left school at 15 and worked as a clerk before joining his mother (who had decamped with her lover and daughters in 1873) in London; he worked as a critic, of art, books, music and theater – he began writing plays in the 1880s; he also became a socialist, and in 1884 joined the Fabian Society. *Candida* (1894) is Ibsenesque; others followed, and he became famous in Europe, but success in England came only in 1904, with the production of *John Bull's Other Island*, and the Royal Court theater staged eleven of his plays between then and 1907. *Pygmalion* (1913) is his most popular, and funniest play, dealing with love and class barriers – it has been filmed, and adapted into a hugely successful musical. Shaw was a master of English prose; his didacticism is balanced by his freshness and wit, and the integrity of his socio-political commitment. Until 1930, he produced a stream of high-quality plays, including *Caesar and Cleopatra* (1901), *Man and Superman* (1903), *Major Barbara* (1905), *Heartbreak House* (1920), and *St Joan* (1923). The last, a superbly moving exemplary drama with soaring lyrical passages, won him the 1925 Nobel Prize.

Sherrington, Charles Scott 1857–1952

British neurophysiologist. After studying in Cambridge and London, Sherrington did physiological research in Germany before becoming professor of physiology at Liverpool in 1895. From 1913 to 1936 he was Waynflete professor of physiology at Oxford. He specialized early in the physiology of the nervous system, and published over three hundred papers on this subject. In the 1890s he mapped the nervous supply to the musculature but from about 1900 became increasingly interested in the physiology of the brain and spinal cord. His *Integrative Action of the Nervous System* (1904) is one of the great classics of medical literature. He was awarded a Nobel prize in 1932.

Sibelius, Jean 1865–1957

Finnish composer. In 1886, Sibelius switched from studying law to studying music, in Helsinki, Berlin (1889), and Vienna (1890). His choral *Kullervo Symphony* (1892) made his name as the supreme Finnish composer. Like most of his works, it draws on the Finnish epic *Kalevala* and on the Finnish landscape. In 1897 he was granted a State pension, and *Finlandia* (1899–1900) brought him international fame. His preoccupation with thematic unity and a severely logical approach to the symphonic form led to his famous disagreement with Mahler, who believed that "the symphony…must contain everything". He produced a series of works inspired by the *Kalevala* – *Pohjola's Daughter* (1906), *The Swan of Tuonela* and *Tapiola* (1925), the latter of which, a bleak, visionary tone-poem, is one of his greatest works. He explored the limits of tonality in the *Fourth Symphony* (1911), but drew back from the atonal abyss; his *Seventh Symphony* (1924) is one of the most structurally perfect of all symphonies. Sibelius fell silent after 1925, and an unfinished *Eighth Symphony* was destroyed before his death.

Smuts, Jan (Christian) 1870–1950

South African prime minister. Smuts was given charge of a commando group in the Boer war, and in 1902 invaded the Cape Colony. He later advocated peace. The Boers lost their two independent republics, and Smuts, together with General Botha, demanded Boer rights. In 1906, the British granted white self-government to the Transvaal, and Smuts was elected to the House of Assembly in 1907. In 1910, four British colonies were merged into the Union of South Africa with Botha as its premier and Smuts as his right-hand man. During World War I, they conquered German-controlled Southwest Africa. Smuts also commanded Allied troops in East Africa, and in 1917 he became Lloyd George's minister for air. He opposed the harshness of the Versailles Treaty, and helped pave the way for the establishment of the League of Nations. Smuts then served as prime minister from 1919–24, and as deputy prime minister in a coalition from 1933–39, when he regained the premiership and declared war on Germany. The South African army helped to overthrow the Axis forces in North Africa, and in 1945 Smuts attended the San Francisco conference at which the United Nations Organization was founded. He lost power to the National party in the 1948 general election.

▼ Jan Christian Smuts

▼ Frederick Soddy

▼ Peter Arkadyevich Stolypin

Soddy, Frederick 1877–1956

British chemist, pioneer of radiochemistry. After graduating at Oxford he worked in Montreal under Ernest Rutherford, who was investigating radioactivity. They deduced that this must be the consequence of spontaneous atomic disintegration and that in the case of radium a product of decay should be helium gas. In 1903, working with William Ramsay in London, Soddy identified helium in the gaseous emanation of radium bromide. In 1913 Soddy closely related the new concept of atomic number to radioactive decay. Emission of a beta particle, he postulated, increases atomic number by one; of an alpha particle diminishes it by two. In the same year he put forward the idea of atoms of different atomic weights having identical chemical properties: to designate such atoms he coined the word isotope. He was awarded a Nobel prize in 1921. He wrote books on the relationship of science and society.

Sorel, Georges 1847–1922

French social philosopher. In 1893, after an engineering career, Sorel wrote a critique of Marxism. He applied to politics many of Nietzsche's ideas, like those of the will to power as the basic drive, science as a creative process, and excessive thinking (suppressing other functions) as decadent. He found Marxism spurious but invigorating. He agreed with Pareto that democracy does not banish elites. He believed that the best way of life must be fought for, and that violence is sometimes a noble expression of individuality. For a time a syndicalist, in 1909 Sorel lost faith in the initiative ability of the workers; he became a nationalist. His advocacy of the "social myth" as a means of activating the masses was appreciated by Mussolini, who fitted to his own purposes many of Sorel's theories.

Stieglitz, Alfred 1864–1946

US photographer and art patron. Stieglitz attended university in Germany from 1881, switching from mechanical engineering to photography. In 1890 he left for the USA, and edited a photographic magazine. In 1902 he founded Photo-secession, the group, and the gallery, later known as 291, and began editing the radical journal, *Camera Work*. He was a technical innovator; he took the first photographs in snow, rain, and darkness. Stieglitz was (from 1908), the first US gallery-owner to show Rodin, Matisse, Cézanne, Picasso, and US painters such as Georgia O'Keeffe, his wife from 1924. 291 broke up after World War I. Stieglitz's own photographs from 1917 to 1937 included portraits of his wife, and pictures of cloud formations. He still exhibited, but only artists who were not already popular. Stieglitz gave many fine artists access to a wide public, brought an unprecedented status to US art in the USA, and took photographs which were the first to be counted as art.

Stolypin, Peter Arkadyevich 1862–1911

Russian Statesman. Governor of Grodno (1902) and Saratov (1903), minister of the interior (1906) and prime minister (1906–11) after the elections to the first Duma in 1906. He combined a policy of harsh repression with systematic reforms. He dissolved the second Duma in 1907 and changed the electoral law to restrict franchise and reduce nationalist representation. His agrarian reforms of 1906–11 broke up the commune. They established hereditary land tenure by heads of families and peasants were permitted to leave village communities and establish separate farms, and encouraged to buy and enclose their land. The amount of resources available to peasant land-banks was increased and education and settlement in less populated areas encouraged. Stolypin's aim was to create a prosperous and conservative kulak class of small and medium farmers and generally improve agriculture. The resultant expanded domestic market would eventually be integrated by the industrialization of the country. Stolypin was assassinated by a socialist revolutionary terrorist in 1911.

Strauss, Richard 1864–1949

German composer. Strauss's earliest pieces were published in 1876. From 1882 he studied philosophy and art history at Munich University, and in 1885 became an assistant conductor; after a month he became the chief conductor at Meiningen. He was among the foremost conductors of his day. He began a series of programmatic tone poems, the finest of which are *Also Sprach Zarathustra* (1895–96) and *Ein Heldenleben* (1898). With *Salome* (1905) and *Elektra* (1909) he reached the bounds of tonality, but this was as far as Strauss went in this direction, and with *Der Rosenkavalier* (1910) he retreated into a Mozartian conservative manner, which made him popular and rich. Approachable works, like the *Alpine Symphony* (1911–15) and *Sinfonia Domestica* (1903), and operas in collaboration with Hugo von Hofmannsthal and Stefan Zweig followed. He remained in Germany after 1933, accepting a post from Hitler, but resigned soon after. *Metamorphosen* (1945) and *Four Last Songs* (1948) are among his last works.

Stravinsky, Igor 1882–1971

Russian composer. In 1905, when Stravinsky graduated in law, he was already composing. He was taught by Rimsky-Korsakov (1903–06), and in 1909 joined Diaghilev's *Ballets Russes*, for whom he wrote *The Firebird* (1910), *Petrushka* (1911) and the seminal *Le Sacre du printemps*, important for its rhythmic innovations – it caused a riot at its first performance. During World War I, Stravinsky lived in Switzerland, moving in 1920 to France, where he composed music in a neoclassical style, such as *Pulcinella* (1920), a reworking of pieces attributed to

Pergolesi. He rejoined the Orthodox Church in 1926 and wrote several Slavonic chorales. In 1939 he settled in the USA, producing two major symphonies, and in 1951, *The Rake's Progress*, with a libretto by Auden and Kallmann. He now moved into the dodecaphony he had previously derided, with pieces like *Threni* (1958), and *Requiem Canticles* (1966). Stravinsky adopted many stylistic masks, repudiating each as he moved on, however all of his music exhibits a conspicuous craftsmanship and inventiveness.

Strindberg, August 1849–1912

Swedish dramatist. After an insecure and impoverished childhood, and failing to graduate from Uppsala University, Strindberg worked as a journalist. His first play, *Mäster Olof* (1872), was rejected by the Royal Theater. In 1877, now a librarian, he married, divorcing in 1891. During this period he wrote novels and plays, and traveled Europe (1883–89). By the time he wrote *The Father* (1877) and *Miss Julie* (1888), his mental stability was slipping, and he was soon an unemployable alcoholic. In 1892 he moved to Berlin and married the following year. After this marriage ended (1895) in separation, he went through a spiritual crisis, recorded in *Inferno* (1898), and conversion. He studied theosophy, returned to Stockholm and wrote a series of historical dramas, and later, inspired by his third, brief (1901–04) marriage, fantastic, experimental works, *The Dance of Death* (1901), and *A Dream Play* (1902), as well as a fine autobiography. Strindberg is considered the greatest Swedish writer; his brooding, disturbing work resembles the paintings of Munch.

Sun Yat-sen 1866–1925

Revolutionary and "Father of Modern China". In 1894, Sun worked for the overthrow of the Manchu dynasty. In 1895 he fled abroad, organized uprisings and promoted the revolutionary cause. In 1905 he became head of the Tokyo-based Alliance Society, a pro-republican coalition, based on 3 principles: People's Rule, People's Authority, and People's Livelihood (often interpreted as nationalism, democracy, and socialism), and in 1911, after 10 unsuccessful uprisings, the Manchus were overthrown. Sun returned to China to become president of the new republic, but soon resigned in favor of the powerful Yuan Shikai. Sun then denounced Yuan's dictatorial ambitions, tried unsuccessfully to overthrow him in 1913, and fled abroad to reorganize the Guomindang (Nationalist Party, founded 1912). After Yuan's death in 1916 China deteriorated into warlordism and the Peking government fell into dictatorial hands. In 1920 he became president of a regime in Guanzhou and later cooperated with the Soviet Union and the Chinese Communist party to work for national unification. Sun died in Beijing after a long winter trek to attend a National Assembly.

▼ Konstantin Tsiolkovsky

▼ Max Weber

▼ Alfred Wegener

Taft, W.H. 1857-1930

US president. The Republican Taft, called to the bar in 1880 and a judge by 1887, was US solicitor-general from 1890 to 1892, when he resumed work as a judge on circuit. Chairman of the second Philippine Commission, he became very popular in the Philippines as their first civilian governor (1901-04). Secretary of war from 1904, in 1908 he succeeded Theodore Roosevelt as US president. Neither clever nor imaginative, he was known for honesty and efficiency. He continued with Roosevelt's anti-trust legislation. But the more radical Roosevelt ran against him in 1912, splitting the Republican vote and letting the Democrat Woodrow Wilson in. Taft then taught law at Yale university (1913-21), chaired the War Labor Board, and in 1921 became US Supreme Court Chief Justice; in this position he did much to improve the efficiency of the judicial system.

Tagore, Rabindranath 1861–1941

Indian poet, philosopher and educationalist who influenced the founders of modern India, its society, and Western attitudes towards the country. Son of the Maharishi Devendranath Tagore. Tagore began to write poems in the 1880s, culminating in *Manasi* (1890), a collection containing some of his best-known poems; Tagore introduced new forms to Bengali, such as the ode, in this collection. From 1891, he managed his father's estates, and his close contact with the peasants resulted in a collection of stories, *Galpaguccha* (1912). The concern with political and social problems first expressed in *Manasi* continued; several collections followed, including *Sonar Tari* "The Golden Boat" (1893), *Caitali* "Late Harvest" (1896) and *Naibedya* "Sacrifice" (1901). The deaths of his wife and son inspired some of his finest poetry: his *Gitanjali* "Song Offering" (1910) won him the Nobel Prize. A believer in constructive nationalism with the village as the base of all nation-building activities, he renounced his knighthood in protest against the Amritsar Massacre (1919). He disagreed with Gandhi's policy of non-cooperation and "selfish nationalism", favoring international cooperation. The two, however, remained close friends and Tagore was a strong influence on Gandhi. In 1901 he founded a school in Santiniketan, to the end of studying the finest of Western and Indian culture, and in 1921 he founded the Visva-Bharati University there also.

Tata, Jamsetji Nasarwanji 1839–1904

Indian industrialist. He joined his father's trading firm in 1858. Recovering from the Indian slump after the American Civil War, they reentered the China trade. Tata then entered the cotton industry, converting the Alexandra Mill in Bombay (1871), building a new mill in Nagpur (1877) and reconditioning other mills. The mills became the pivot of the family fortune and were reputed for their efficiency, advanced labor policies and use of finer grade of fiber. Tata diversified his interest in the 1890s, buying property in Bombay, entering the Bombay money market, building the Taj Mahal Hotel and promoting silk production in Mysore state. Most importantly, in 1901 he began to develop India's first large-scale ironworks, incorporated as Tata Iron and Steel Company in 1907, and later one of the world's largest steelworks. It was the center of a vast and various industrial empire. Tata also planned the hydro-electric plants near Bombay which became the Tata Power companies after his death.

Taylor, Frederick Winslow 1856–1915

US inventor and engineer. Taylor trained as a pattern maker and machinist (1875–78), joined the Midvale Steel Company (1878), where he became chief engineer (1884), and obtained a degree in mechanical engineering through night school (1883). He successfully introduced a "time and motion" study at the Midvale plant in 1881 which provided the basis for his future theories of management science. Taylor believed efficiency of production could be increased by observation of workers and disposing of wasted time and motion in their jobs. Such rationalization of production methods, or "Taylorization", had a tremendous impact upon modern industry throughout the world. Taylor worked at a number of other firms including the Bethlehem Steel Corporation (1889–1901) where he developed high-speed steel and other innovations concerning metal production. Despite his skill as an engineer, he resigned in 1901 to devote more time to the spread of his ideas on scientific management.

Thomson, Joseph John 1856–1940

British physicist, discoverer of the electron. After winning a scholarship to Trinity College, Cambridge, in 1876 he graduated in mathematics in 1880. He then joined the staff of the Cavendish Laboratory, Cambridge, latterly as Cavendish Professor (1884–1919). Under his direction it became the world's leading center for research in atomic physics. In 1883 he began to investigate radiation generated by electric discharges through gases at low pressures. The nature of this radiation was uncertain: many physicists believed it to consist of electromagnetic waves, but in 1897 Thomson proved that it was in fact a stream of charged particles. By measuring their deflection in combined electric and magnetic fields he was able to measure the ratio of charge to mass. Subsequently he found the mass to be about one-thousandth of that of an atom of hydrogen, the lightest element. This was an epoch-making discovery, overturning the accepted belief that atoms were the smallest particles existing in nature. He was awarded a Nobel prize in 1906.

Thorpe, Jim 1886–1953

US athlete. Judged the greatest American all-round athlete and footballer of the first half of the century, he was primarily of American Indian descent. He played semi-professional baseball in 1909–10, was chosen for the All-America football team in 1911–12 and won gold for the decathlon and pentathlon at the 1912 Olympics. A relatively unsuccessful National League baseball player (1913–19), he was a star of professional football from 1919 to 1926. He also excelled in basketball, boxing, lacrosse, swimming and hockey.

Tiffany, Louis Comfort 1848–1933

US artist and designer. After studying art in Paris and America, Tiffany began in 1875 to work in stained glass. In 1877 he cofounded The Society of American Artists; in 1878 he opened his own glass factory, and by the 1890s his iridescent, sculptured "favrile" glass was world famous. Seeing Emile Gallé's glass in 1889 inspired him to try glass-blowing. He was now producing his magical "favrile " items in huge quantities, and was an Art Nouveau leader. In 1900 he opened Tiffany Studios, producing lamps and jewelry; in 1911 he made a vast glass curtain for Mexico City's Palacio de Bellas Artes. He was made a Chevalier de la Légion d'Honneur, member of the Société Nationale des Beaux-Arts, and of Tokyo Imperial Society of Fine Arts. In 1919 Tiffany established a foundation for art students.

Tilak, Bal Gangadhar 1856-1920

Indian philosopher and "maker of modern India" (M.K. Gandhi). Tilak, originally a math teacher, published his opposition to British rule, in order to politicize his fellowcountrymen, in two weekly papers he produced. In 1893 and 1895 he organized big Hindi religious festivals, to arouse and deepen nationalist sentiments. Jailed by the British in 1897 for sedition, he won the name Lokamanya (beloved leader of the people). In 1905, opposing Curzon's partition of Bengal, he started a boycott of British goods which spread nationwide. He then initiated a program of passive resistance to British rule. Imprisoned again in 1907, he wrote a massive exposition of the Bhagavad Gita, the Hindu holy book. On his release in 1914, he launched the Home Rule League, and in 1916, back in Congress, signed the Lucknow Pact. In 1918, visiting Britain, he formed ties with the rising Labour Party. Latterly he slightly moderated his methodology, questioning Gandhi's advocacy of council election boycotts. Nehru, as well as Gandhi, loved and revered him.

Tsiolkovsky, Konstantin 1857–1935

Russian physicist. During his years as a (self-taught) teacher he devoted his spare time to studying the problems of aerial travel, beginning with a metal-skinned dirigible (1892) and an

aeroplane with twin propellers (1894). In 1897 he constructed Russia's first experimental wind tunnel. From 1896 he began to explore the possibility of interplanetary travel with rockets and from 1903 to 1917 put forward various plans for the construction of rocket ships, embodying many ideas now widely adopted. However, his work was ignored until the Bolshevik Revolution in 1917. Thereafter he became a pensioned member of the Academy, and was internationally known and respected. In his last years he worked on formulating specifications for rocket fuels.

Twort, Frederick William 1877–1950

British physician. After qualifying he held posts at St Thomas's Hospital, London; the London Hospital; and, as director, the Brown Institution, an animal dispensary (1909). He made many contributions to bacteriology, including identification of the causative agent of Johne's disease, a serious ailment of cattle. His major contribution, however, was made in 1915 when he discovered viruses which infect and destroy bacteria. Felix d'Hérelle in France gave such viruses the generic name bacteriophage. This interaction is, therefore, generally known as the Twort-d'Hérelle phenomenon.

Veblen, Thorstein 1857–1929

American economist and social critic. Hailing from an impoverished family of Norwegian immigrants, he took his PhD at Yale University in 1884. After several years of penury, he was finally given a teaching post at the University of Chicago from 1892 to 1906, where he produced his critique of capitalism, *The Theory of the Leisure Class* (1899). This study came to have great significance for later theorists such as Galbraith, particularly in its identification and critique of "conspicuous consumption".

Venizelos, Eleutherios 1864-1936

Greek prime minister and statesman. Venizelos, son of a Cretan revolutionary, educated in Athens, practiced law in Crete. As Liberal Party Leader he fought for union with Greece. After leading a revolt against the Turks (1897), he became Cretan justice minister (1899-1901); and in 1904 he led a successful coup against the high commissioner, Prince George. Invited to Athens to lead a revolutionary movement, he entered parliament in 1910, and became prime minister the same year. In office until 1933 (8 terms), he established the Balkan League and expelled the Turks, doubling Greece's territory and population. The king prevented him from supporting the Allies in World War l until the Germans invaded Macedonia; Venizelos then ousted and exiled the king and entered the war. He won international renown during and after the Versailles Peace Conference as a great statesman. In 1920 King Constantine was

recalled and Venizelos went to Paris, returning to his premiership in 1923 after the king was dethroned and his son exiled. In 1928, now also Liberal Party leader, he was re-elected with a huge majority, but the Great Depression undermined him at home, and he lost the 1932 election. In 1935 he fled Greece after a failed anti-monarchist uprising, and died in Paris.

Weber, Max 1864–1920

German sociologist and political economist. Seen as one of the founders of modern sociology, Weber held professional positions at Freiburg, Heidelberg and Munich. His work addressed both sociology's methodology and many issues within the discipline. Weber rejected the view that sociological study should be carried out in a way comparable to that of the natural sciences. Instead he emphasized the need to understand the meanings behind people's actions, from which sociology could work towards formal models of action. Weber saw the process of "rationalization" as the dominant trend in society, with every area of human behavior being increasingly subject to both calculation and administration. In *The Protestant Ethic and the Spirit of Capitalism* (1920) he traced the development of modern capitalism back to the influence of the Calvinist religion in Western Europe. This text, along with much of Weber's other work, is seen as a response to Marx's economic rationalization.

Wegener, Alfred Lothar 1880–1930

German meteorologist and geophysicist, formulator of the theory of Continental Drift. After an academic appointment at Marburg, he joined the meteorological research department of the *Deutsche Seewarte* (Marine Observatory) in 1919. In pursuit of his meteorological studies, Wegener joined, in all, four expeditions to Greenland, on the last of which he lost his life. His *Thermodynamik der Atmosphäre* (Thermodynamics of the Atmosphere, 1911) was a standard textbook. He is, however, best known in respect of a secondary interest, deriving from meteorology. Unable to reconcile evidence about climates in the geological past with the existing pattern of the continents, he suggested that over geological time an original supercontinent, Pangaea, had broken up and the fragments had drifted in a sea of molten magma to their present positions. At the time this radical theory found little support, mainly because no appropriate source of power could be discerned, but it is now generally accepted.

Wilhelm II 1859–1941

German emperor. Wilhelm succeeded to the throne in 1888, and in 1890 forced Bismarck to resign as chancellor. In the same year, Germany refused to renew the Reinsurance Treaty with Russia, which then strengthened its ties with France. In 1896,

Wilhelm damaged relations with Britain by congratulating the South African President Kruger on the defeat of the British- inspired Jameson raid; and also by building up the German navy. In 1905, he attempted unsuccessfully to subvert the Franco-British Entente (1904) by siding with Britain against French domination of Morocco. The Triple Entente of France, Britain and Russia was formed in 1907, and in 1908 Wilhelm again caused alarm in Britain by telling a newspaper reporter that many Germans were antiEnglish. In 1911 he tried to intervene in Morocco once more, and so Britain agreed to send troops to the French front in the event of war with Germany. Wilhelm delegated all major decision-making during World War I. A few days before the armistice was signed, he was forced by internal unrest to abdicate, and fled to the Netherlands.

Wright, Orville (1871–1948) and Wilbur (1867–1912)

US pioneer aviators. Talented and self-taught mechanics, they became interested in aviation through the gliding experiments of Otto Lilienthals and established a bicycle business which financed their early aviation experiments. The brothers developed a three-axis control system for a biplane kite and in 1900 moved on to testing a series of gliders with moveable wing-tips that gave total control. For their experiments they designed a wind tunnel and also undertook much theoretical work. In 1903 they made the first powered airplane flight at Kitty Hawk. The "Flyer II" was flown in 1904 and in 1905 "Flyer III" undertook a flight of 24 miles lasting over half an hour. The Wrights lacked sponsorship but continued to develop aircraft. In 1908 they acquired a licence to produce airplanes in Europe and won a US Army contract to produce the world's first military airplane. In 1909 they gave up their cycle business and established an aircraft production company, of which Wilbur was president until his death. Orville devoted the remainder of his life to research.

Zeppelin, Ferdinand, Count von 1838–1917

German pioneer of airships. As a soldier (from 1858) he was much impressed by the military use of balloons for observation in the American Civil War (during which he made his own first flight) and the siege of Paris (1870–71). He failed, however, to interest his superiors but when he retired in 1891, as a general, he began experiments on his own. His first airship (LZ1) made its maiden flight in 1900. The poor development of airplane technology was influential in the German government's decision to commission an entire fleet of airships after Zeppelin achieved a twenty-four hour flight in 1906 and between 1910 and 1914 carried over 30,000 passengers without accident. Zeppelins were deployed in World War I, but they had limited military success.

ACKNOWLEDGEMENTS

Picture credits

1 US President Theodore Roosevelt on the campaign trail in 1903 LC

2–3 Military training in Russia in the 1900s BPK

4–5 Mexican women in 1911 Museum of Modern Art, Oxford/Casasola Archives

10–11 Funeral of Queen Victoria HDC

44–45 Workers leave the Belfast shipyards after a shift constructing SS Titanic, 1911: Ulster Museum

82–83 A street market in East London, c.1910: HDC

120–121 The Paris Exhibition, 1900: RV

7 RV, Paris 8–9 LC 15 CP/IWM 16tl Edimedia 16br MEPL 16–17 Royal Commonwealth Institute, London 17br Staatsgalerie, Stuttgart 18t MEPL 18b UB 18–19 CPI 21tl DKC 21tr Victoria and Albert Museum, London 21br Picturepoint 22 JH 24t LC 24b IWM 24–25 Bibliothèque Nationale, Paris 25t Alexander Meledin 25b PF 27 HDC 28–29t BPK 28–29b SV 30–31t JH 30b TPS 31 MEPL 32–33 SV 33t TPS 34t, 34–35 IKON/USPG 35tl, 35cr MEPL 35bl RF 37 PF 38 *Illustrated London News* 39 DKC 40 LC 41t HDC 41b MEPL 42 LC 49 International Museum of Photography at George Eastman House 50, 51t HDC/Bettman Archive 51b TPS 52–53 AEG Aktiengesellschaft 53 TPS 54 UB 55t HDC 55bl Siemens Institut, München 55br MEPL 56t Joseph Byron 56b HDC 57l Unilever Information Services 57r MEPL 58 Staatliche Landesbildstelle, Hamburg 59 Ulster Museum 60t Chicago Historical Society 60–61 City of Toronto Archives 61t PF 62t, 62–63, 62c Henry Ford Museum 63t PF 63tr Minnesota Historical Society 63br M/René Burri 64–65 PF 66 RV 67t HDC 67b Mansell Collection 68t De Beers Consolidated Mines 68b Angela Murphy 69 PF 70t MEPL 70b Foreign and Commonwealth Office Library 70–71 TPS 71tr RV 71 HDC 72–73 Foreign and Commonwealth Office Library 74 PF 75t Fotomas Index 75c MEPL 75b Foreign and Commonwealth Office Library 76t Zefa/Orion Press 76b City of Toronto Archives 78l, 78r Bell Canada Telephone Historical Collection 79 AEG Aktiengesellschaft 80–81 Smithsonian Institution 80t AA 80b Rank Xerox Ltd 81t Henry Ford Museum, Dearborn, Michigan 81c CP 81b SPL/Heini Schneebeli 87 Ford Motor Co. 88 RV 89 Victoria and Albert Museum 90t Cadbury Ltd 90b AA 91t RV 91b Musée de l'Elysée, Lausanne 92t Private Collection 92b Cleveland Museum of Art, gift of Hanna Fund © ADAGP, Paris and DACS, London 1990 92–93 Clovis Prévost 93t Francisco Valls 93b Sonia Halliday Photographs © ADAGP, Paris and DACS, London 1990 95 HDC 96–97, 97tr LC 97tl SV 98–99 Greater London Photograph Library 98 HDC 99 SV 100 MEPL 100–101 RV 102–103, 102t HDC 102b PF 103t RV 103b M/Pinkhassov 105 Mansell Collection 105t, 106b International Museum of Photography at George Eastman House 107 Hapag-Lloyd AG 108 RV 109t MEPL 109c AA 109b HDC 110t MEPL 110b PF 110–111 State Historical Society of Wisconsin 111, 112–113 SV 112, 113t HDC 113c FSP 113c Sally and Richard Greenhill 114–115 RV 115 MEPL 116t HDC 116b RV 118t Society for Oriental and African Studies, London 118b SV 119 Museum of Modern Art, Oxford/Casasola Archives 125 PF 126–127 CPI 127t AA 128l Mander and Mitchenson Theatre Collection 128r Missouri Historical Society 129, 130t MEPL 130–131b Bulloz 131t AA 131br MEPL 133 W.H. Smith 134 FPG International 135t AA 135c FP 135b Museum of the City of New York 136t Michael Holford 136b CPI 137t NFA, London 137c KC 137b Museum of Modern Art, New York/Film Stills Archive 138–139, 139b KC 139t AA 140 National Film and Sound Archive, Australia 140–141 CPI 141t APL 142t CPI 142–143b CPI 142–143c AA 143 Süddeutscher Verlag 144l The Circus World Museum, Wisconsin 144tr, 144br HDC 144 (background) Mander and Mitchenson 145t Liverpool Walker Art Gallery 145b Süddeutscher Verlag 146–147 KC 146t AA 146b NFA, London 147l National Archives, Washington

147cr CPI 147br KC 149t Le Comité International Olympique, Switzerland 149b, 150 HDC 150–151 JH 151t CPI 152t HDC 152b CPI 153t LC 153b Colorsport 154l M/Elliott Erwitt 154c PF 154r HDC 155l AA 155c, 155r HDC 156l PF 156c HDC/Bettman Archive 156r PF 157l M/Herbert List 157c PF 157r, 158r HDC 158l AA 158c Yale University Art Gallery 159l HDC 159c APL 159r Brown Brothers 160l, 160c PF 160r HDC 161l, 161c PF 161r HDC 162l AA 162c, 162r HDC 163l, 163c HDC 163r PF 164l RV 164c HDC 164r PF 165l, 165c, 166l, 166r HDC 166c AA 167l, 167c, 167r PF 168l, 168c, 168r PF 169l HDC 169c TPS 169r PF 170l Novosti Press Agency 170c UB 170r PF 171l HDC/Bettman Archive 171r PF

Abbreviations

APL	Aquarius Picture Library
AA	Andromeda Archive
BPK	Bildarchiv Preussischer Kulturbesitz, Berlin
CP	Camera Press, London
CPI	Culver Pictures Inc, New York
DKC	David King Collection
FP	The Futile Press
FSP	Frank Spooner Pictures, London
HDC	Hulton Deutsch Collection, London
IWM	Imperial War Museum, London
JH	John Hillelson Agency, London
KC	Kobal Collection
LC	Library of Congress, Washington D.C.
M	Magnum Photos, London
MEPL	Mary Evans Picture Library
NFA	National Film Archive
PF	Popperfoto, London
RF	Rex Features
RV	Roger-Viollet, Paris
SPL	Science Photo Library, London
SV	Süddeutscher Verlag, Munich
TPS	Topham Picture Source, Kent, UK
UB	Ullstein Bilderdienst, Berlin

t = top, tl = top left, tr = top right, c = center, b = bottom etc

Editorial and Research Assistance
Steven Chapman, Mary Davies, Robert Dewey Jnr, Jackie Gaff, John Horgan, Louise Jones, Nick Law, Andy Overs, Mike Pincombe, Maria Quantrill, Graham Speake, Michelle von Ahn

Artists
Alan Hollingberry, Ayala Kingsley, Kevin Maddison, Colin Salmon

Design Assistance
Cyndy Gossert, Dave Smith, Del Tolton

Photographs
Shirley Jamieson, David Pratt, Joanne Rapley

Typesetting
Brian Blackmore, Catherine Boyd, Anita Wright

Production
Stephen Elliott, Clive Sparling

Cartography
Sarah Rhodes
Maps drafted by Euromap, Pangbourne; Lovell Johns, Oxford; Alan Mais (Hornchurch)

Color Origination
J. Film Process, Bangkok; Scantrans, Singapore; Wing King Tong Co., Ltd, Hong Kong

Index
Ann Barrett

INDEX

standardization 54, 94, 128; education *99*; time 78; weights and measures 77–78
steel industry 54, 55, 72, 116
Stieglitz, Alfred 169
Stolypin, Peter Arkadyevich **20**, 169
Strauss, Richard 169
Stravinsky, Igor 169
strikes **36**, 40, 97
Strindberg, August 169
Sudan 70
Suez Canal **72**
suffrage 36, **36**, 37, 40, **40**, **43**, 94–95; women's 40, **40**, *41*, 94
suffragettes 40, *40*, **40**
Sun Yixian (Sun Yat-sen) 119, 169
Sundback, Gideon *80*
Sweden **48**, 53, 54, 97, 101
Switzerland 49, **53**, 77

T

Taft, William H. 23, **36**, 170
Tagore, Rabindranath 170
Tanganyika *70*, 115
Tata, Jamsetji Nasarwanji 170
Taylor, Frederick Winslow 91, 170
tea industry 65, 67, 69
telegraph 78
telephone *78*, *79*
television 136
textile industry 66, 69, 73, 74, 116
Thailand, exports 66
Thaubault, R. 89
theater *144*, **144**, *145*
Theodore (emperor of Ethiopia) **34**
Third World *114*, **114**, 115–17
Thompson, Flora 99
Thomson, Joseph John 170
Thorpe, Jim *148*, 170
Tiffany, Louis Comfort 170
Tilak, Bal Gangadhar 170
Tirpitz, Admiral Alfred von 18, 22, 28, 31
Tobey, Mark **92**
Tocqueville, Alexis de 94
Togo *70*
trade; colonies and primary producers 64–69, **64**, *70*, **70**, *71*, 76; commodity markets 77; cotton industry *66*; economic interdependence 72–79, **72**; European 73; European influences 65; international exchange rate 77; multinational companies 75; "new imperialism" 68; overseas development 67–68; protective tariffs 69; South America 69; Suez and Panama Canals *72*; Third World **114**; transfers of labor 65; transportaion 66–67, *70*, 72. *see also* transportation; weights and measures standardization 77–78
trade unions **36**, 40, 42, *94*, **94**, 96, *96*, 97
tramways 60, *61*
transistor 80
transportation **14**, **89**; aircraft *80*, **80**; commuting 60; economic development **14**; economic interdependence *72*; omnibus 60; steam tramp 72; Suez and Panama Canals *72*; time standardization 78; and trade 66–67, *70*, 72; tramways 60, *61*; underground railroads 60; urban transport systems 60, *61*; *see also* automobile; rail transportation; shipping
Triple Alliance 15, 18, 21
Triploi, annexation 15
Tsiolkovsky, Konstantin 170–71
Turkey 29, *110*; Atatürk **28**; Balkan wars 32–33, *32*, *33*; Italy declares war 32; Young Turks 29, *32*, *33*
turret lathe 55
Twort, Frederick William 171
typewriter 54, *55*, 91, 127

U

Uganda, missionary movement *34*
Ukraine **28**, 101
Union of Soviet Socialist Republics; suffrage 40; *see also* Russia
United Kingdom; Anglo–French agreement (1912) 32; Anglo–German alliance 18; Anglo–German naval race 27, 28–29, *28*, 31; Anglo–Japanese alliance 18; Asian entente 22–23; Australia 16; Balkan crisis 31; banking *72*, 74, 76, **86**; Birmingham 59; Boer War 15, 17, 133, 151; Boy Scouts 151; British mercantile houses 66–67; Canada 16, 17; canning industry *55*; capital exports 53, *72*; colonial preferences 74; colonialism 15, 16, 21–22, 68, **70**; constitutional government 39, **43**; cooperative societies 56, *56*, 57; department stores 57; diet **97**; Dogger Bank incident 20; Dominions 16, 39; economic development 52–53; emigration 72; exports *72*, 73; film industry **137**; foreign debtors 76; foreign investment 74–75; Franco–British settlement 21–22; gold standard 76, 77; Greenwich Mean Time 78; Imperial General Staff 22; imports 73, 74; India 16, 23, 114, *114*, 117–18, *118*; industrialization **26**, **36**, **48**, 49, 61, 86, **86**; investment **48**, 52–53; Ireland 16, **28**, 101; labor force 51; labor movement 97; Labour party 42; Lloyd George's Mansion House speech 31; London underground 60, *61*; military strength **26**; mining industry 54, 95, *95*; monarchy 39; Moroccan crisis 31; multinational companies 75; music hall *144*, **144**, *145*; National Insurance Act 98; navy 17, **26**, 27, 28, 28–29, *28*, 31; old age pension 98, *98*; Panama Canal 17; Parliament 36, *38*, 39, **43**; *Pax Britannica* 28, 29; and Persia 17, 23; press 132–35; retailing 56–57, *56*, *57*; shipping *58*, **86**; social inequality *94*; social welfare 98, *98*; "splendid isolation" policy 17, 18; sport 49, 148–49, 152, *152*; suffrage 36, **36**, 40, **43**; suffragettes 40, *40*, **40**; textile industry 73; trade 73; trade unions **36**, 40, 42, 97; underground railroads 60, *61*; and United States 17; urban transport systems 60; urbanization 58, *58*, 59; World War I 31; Young Men's Christian Association 151
United States of America; Alaska–British Columbia border claims 17; American Federation of Labor *94*, 97; birth rate *104*; canning industry *55*; capital exports *72*; capital imports 53; child labor 98; colonialism 15, 16; commodity markets 77; Congress **43**; constitutional government 36, 40, 42, **43**; copyright protection 79; department stores 57; economic growth 53; education 52, 94; ethnic minorities 105, **106–07**, *106*, *107*; exports 74; film industry 137, 139–40; Ford Model T 56; foreign investment 74, 75; gold standard 77; Great Atlantic and Pacific Tea Company 56–57; Hollywood *146*, **146**; immigration **48**, 50–52, *50*, *51*, *59*, 72, 91, *104*, 105, *106*, **106–07**, 107, *107*, 132, **132**, *134*; industrialization **14**, **26**, **48**, 54, 61, 86, **86**; investment 53; Jews *51*, *106*; labor movement 40, *40*; labor unrest 91; mail-order retailing 57; Mexico *114*; migration **14**; military strength **26**; mining industry 53, 54, 96; "monopoly capitalism" 89–90; multinational companies 75; navy 28; newspapers 132–33; oil industry 90; Panama Canal 17, *24*, 74; per capita income **124**; Philippines 15; popular music 142–43, *144*, **144**; population **48**; press 132–35; Republicans **36**; retailing 56–57, *56*; social inequality *94*; Spanish–American War 17, *74*, 133; suffrage 40, **40**; suffragettes **40**; telephone communications *78*; trade unions 40, *94*, 96, *96*, 97; and United Kingdom 17; urban transport systems 60; urbanization 58, 59, *59*, 86; Wild West show *144*; World War I **28**
Uraguay, average income 64
urbanization **14**, 58–59, *58*, *59*, 69, **86**, 96–97, 104–05, 107–10, 132–34; transport systems 60, *61*

V

vacuum cleaner 127
Vall, Theodore *78*
Valls, Francisco *93*
Vanderbilt, Cornelius 90
Veblen, Thorstein 100, 171
Venizelos, Eleutherios 171
Villa, Pancho 119
Vionnet **131**
Vitagraph 137
Volga Tatars 100

W

Wanamaker, John 57, 127
Ward, A. Montgomery 57, 127
Weber, Eugen 89
Weber, Max **91**, 171
Wegener, Alfred Lothar 171
weights and measures 77–78
Welles, Orson 133
Weltpolitik 15, 23
West Africa, exports 66
West Indies, French colonies 16
Westernization 118–19
Wilhelm II (kaiser of Germany) 18, 21, 22, 171
Wills, Harold C. **62**
Wilson, Thomas Woodrow **28**, **36**
women 107–08; birth rate 110; clothing *see* fashion and clothing; domestic service 100, 108, 109; education 108, **112**; emancipation 104, *105*; employment *100*, 108, 109, 116, 128; feminism **110–11**, *111*; medical care *109*; migration *107*; newspapers and magazines 134; political mobilization 104; prostitution 109; sport 130, 151–52, *151*; suffrage 40, **40**, *41*, 94; wages 109; Women's Liberation movement **111**
World War I; Anglo–French agreement 32; arms race 25, **26**; Austria–Hungary 31; education *111*; France 31; Germany 25, 31; industrialization *24*, 25; military strength 24; nationalism **28**; Russia 31; Schlieffen plan 31; United Kingdom 31; United States of America **28**
Wozniak, Stephen 80
Wright, Orville and Wilbur 80, 171, **180**

Y

Young Turks 29, *32*, *33*
Yuan Shikai **19**
Yugoslavia **28**

Z

Zambia *see* Rhodesia
Zapata, Emiliano 119
Zenardelli, Giuseppe 39
Zeppelin, Ferdinand, Count von 171
Zetkin, Clara **111**
Zimbabwe *see* Rhodesia
Zimmermann, W. 57
Zionism 16
zipper fastener *80*
Zukor, Adolph 140